Child Soldiers in the
Western Imagination

D1065861

The Rutgers Series in Childhood Studies

The Rutgers Series in Childhood Studies is dedicated to increasing our understanding of children and childhoods, past and present, throughout the world. Children's voices and experiences are central. Authors come from a variety of fields, including anthropology, criminal justice, history, literature, psychology, religion, and sociology. The books in this series are intended for students, scholars, practitioners, and those who formulate policies that affect children's everyday lives and futures.

Edited by Myra Bluebond-Langner, Board of Governors Professor of Anthropology, Rutgers University and True Colours Chair in Palliative Care for Children and Young People, University College London, Institute of Child Health.

Advisory Board

Perri Klass, New York University
Jill Korbin, Case Western Reserve University
Bambi Schieffelin, New York University
Enid Schildkraut, American Museum of Natural History and Museum for
  African Art

Child Soldiers in the Western Imagination

From Patriots to Victims

DAVID M. ROSEN

RUTGERS UNIVERSITY PRESS

NEW BRUNSWICK, NEW JERSEY AND LONDON

LIBRARY OF CONGRESS CATALOGING-IN-PUBLICATION DATA

Rosen, David M., 1944–
    Child soldiers in the Western imagination : from patriots to victims / David M.
Rosen.
        pages cm. — (The Rutgers series in childhood studies)
        Includes bibliographical references and index.
        ISBN 978–0–8135–6371–8 (hardcover : alk. paper) — ISBN 978–0–8135–6370–1
(pbk. : alk. paper) — ISBN 978–0–8135–6372–5 (pdf) — ISBN 978–0–8135–7289–5
(epub)
        1. Child soldiers. 2. Children and war. 3. Child soldiers—History. 4. Children
and war—History. 5. Child soldiers—Case studies. 6. Children and war—Case
studies. 7. Childhood—Cross-cultural studies. I. Title. II. Title: From patriots to
victims.
    UB418.C45R68 2014
    355.0083—dc23   2014049320

A British Cataloging-in-Publication record for this book is available
from the British Library.

Visit our website: http://rutgerspress.rutgers.edu

Manufactured in the United States of America

For Tori and Sarah

CONTENTS

PREFACE AND ACKNOWLEDGMENTS

Child soldiers have captured my attention and imagination for the past decade and a half, and have been the focus of much of my scholarly work. In an era when the "child soldier problem" emerged as a central concern for international humanitarian and children's rights organizations, I came to realize that there had been "child soldiers" throughout history and across the globe: what was new was the perception that they constituted a "problem." My first book, *Armies of the Young*, complicated the picture of child soldiers presented by humanitarian and human rights organizations by looking at some of the specific instances in which children played a role in armed conflict. I highlighted the varieties of circumstances and motivations that could bring children into battle.

This book explores child soldiers through a different lens, and frames the question in another way: What has changed in our cultural imagination that has so profoundly altered our understanding of the compatibility—or rather, incompatibility—of children, the military, and war? It examines the transformation of our understanding of child soldiers over the past two centuries, by looking both at the presence of children in the military and how they have been imagined in politics, popular culture, literature, and the arts. Though my focus is primarily on the West, especially Great Britain and the United States, I also examine how this transformation has influenced common understandings of child soldiers throughout the international community.

Throughout much of the eighteenth and nineteenth centuries, children and youth were an unremarkable feature of military life. By the middle of the nineteenth century, powerful new ideas about children and childhood began to put pressure on the military recruitment of youngsters. These ideas, that childhood is a highly distinct stage of life characterized by innocence, vulnerability, and the need for protection, remain central to Western understandings of the child, and have increasingly rendered childhood and military life incompatible. By the late twentieth century, humanitarian and human rights groups invented the concept of the "child soldier," a term that, in its contemporary sense, denotes a person too young to serve legitimately in the military.

This understanding of children as innocent and vulnerable is a powerful and pervasive idea. It has served as a general platform for social reform in many areas of children's lives. It was the basis of the nineteenth-century Child Saver movement, which sought to rescue working-class children in Great Britain and America from the evils of their environment. Not long afterward, it was exported to the colonial world, where it became the template for saving innocent children from the "evils" of their own societies and cultures. This view of children has become the foundation stone of virtually all contemporary international legal, humanitarian, and human rights efforts to improve the lives of children, including severing any links between childhood and military service. There is little or no room for diversity or pluralism in this essentially monist model, which renders all child soldiers as victims and all recruiters of children as deviant and criminal abusers of children.

The contemporary cultural construction of the child soldier is grounded in the discourse of humanitarian, human rights, and children's rights advocacy, and law. This discourse imagines and posits the existence of a universal child whose development, needs, and well-being are all indifferent to context. The most striking features of this image of the child are its mobility, transferability, and disconnectedness from history. Using this cultural model, children's rights advocates have little difficulty in codifying simple, universally applicable, bright-line distinctions between childhood and adulthood. In contrast, many fields involved in the study or representation of children, such as anthropology, history, and literature, take as their central orientation the idea that there are a multiplicity of concepts of childhood and adulthood, each codified and defined by age, ethnicity, gender, history, location, and numerous other factors. Whereas the idea of the "rights of the child," a concept based upon a putative universal child, seems self-evident and obvious to modern-day children's rights advocates, it often seems facile, overly simplistic, and ethnocentric to anthropologists and historians. Concerns about childhood, cast in the language of human rights and humanitarian imperative, pay little attention to the enormity of the issues of social and cultural changes contained in the transnational restructuring of age categories. Like many other avowed human rights imperatives, it tends to ignore or demonize the historical experiences and moral and legal imperatives of other cultures.

For rights advocates, aversion to the idea of the child soldier is a simple and logical extension of the concept of a universal child. Indeed, the very concept of the "child soldier" appears intentionally constructed to conflate two contradictory and incompatible terms. The first, "child," typically refers to a young person between infancy and youth and connotes immaturity, simplicity, and an absence of full physical, mental, or emotional development. The second, "soldier," in the context of contemporary professional armies in the West, generally refers to men and women who are skilled warriors. As a result it melds together two very contradictory and powerful ideas, namely the "innocence" of childhood and the "evil" of warfare. Thus, from the outset, in the modern Western imagination the very idea of the child soldier seems both aberrant and abhorrent.

Beyond this, anyone who studies child soldiers enters into a conceptual as well as legal and moral minefield. Currently, international criminal law makes the recruitment of children under age fifteen a war crime. But a variety of children's rights treaties, including the Convention on the Rights of the Child and its progeny, use the term "child" to mean any person younger than eighteen. Virtually all human rights and children's rights groups adopt this position. Accordingly, the vast majority of so-called child soldiers are in reality adolescents and youth who are defined as children by international treaties. These treaties are the fruit of the international children's rights movement, which in essence is a movement for directed social change that seeks the universal transformation of age categories and with it the reformulation of the rights and duties of children and adults. What this also means is that many child soldiers are persons who both historically and cross-culturally were not regarded as children at all. It is easy to lose sight of the fact that the term "child soldier" was not created by historians or social scientists as a guide to empirical research and analysis but is a legal and moral concept created by humanitarian and human rights organizations, law enforcement, criminal law codes, and political leaders. This language is now so deeply embedded in a Western discourse of deviancy that it is virtually impossible to treat it as a socially constructed codification, often divorced from the experiences of real children and youth and clashing with local understandings about the involvement of young people in war.

Without doubt there are many circumstances where the recruitment of children has been criminal and cruel by any standard. The cases of Joseph Kony and the Lord's Resistance Army as well as that of Sierra Leone's Revolutionary United Front easily come to mind. But over the centuries many children—heroes, villains, patriots, and victims—have been child soldiers. Joan of Arc, Carl von Clausewitz, Andrew Jackson, Moshe Dayan, Yasser Arafat, Ishmael Beah, and even Dr. Ruth Westheimer were child soldiers. Their stories cannot be reduced to simple formulas of abuse and exploitation. This book is a partial attempt to show how history, culture, and circumstance shape our understanding of their participation in war.

Many of the ideas in this book emerged out of numerous presentations and talks I have given about child soldiers. Early versions of my ideas were presented at the National Endowment for the Humanities Institute, Human Rights in Conflict—Interdisciplinary Perspectives, at the Graduate Center, City University of New York, June–July 2006; the African Studies "Sandwich Seminar" at the University of Wisconsin–Madison in 2007; the research seminar on Root Causes of Child Soldiering, hosted by Radhika Coomaraswamy, UN Special Representative of the Secretary-General on Children Affected by Armed Conflict at the United Nations in 2008; the Commodification of Human Beings: Exploring the Reality and Future of Modern-Day Slavery seminar at the University of Connecticut School of Law in 2009; the Slavery Then and Now interdisciplinary faculty workshop sponsored by the Human Rights Institute of the University of Connecticut in 2010; and the Childhood and Violence: International and Comparative Perspectives seminar series at Birbeck College, University of London, in 2011. I also presented a series of lectures at the University of Milano Bicocca and the University of Bologna in 2008. I am pleased to acknowledge the contribution of Susan Rakosi Rosenbloom to my thinking and early development of the ideas in this book. She is especially interested in how the experiences of child soldiers are crafted into humanitarian accounts of innocence and victimization, and I have greatly benefitted from our conversations. I have profited from the numerous comments of friends, colleagues, and critics, including David Blight, Radhika Coomaraswamy, Lorenzo D'Angelo, Antonio de Lauri, Anna May Duane, Luca Jourdan, Ginny Murrow, John Wallach, Jo Boyden, Myra Bluebond-Langner, and Jill Korbin. I would like to greatly thank my friend David Fleischmann for bringing to my attention the drawing *Young Soldier* by Winslow Homer, which is on the cover of this book.

Over the last number of years I have also received release time from my teaching duties at Becton College of Fairleigh Dickinson University. I thank Dean Geoffrey Weinman for his continuous support of my research and writing. I also thank the librarians and staff at the London Metropolitan Archives, the archives of the London School of Economics, and the Monninger Center for Learning and Research at Fairleigh Dickinson University. An earlier version of portions of chapter 4 was published in *Restaging War in the Western World: Non Combatant Experiences, 1890–Present* edited by Maartje Abbenhuis and Sara Buttsworth, and is published with the permission of Palgrave Macmillan. Other parts of this chapter also contain portions of my coauthored article "Representing Child Soldiers in Fiction and Film," by Sarah Rosen and David M. Rosen, published in *Peace Review: A Journal of Social Justice* 24 (July 2012), and are published with the permission of Taylor and Francis.

I cannot adequately thank my wife, Tori Rosen, for her guidance, practical judgment, editorial skill and imagination, personal support, and everything else that goes into writing a book. She is a person of exceptional grace, kindness, and keen and swift intelligence. I just consider myself very lucky. My daughter, Sarah Maya Rosen, is my sometime coauthor and copresenter and an avid Harry Potter fan who introduced me to Dumbledore's Army in the Harry Potter series. We have both written about the rebirth of the child soldier in contemporary Western literature, and I am delighted that she is both my daughter and my colleague.

Child Soldiers in the
Western Imagination

1

A Tale of Two Orphans

The lives of two thirteen-year-old boys, separated by over two centuries, reveal both the history of child soldiers and the profound transformation of cultural attitudes toward children in armed conflict. The first was born in 1767 and the second in 1980. Both were thirteen years old when they became soldiers. Both fought in brutal partisan conflicts that pitted neighbor against neighbor and in which soldiers and civilians were massacred, murdered, and mutilated. Both became orphans during the war. Both survived and continued their studies after the war: one studied law and was admitted to the bar in North Carolina, the other finished a degree in politics at Oberlin College in Ohio. Both were the subjects of very successful books—national best sellers. But one was celebrated as a great American hero and patriot while the other attained international fame as a survivor and victim of war.

Two hundred thirteen years separate the birth of Andrew Jackson— child soldier, hero of the American Revolution, and seventh president of the United States—and Ishmael Beah—child soldier, victim of the civil war in Sierra Leone, and spokesman for the plight of child soldiers everywhere. John Eaton's 1824 book *The Life of Andrew Jackson* caught the attention of the nation as the first presidential campaign biography ever written and the model for every one written since.[1] Ishmael Beah's autobiography *A Long Way Gone: Memoirs of a Child Soldier* was a best seller in the United States in 2007 and was distributed nationally through the Starbucks coffee chain. Why was Andrew Jackson lionized as a hero, and why is Ishmael commiserated with and valorized as a victim of adult abuse? What processes turned the heroes of yesteryear into the victims of today? Understanding the stories of these two child soldiers, and the differences in the ways their societies viewed them, will illustrate the dramatic cultural shifts that have occurred in the West in our attitudes about the nature of war, the nature of children, and the responsibilities of society to its children in the context of armed conflict.

Andrew Jackson: Child Soldier of the American Revolution

Andrew Jackson, the youngest of three sons of Scots-Irish immigrants, was born in 1767 in the Waxhaw Settlement in the Piedmont region that straddles the border between North and South Carolina. Jackson's father died shortly after his birth. His mother, a staunch opponent of the British, apparently impressed her sons with her tales of British tyranny and the oppression of the poor in Ireland. According John Eaton, Jackson's first biographer, she held that the "first duty" of her children was "to expend their lives . . . in defending and supporting the natural rights of man."[2]

Jackson was nine years old when the Declaration of Independence was signed. By the time he was thirteen, the Revolutionary War was raging across the South. His older brother Hugh was already dead, a victim of heat exhaustion during the 1779 Battle of Stono Ferry, near Charleston. The American Revolution was as much a civil war as it was a war of national independence from England. This was especially so in the Carolinas, where the citizenry was radically divided between Patriots (Whigs) and Loyalists (Tories). Indeed, North Carolina had the largest number of Loyalists of any of the American colonies, which meant that the war was not simply one of contending armies, but was fought among a local population with fiercely divided factions and loyalties.[3] The war between Patriots and Loyalists was also an internal domestic conflict that set neighbor against neighbor, brother against brother, and father against son.[4]

By 1780, when Jackson was thirteen, the British seemed to have the upper hand in the battlegrounds of North and South Carolina. Charleston, South Carolina, fell on May 12, 1780. The defeated forces of the Continental Army retreated northward toward North Carolina, but were routed by British forces under the command of Banastre Tarleton on May 29, 1780, in the

Battle of the Waxhaws. Jackson got his first taste of the sheer brutality of warfare at this battle, although he was not yet a soldier. During the battle, Tarleton's largely Loyalist forces killed 113 members of the Patriot militia and wounded 150. More important, the battle was noted for the way in which Loyalists deliberately killed surrendering Patriots. Dr. Robert Brownfield, a surgeon who treated the wounded, described it as "indiscriminate carnage never surpassed by the most ruthless atrocities of the most barbarous savages."[5] The surviving wounded soldiers were abandoned to the care of the settlers at a church meeting house converted into a hospital. Jackson's mother was among those who ministered to the wounded soldiers, and both Jackson and his sixteen-year-old brother Robert helped their mother treat the wounded, many of whom were horribly mangled with multiple wounds.[6]

A War of Revenge, Murder, and Mayhem

The so-called Waxhaws Massacre catalyzed an emerging rhetoric of atrocity and revenge that defined the way in which Patriots and Tories viewed one another.[7] Although it is sometimes difficult to sort out myth from reality, personal revenge was a powerful motive for many of the rebels.[8] One young patriot, Major Thomas Young, who joined the Patriot militia at age sixteen, was clear that he enlisted to avenge the murder of his brother John. In revenge, he claimed, more than one hundred Tories "felt the weight of his arm" and he personally hanged a local and reviled Tory named Adam Steedham.[9]

Like Young, Jackson and his brothers burned to avenge the dead and the wounded, particularly their brother who had been killed in the melee.[10] "Men hunted each other," said Amos Kendall, "like beasts of prey."[11] The main objective of both parties was to kill the fighting men, and thereby avenge the slaying of partisans.[12] The historian Augustus Buell called it a "savage carnival of internecine murder, where neighbor destroyed neighbor and families exterminated families."[13] Without first enlisting in any organized corps Jackson and his brother, along with many others, formed small parties that went out on single enterprises of retaliation, using their own horses and weapons.[14] In this murderous cauldron the laws and customs of war were routinely disregarded. There were few distinctions between soldiers and civilians, and even where different groups wore distinguishing signs or badges, they often used each other's badges as a mode of disguise.[15] Later in life, Jackson spoke about the madness of war during that time, particularly citing the case of one Patriot who, having found a friend murdered and mutilated, devoted himself to killing Tories. According to Jackson, he lay in wait for them and had killed twenty by war's end.[16]

Not long after setting out for war, Jackson and his brother Robert joined a cavalry unit under the command of Colonel William Davies, who made Jackson a mounted orderly (messenger) and gave him a pistol. Jackson also carried a small shotgun given to him by an uncle.[17] But the forces in which Jackson served were routed by a group of armed Loyalists dressed as Patriots, who were backed by a troop of British dragoons.[18] Jackson and his brother fled to a nearby house, but were soon discovered and captured. What followed became one of the most important episodes in Jackson's life. Not long after Jackson's capture, the officer in charge ordered him to clean the officer's boots. Jackson refused, demanding to be treated as a prisoner of war. Jackson's biographer James Parton described the scene: "The officer glared at him like a wild beast, and aimed a desperate blow at the boy's head with his sword. Andrew broke the force of the blow with his hand, and thus received two wounds—one deep gash on his head and another on his hand, the marks of which he carried to his grave. The officer, after achieving this gallant feat, turned to Robert Jackson, and ordered him to clean his boots. Robert also refused. The valiant Briton struck the young man so violent a sword blow upon the head, so as to prostrate and disable him."[19]

Jackson and his brother were nearly starved as prisoners of war and his brother's condition worsened. Ultimately both captives were released in a prisoner exchange, but Robert died a few days later, possibly of his wounds or of smallpox.[20] Not long after this, Jackson's mother and other women brought food and medicine to those held in the prison ships in Charleston (the prisoners included the sons of Mrs. Jackson's sister), where Mrs. Jackson caught fever and died.[21] Thus by age fifteen, his brothers and parents all dead, Jackson became an orphan of the American Revolution.[22]

Child Prisoners of War

The British soldiers' brutal treatment of Jackson and his brother was a commonplace experience for captured rebels during the war. Captured rebels were treated not as prisoners of war, but as traitors and criminals "destined to the cord," that is, the hangman's noose. Rebellion, in British eyes, was a capital offense and execution the just fate of rebels. Prisoners were routinely abused and beaten, and robberies, murders, and mock executions were common.[23] The worst excesses took place in New York, the center of British wartime operations during the Revolutionary War. Here the British created a notorious system of prison ships at Wallabout Bay in Brooklyn, just across the East River from Manhattan Island.[24] The British interned between 24,850 and 32,000 Americans in these prison ships and other places in New York, and between 15,575 and 18,000 of those prisoners died in captivity.

The majority of Revolutionary War soldiers came from the white male population aged sixteen and above, although by 1778 a large number of black volunteers and bondsmen serving as substitutes for their white masters were added to the ranks of the Continental Army.[25] During the American Revolution a total of 68,024 Americans were killed in action and other 10,000 died of wounds or disease. The death rate for captive prisoners was horrifying: the number of captives who died from systemic abuse and ill treatment was two or three times the number actually killed in battle.[26]

Age appears to have had little or no impact upon whether a person was interned as a prisoner. A twelve-year-old boy named Palmer served as the youngest crew member of the American privateer *Chance*; but when the British captured the ship they confined Palmer on the prison ship *Jersey* along with the rest of the *Chance*'s crew. Palmer apparently died of smallpox on the prison ship. On the night of his death, his captain, Thomas Dring, whom Palmer had always regarded as his protector, held onto Palmer during his convulsions as he screamed and begged for his mother and family.[27] Another boy, Daniel Bedinger, age fifteen, was one of about twenty-eight hundred prisoners captured by the British in the Battle of Fort Washington in Upper Manhattan in November 1776. He was first held in a sugar refinery in Lower Manhattan that had been converted into a prison, where many prisoners died of sickness, starvation, and exposure to the cold. He was ultimately transferred to one of the prison ships in Wallabout Bay, and was later released in a prisoner exchange, but never fully regained his health. Bedinger was lucky; only eight hundred of the prisoners captured at Fort Washington survived their imprisonment.[28]

Heroism and National Celebrity

The horrifying conditions of capture and imprisonment of American soldiers by the British were well known. Indeed, many who served in the Continental Army remained as living witnesses to the brutality of warfare, so Jackson's story no doubt rang true to many Americans in the early nineteenth century. The episode of Jackson's service and capture became central to Eaton's *Life of Andrew Jackson*. With the book in print, Jackson structured his presidential campaign around his story; and the heart of the story was the brave thirteen-year-old soldier who refused to bow down to a tyrant. Jackson himself seems to have been somewhat circumspect about his military service, but by the time he ran for president he was celebrated as the hero of two wars—the American Revolution and the War of 1812. Arguably, Jackson was the first president of the United States to be democratically elected.[29] As Jill Lepore has put it, "Americans first voted for a President whose campaign touted him as a rugged, stubborn, hot-tempered war hero";[30] Jackson the war hero was a child soldier.

Ishmael Beah: Child Soldier of the Civil War in Sierra Leone

Ishmael Beah was born on November 23, 1980, in a fishing village in Bonthe District in southern Sierra Leone. Beah's memoir of his recruitment and service as a child soldier sold over a million and a half copies, and the book was studied on college campuses across America. He is regarded as one of the most widely read contemporary African writers. According to his memoir, in 1993 his village was attacked by rebel soldiers of the Revolutionary United Front (RUF), the Sierra Leonean rebel group known for its murderous cruelty in the treatment of the civilian population, including the widespread amputation of civilians' hands and arms. The attack on his village was the beginning of Beah's odyssey of flight, recruitment, and rehabilitation, a journey punctuated by a series of horrifying episodes that shaped his life's narrative.

Beah's account begins with his visit in 1993 to the village of Matter Jong, which came under sudden attack by the forces of the RUF. Beah and several companions fled, but soon realized they would not be able to feed themselves without money, so they sneaked back into the village to retrieve funds. After they escaped again from the village, they wandered through the countryside looking for a zone of safety and hoping perhaps to reconnect with Beah's parents. The boys were briefly captured by rebels, witnessed the torture and mock execution of an old man by rebel fighters, and were forcibly recruited into the rebel ranks. Beah learned that those not selected for recruitment would be marched to a river and shot, but the whole episode was interrupted by gunfire and he again fled. He wandered through an apocalyptic countryside of burned villages, piled high with dead and mutilated bodies and full of fearful and hostile survivors who sometimes threatened and robbed him. He saw rebel soldiers who had just burned down villages, carrying the severed head of one of their victims. Finally, after a long journey, Beah was captured by Sierra Leone Army (SLA) government soldiers and believed he had found safety; instead, he was forced into service as a child soldier.

Civil War in Sierra Leone

The war in which Beah was compelled to fight was a brutal civil war, with vicious cruelty exercised by all sides of the conflict. Though the RUF was marked by its extreme brutality toward civilians, the SLA was also a predatory force and was ruthless in its treatment of enemy combatants. The army killed virtually all enemy soldiers and offered no quarter to the wounded or captured. As Beah's commanding officer, the "Lieutenant," explains, all rebels must be killed: "We are not like the rebels," he says, "those riffraff's who kill people for no reason. We kill them for the good and betterment of the country."[31] The army gives Beah an AK-47 assault rifle, trains him to use the bayonet, and orders him to kill all rebels and leave none alive. He is introduced to the use of drugs, including marijuana, brown-brown (a mixture of cocaine and gunpowder), and white capsules (probably amphetamines), and attacks a village where he shoots and kills "everything that moves" and watches as swamp crabs feast on the eyes of the dead.[32]

But this is only the beginning of his descent into violence and the commission of horrible war crimes. His troop raids both enemy camps and civilian villages to capture recruits. They force other civilians to carry loot. He and his fellow SLA soldiers kill all the wounded, and round up prisoners for hideous and gruesome executions. In one instance, Beah wins a killing exhibition and contest that involves slitting the throats of captured rebels to see who dies first. In another, prisoners are forced to dig their own graves, and Beah joins in tying them up, bayoneting them in the legs, and burying the screaming captives alive as he and his companions laugh and joke.

Victimization and Celebrity

The violence of Beah's life carries over into his demobilization experience. The SLA agrees to comply with UN demands, and suddenly Beah is demobilized as a child soldier and turned over to UNICEF. Although he should have surrendered his weapons, Beah hides a hand grenade and a knife in his clothing. Later, in a camp for former child soldiers, he and his SLA comrades enter into a pitched battle with former child soldiers of the RUF, and six child soldiers are killed before order is restored. Beah makes plain in his memoirs that he wholeheartedly participated in these and many other atrocities. To Beah's credit, he casts a gimlet eye on the parade of humanitarian and human rights workers who keep telling him that no matter what he did it was "not his fault." He is quite aware of his complicity in the war crimes he willfully committed and of his personal culpability for murder.

But Beah was also quite lucky. He is charming and charismatic, and people like him. He gained the personal attention of Esther, a nurse at a mini-hospital associated with the UNICEF rehabilitation center, who continued to emphasize that nothing he did was his fault. Beah states that "even though I had heard that phrase from every staff member—and frankly I had always hated it—I began that day to believe it." From then on there was a rapid change in the course of Beah's life. Visitors from UNICEF and the European Commission came to the center and in a talent show for the visiting dignitaries Beah read from Shakespeare's *Julius Caesar* and performed a short hip-hop play about the redemption of a child soldier that he had written with Esther's encouragement.[33] Soon afterward, he was selected as a spokesman for the center and began talking to gatherings in Freetown about how to end child soldiering and rehabilitate former child soldiers. Not long after that, he was interviewed and selected by the UN to travel to New York to participate in the First International Children's Parliament and to speak before the UN Economic and Social Council. He returned to Sierra Leone and then ultimately fled the country. While in New York, he met Laura Simms, who eventually adopted him when he returned to the United States in 1998 at the age of seventeen.

Beah completed high school at the United Nations International School and went on to Oberlin College, where he wrote the original drafts of his memoirs and graduated in 2004. He became an internationally known spokesman and advocate for the plight of child soldiers and children in conflict zones. He was appointed UNICEF's first advocate on children affected by war. He served on Human Rights Watch's Children's Rights Division Advisory Committee. He testified before the U.S. Congress and regularly speaks on college campuses across the United States and in many other key policy venues, such as the Aspen Institute, the Council on Foreign Relations, and the U.S. Marine Corps' Warfighting Laboratory. He has also founded the Ishmael Beah Foundation, which provides direct assistance to war-affected children in Sierra Leone to help them further their education and reintegrate them into Sierra Leone society.

In this age of fact-checking, Beah's memoirs have been subject to intense scrutiny. The Sydney, Australia, newspaper the *Australian* raised a number of questions about the accuracy of his story and whether or not some of the events portrayed happened at all. UNICEF, for example, could not verify the deadly incident in its camp that resulted in the death of six teenagers that is described in Beah's memoirs. Likewise, the *Australian* could not find anyone who remembered this incident or who filed a report about it. Nevertheless, UNICEF maintained that *Long Way Gone* is "a credible account of the tragedy of recruitment of children into armed groups, told by one who undoubtedly experienced this abuse firsthand."[34] Nonetheless, the negative reporting on the book has inflicted damage. Chris Blattman, who extensively researched child soldiers in Uganda, doubts the accuracy of Beah's book. He states, "We are told what we want and expect to hear when we ask for desperate and tragic tales. The truth is of secondary importance."[35] Neil Boothbay, who has had extensive experience with child soldiers, has also cast some doubt on the veracity of the book. Boothbay's criticism stems from the fact that Beah's account includes almost every possible trauma that could ever occur to a child soldier, and suggests that it would be unlikely for all of these to have happened to a single person. Like Blattman, he suggests that Beah was egged on by UNICEF, psychologists, and journalists to produce a sensationalist account of trauma and rehabilitation. Despite this, both Beah and his publisher have insisted on the truthfulness or at least the "truthiness" of the accounts.[36] Nowadays Beah maintains an ironic distance from attempts to portray him as a brainwashed and traumatized victim of war. He recently regaled an audience of appreciative anthropologists with tales about how his glassy-eyed teenage boredom during endless meetings with humanitarian and human rights officials was invariably described by these officials as the effect of "trauma."[37] Despite all these difficulties, like Andrew Jackson, Beah has emerged from war as a star. But instead of serving as a symbol of militant patriotism, his experience as a child soldier serves as a symbolic proxy of all that is wrong with war.

Boy Soldiers in the American Revolution

This chapter began with the particular story of Andrew Jackson, but his experience as a child soldier was hardly unique. During the American Revolution the armies, militias, and partisan groups of both sides were filled with children. Colonial militias played a vital role in the emerging youth culture in America. Organized in opposition to dominant Puritan values, youth culture began to take shape around militia training days, which afforded young people the opportunity to congregate and, to the alarm of many adults, allowed youngsters to meet, smoke, carouse, and swagger.[38] Between 30 and 40 percent of adolescent males participated in armed conflict between 1740 and 1781.[39] Indeed, American Revolutionary leaders were much younger than Loyalist leaders, and local militias were often organized at college campuses, which were themselves cauldrons of revolutionary thinking.[40] Teenagers played a major role in American resistance to British rule. Between 1765 and 1760, there were at least 150 anti-British riots in the American colonies, and the rioting mobs were filled with teenage apprentices and youthful laborers. Not surprisingly, these teenagers filled the ranks of the Continental Army. The army itself was composed largely of men and boys drawn from the poor, the young, the marginal, and the unfree. With half the American population under age sixteen, it is not surprising that the Continental Army was filled with boys of every age.[41]

One of the best descriptions of life in the Continental Army during the American Revolution was written by Joseph Plumb Martin, only fifteen years old when he enlisted along with many of his peers.[42] Daniel Granger, another thirteen-year-old Revolutionary War soldier, penned a lengthy memoir of his service.[43] Granger was involved in several battles, witnessed the execution of deserters and others, and otherwise experienced all the pleasures and privations of an ordinary soldier. What is remarkable about Granger's memoir is how unremarkable the issue of his age was. Granger enlisted when his older brother was already in the army but had been taken ill. Granger's parents sent him to the barracks to bring his brother back home to recuperate and, if possible, substitute for him. When he arrived, several officers questioned him as to whether he could perform the duties of a soldier and recruited him on the spot.[44] Following the war, he settled in Sasco, Maine, where he served as a customs agent during the Jefferson and Monroe administrations and became commissioner of prisoners during the War of 1812.[45]

Another boy soldier, Peter Francisco, joined the Tenth Virginia Regiment at age sixteen and became a widely known hero of the American Revolution. Francisco was from the Azores and may have been forcibly brought to America as an indentured servant. As a child he was bound out to the estate of an uncle of Patrick Henry. Because of his great strength and size he was called the Virginia Giant or the Virginian Hercules, and he fought in many battles of the American Revolution, including Brandywine, Germantown, Monmouth, and most notably Guilford Courthouse in Greensboro, North Carolina.[46] When he died in 1831 he was a widely celebrated hero and folk legend of the American Revolution, although today—along with most of the common soldiers of the American Revolution—he is largely forgotten.[47] Nevertheless, in the United States at least four monuments have been erected in his honor—in Hopewell, Virginia; Newark, New Jersey; Greensboro, North Carolina; and New Bedford, Massachusetts, where he is celebrated as a Revolutionary hero of Portuguese descent. In 1976, the two hundredth anniversary of the Revolution, the U.S. Postal Service issued a commemorative stamp in his honor. In 2009, a fictional account of his life was published, titled *Hercules of the Revolution*.[48]

These are but a few examples of a widespread phenomenon. Given the pull of adventure and the clamor for patriotism, it is little wonder that so many youngsters fought in the Revolution. Caroline Cox's recent analysis of pension applications and memoirs of former Revolutionary soldiers reveals the pervasive presence of boy soldiers under age sixteen in the American Revolution.[49] The available records of the many regiments camped at Valley Forge with Washington during the winter of 1777–1778 show that there were many youngsters in regiments from all over the county. In the First to Eight Connecticut regiments, 179 of 655 soldiers (27.3 percent) were between ages twelve and seventeen. In the nine companies of the New York Second Regiment, 52 of 188 soldiers (27.6 percent) were between ages twelve and seventeen. In Rhode Island's First and Second Regiments, 35 of 109 (32 percent) were between the ages of thirteen and seventeen. Of the 922 soldiers of the Pennsylvania Line of the Continental Army between 1775 and 1783, 113 (12 percent) were ten to seventeen. The age range of soldiers serving in the Revolutionary War was far greater than is the case with modern armies. In the Pennsylvania Line there were four youngsters aged ten and one man who was seventy-three. The vast majority of young soldiers across the militias and regiments of the revolutionary forces were fifteen, sixteen, or seventeen years old. Many of the youngest were fifers and drummers, but many were also ordinary private soldiers. The age ranges differ to some degree by regional and other circumstances, but it is clear that the armies of the Revolution were filled with youngsters from ages twelve to seventeen.[50] What all this makes clear is that children and teenagers were a regular and unremarkable part of the armed forces of the American Revolution.

The eighteenth century was clearly a time when ideas about childhood were undergoing many transformations and the boundaries between childhood and adulthood were not settled. Age sixteen often distinguished between children and adults, but a strong child of fourteen was often a more desired recruit than an older child. Boys regularly enlisted either independently or as substitutes for drafted fathers, brothers, neighbors, or even strangers. Younger children often substituted for older children or fathers, whose labor was more significant to the family.[51] Neither the family nor the state was able to exert consistent control over boys, who like others in the era of the American Revolution saw military service as a way to become masters of their own fate.[52]

Boy Soldiers in the American Civil War

Boy soldiers also figured prominently both in reality and in legend in the American Civil War.[53] Throughout that war, youngsters followed brothers, fathers, and teachers into the army. They often had support roles, but quickly graduated into combat roles. They were sometimes recruited at school, and when necessary, they were issued weapons that had been cut down and adapted for use by younger people. There are numerous examples of famous boy soldiers: David Baily Freemen, "Little Dave," enlisted in the Confederate Army at age eleven, first accompanying his older brother as an aide-de-camp and then as a marker for a survey team, before finally fighting against Sherman's army.[54] Avery Brown enlisted at the age of eight years, eleven months, and thirteen days in the Ohio Volunteer Infantry. Known as the "Drummer Boy of the Cumberland," he lied about his age on his enlistment papers, claiming to be twelve years old.[55]

Perhaps the most famous boy soldier of the Civil War was John Lincoln Clem (August 13, 1851—May 13, 1937). Known as the Drummer Boy of Chickamauga, Clem was ten years old when President Abraham Lincoln issued his first call for volunteers in May 1861. He tried to enlist in the Third Ohio Infantry, but was rejected because of his age and size. In June 1861, after much persistence, he was accepted into the Twenty-Second Michigan Infantry as a combination regimental mascot and emergency drummer boy. He was provided with a uniform, a drum, and—to enable him to carry a gun—a sawed-off musket. He distinguished himself in the fighting—firing his gun—at the Battle of Chickamauga in 1863, and was promoted to sergeant, becoming, at age twelve, the youngest noncommissioned officer ever to have served in the U.S. Army. He spent his entire life in the army and at age sixty-four, at the beginning of World War I, retired as a major general and the last Civil War veteran on active duty.[56] Clem died in 1937 and was buried in Arlington National Cemetery.

National Honors for Child Soldiers

The history of recipients of the Congressional Medal of Honor in the United States also attests to the presence of children on the battlefield. For example, the youngest award winner was William "Willie" Johnson, a musician in the Vermont Infantry who, at the request of Abraham Lincoln, received his award for his bravery under fire at age twelve.[57] There were numerous other Civil War recipients, including Benjamin Levy, a private in the First New York Infantry. He enlisted as a drummer boy, but he took the gun of a sick comrade and went into battle at Glendale, Virginia, in 1862. He was cited for bravery for saving the colors from capture when the color bearers were shot down.[58] Another example is James Machon, who was born in England in 1848. He held the rank of "boy" on the USS *Brooklyn* and received his medal at age sixteen for his bravery during the 1864 attack on Fort Morgan in Mobile Bay, Alabama. His citation describes him as having "remained steadfast at his post and performed his duties in the powder division throughout the furious action."[59] Similarly, John Angling, born in 1850 and a cabin boy aboard the USS *Pontoosuc* in December 1864, was recommended for "gallantry and skill and for his cool courage while under the fire of the enemy."[60] Orion P. Howe received the medal for heroic action at age fourteen at the siege of Vicksburg, Mississippi. John Kountz, who enlisted at age fourteen, received his medal for heroic action at age sixteen in the Battle of Missionary Ridge. Robinson Barr Murphy enlisted at age thirteen as an orderly and was awarded the medal for heroic action under fire at age fifteen, when he led two regiments into battle near Atlanta. James Snedden, age fifteen, received his medal for heroic action under fire at Piedmont, Virginia, and Julian Scott received his for heroic action under fire when he was age fifteen at the Battle at Lee's Mill, Virginia, in 1862. His younger brother also enlisted, at age thirteen. William Horsfall was honored for his heroic action under fire at age fifteen during the siege of Corinth, Mississippi, and William Magee was awarded the medal for heroic action under fire at Murfreesboro, Tennessee, in 1864, when he was fifteen years old.

There were other honorees who enlisted as boys and grew to adulthood while under arms. These include Galusha Pennypacker, who enlisted in the Ninth Pennsylvania infantry regiment at age sixteen, and by age twenty became the youngest person ever to hold the rank of brigadier general in the U.S. Army.[61] Of course the vast majority of boy soldiers were not medal winners. These include Alfred Woolsey, who was born in 1850 and enlisted at age fourteen as a drummer boy in the First Minnesota Heavy Artillery Regiment after his father was wounded at the Battle of Shiloh. He was discharged after the war and lived to become the oldest surviving

Union soldier of the Civil War. When he died in 1956, President Dwight David Eisenhower eulogized him, stating that "the American people have lost the last personal link with the Union Army. . . . His passing brings sorrow to the hearts of all of us who cherished the memory of the brave men on both sides of the War Between the States."[62]

How Many Boys?

How many youngsters served in the military during the American Civil War? It is generally accepted that about 2.1 million soldiers and sailors served in the Union forces during the Civil War and that about 882,000 soldiers and sailors served in the Confederate forces.[63] During the war, Benjamin Gould of the U.S. Sanitary Commission undertook a statistical analysis of the ages of soldiers in the Union Army as of 1864. He examined the recorded ages in military rosters of 1,049,457 soldiers, which showed that 1.2 percent of the soldiers were under eighteen years of age.[64] George Kilmer, a former Union officer and military historian, believed Gould's figures were unreliable because of the large numbers of volunteers who misrepresented their age. In 1905, Kilmer reviewed Gould's data and pointed out a number of statistical anomalies that led him to assert that at least 100,000 boys who were listed as being age eighteen were not even sixteen or seventeen. This did not include the thousands who were officially listed as sixteen or seventeen or younger.[65] In 1911, Charles King, a career military officer, asserted that the Civil War was fought by a "grand army of boys." He claimed that 800,000 soldiers were below age seventeen, 200,000 were under sixteen, and another 100,000 were no more than fifteen.[66] King did not explain how he obtained these figures, and we have no way of fully judging the accuracy of his claims. King had a long and distinguished career in the U.S. military; he was a West Point graduate who participated in the Civil War and retired from active service in 1879, but continued on in the military through the Spanish-American War and World War I. It may well be that he had a good understanding of the general age and composition of military units. Nevertheless, if King's figures are taken at face value, more than half the Union Army of 2.1 million would have been below age eighteen, a figure that seems somewhat exaggerated.

However, more accurate recent evidence points to a very large number of children in the armies of the Civil War, even if not quite the huge percentage claimed by King. In 2006, Judith Pizzaro, Roxanne Cohen Silver, and JoAnn Prause examined the full medical records of recruits from 303 randomly selected companies of the Union Army. The data were drawn from the descriptive roll books in the U.S. National Archives, and yielded a sample of 35,730 individuals. Of this larger sample, 15,027 recruits who lived until at least 1890 were selected for the analysis of their medical histories, which showed that 3,013 (20 percent) were recruited into the Union ranks between the ages of nine and seventeen.[67] Assuming the random sample is representative of all recruits across the armed forces, approximately 420,000 of the 2.1 million soldiers in the Union forces were between nine and seventeen. While this number is less than half of what King suggested, it still represents a very significant number of child soldiers. The number of youngsters in the Union forces alone would have been greater than the numbers of child soldiers said to exist in the world today, usually estimated between 250,000 and 300,000 soldiers under eighteen. While we do not have comparable data for the armies of the Confederacy, it is not unreasonable to assume that the figures would be proportionately similar. There is no reason to believe that the Confederacy was more lax in this respect, despite General U. S. Grant's charges that the Confederacy in particular had robbed both the cradle and the grave to sustain its forces.[68] So even if it is impossible to pin down exact numbers, the presence of underage recruits throughout the army was a well-known and accepted fact of life throughout the Civil War.

Boy Soldiers as Noble Patriots

It is important not only to note the presence of these boy soldiers in the Civil War, but also to understand how their participation in the war was understood at the time. Writings about boy soldiers in the aftermath of the Civil War constitute a hagiographic genre celebrating the nobility and sacrifice of young boys in battle. Testimonials collected by Susan Hull in 1905 describe Confederate boy soldiers as enduring battle with "patience and gaiety" and those who died as having "made their peace with God." Equally important, the experience of battle, however horrible, was understood not as destroying the lives of children but as ennobling them. Boy soldiers who survived intact were described as respected citizens whose contribution to civic life was enhanced by their experience of war.[69] While it may not be

possible to verify the accuracy of these accounts, they are significant precisely because they highlight radically different views of children in battle
than those of contemporary humanitarian accounts.

In a similar vein, former boy soldier John Lincoln Clem, writing shortly
before his retirement from the U.S. Army in 1915, applauded the idea of
boy soldiers. He wrote that the thousands of underage boys who enlisted
in the Union Army were very welcome in the regiments, were prized for
their youthful enthusiasm, and made excellent soldiers. Boys, he added,
were good for the army, and the training and experience were valuable for
them. Most importantly, he argued that of all soldiers they had the highest
degree of élan because of their ambition, skill, endurance, fearlessness,
and willingness to obey orders. His one caveat was that he did not believe
that boys had sufficient judgment to command. Clem did not gloss over
the horrors of war, but he also thought that boys, by their very nature,
were especially well suited for combat. "War," he wrote, "is bald, naked
savagery. Disguise the fact though we may try, it properly bears that definition. As compared with the adult man, the boy is near to the savage."[70]

Developmental differences between boys and men were widely recognized but understood rather differently than they would be today.
Although young boys were regarded as impulsive and less mature than
older men, these qualities were interpreted as grand and heroic. Today,
most humanitarian accounts of child soldiers cite their fearlessness, lack
of caution, and willingness to obey orders as reasons for excluding them
from combat. In the Civil War these were precisely the qualities that made
them prized combatants in both armies.

The Rites of Martyrdom: Memorializing Child Soldiers

Another way to begin to understand nineteenth-century attitudes toward
child soldiers is by examining the rituals and ceremonies that accompanied
the death of young soldiers. Funerals and other forms of commemoration
for fallen soldiers usually involve rituals that shape and reflect community
and national solidarity.[71] Such funerals not only memorialize the dead, but
also give meaning to their deaths and their individual sacrifices within a
narrative of communal history and solidarity. As with all types of mortuary
ceremonies, even the emotions of the bereaved are shaped by cultural and

social conventions.[72] In large-scale societies, where most people are strangers to one another, such ceremonies can create, at least for a moment in time, a collective intimacy among citizens.[73] In most instances, the dead soldier is one of many thousands of ordinary and nearly anonymous private individuals. But in death, the deceased can achieve personal and collective recognition and a kind of social immortality.[74]

During the Civil War, these key public rituals also incorporated and embodied particularly American concepts of what Drew Gilpin Faust has described as the "good death."[75] Ideas about the good death were deeply embedded in nineteenth-century American culture. They transcended religious and denominational boundaries and became a general system of beliefs about life's meaning. The good death was a final and powerful personal demonstration, and socially significant symbol, of the way the deceased's life had been lived and his or her belief, hope, and salvation. Ideas about how to die spread broadly, and were even distributed in Sunday school tracts across the nation. In many ways, nineteenth-century ideas of the good death stand in opposition to modern ideas about dying. In the nineteenth century, the ideal death involved consciousness and the ability to contemplate one's demise. Few people living around the time of the Civil War would have embraced sudden death in war or in peace, even one without pain, as ideal. Death required both preparation and performance, because it "epitomized a life already led and predicted the quality of life everlasting." As a result, the ideal death was "witnessed, scrutinized, narrated, and interpreted."[76]

The Civil War fused cultural and theological notions of the good death with powerful strains of patriotism. The good death was central to the songs, stories, and poetry of the Civil War.[77] In wartime, families could rarely, if ever, witness the final moments of a loved one. In the aftermath of battle, those among the dying who were able were encouraged to write letters home. More frequently, conveying the details of action and words of the dying to their family member by letter was a powerfully felt duty, accepted by friends, comrades, physicians, nurses, even enemy soldiers. The last words of the dying person were central to the idea of a good death. They were cherished in particular because they were signs of salvation and imposed meaning on the life narrative of the dying. And because they could survive as teachings, the last words served as a continuous link between the living and the dead.[78] The image of the Christian soldier's sacrifice combined the elements of patriotism and faith. But the death of a Christian boy soldier magnified these elements tenfold.

Luther Ladd (1843–1861)

The first Union soldier to be killed in the Civil War was seventeen-year-old Luther Ladd of the Lowell City Guards, part of the Sixth Regiment of the Massachusetts Volunteer Militia. Ladd was killed in the secessionist riots in Baltimore on April 19, 1861.[79] Born in Bristol, New Hampshire, on December 22, 1843, at his father's farm, Ladd spent much of his early life doing farm work and attending school. By 1860, he had migrated to Lowell, Massachusetts, one of the largest industrial and textile centers in the United States. By 1852, Lowell was the home to the "mile of mills" along the Merrimac River, where more than twelve thousand workers and thousands of looms produced millions of yards of cloth each year. Most of the textile mill workers in Lowell were girls and young women from rural New England, some as young as ten years old, but men and boys also found work in the many machine shops that serviced the mills. Like many young women and girls, Ladd's sisters found work in the mills; Ladd went to work in the Lowell Machine Shop.[80] Lowell itself was a staunchly abolitionist town, but it was dependent on cotton from the South. After the war began, the supply of cotton dwindled, many of the mills were idled, and many men and boys went to war.

On April 15, 1861, President Lincoln issued his first call for seventy-five thousand volunteers from the state militias, and Ladd's regiment was sent to Washington, D.C. On April 19, only a week after the Confederate attack on Fort Sumter, the regiment was attacked by a mob as it marched through Baltimore on the way to board the train to Washington. Ladd was the first to fall, followed by several others, including another soldier from Lowell, Addison Whitney. Ladd's skull was fractured and a bullet severed an artery in his thigh. He bled to death from his wounds. Within a few days, the bodies of Ladd and Whitney were taken by train to Lowell. No one had been killed in battle at Fort Sumter, so these were the first deaths of the Civil War; the funeral, held at Lowell's main public venue Huntington Hall, was densely packed. Business was generally suspended and mills were shut down. Thousands tried to attend but were unable to squeeze into the hall.[81]

The story of Luther Ladd was widely told in the press and repeated at the funeral. Ladd was described as a young farmer who, along with all the patriotic citizens of Massachusetts, anxiously watched the progress of the southern rebellion and was determined to defend his country. The fact that he was a minor was deemed no barrier to his enlistment. His sisters were said to be "too patriotic themselves to try to dissuade him from responding to his country's call."[82] On the eve of his departure, his brother-in-law is said to have offered to intercede on his behalf because of his age, but only to "test his resolution." Most significantly, it was declared that at the very moment of his death, he cast "a farewell look at the flag that waved over him" and "with glassy eyes, fainting from loss of blood, he fell, exclaiming with his dying breath, 'All Hail To the Stars and Stripes!'"

Whether Ladd actually uttered these dying words is unknown. The situation in Baltimore was chaotic. Ladd's regiment fought its way through the armed mob to reach the train station and board the train to Washington. The mob fired on the troops, killing and wounding some and using the weapons of the fallen against the remaining troops. The troops were not well disciplined and were described as rushing along "pell-mell."[83] There were difficulties in identifying the bodies of the deceased when they were packed in ice and shipped to Boston from Baltimore. Whitney, who had been a spinner in the Middlesex Mills in Lowell, was identified by friends. Ladd, however, had not been seen since the battle in Baltimore, and it was only a letter from Ladd's brother, who was in the same regiment in Washington, that alerted authorities that Ladd's body might be on the train. In Lowell, Ladd's body was identified by his brother-in-law, and although he was shot in the thigh and had bled to death from the wound, it was reported that his "face was somewhat swollen, and gave evidence of rough usage."[84] Given these circumstances, it is by no means certain who, if anyone, was on hand to witness Ladd's famous last words or report them. Fictional or not, they carried great cultural weight. Such dying declarations were believed to be the truth, and for families to be deprived of the last words of their kinsmen was a source of unbearable grief.[85] Whatever the true source of Ladd's last words, by the time the funeral was held in Lowell, they were fixed in the public imagination of Ladd's final moments of life and publicly displayed at the ceremonies on banners hung above the crowd.

The funeral itself was a fiery exercise in patriotism and northern anger at the death of its first soldiers. The rioters and the rebels in general were regarded as murderers. In his funeral address the Reverend R. W. Clark charged that "every American should love his country with unparalleled ardor as the grand pioneer of Christian civilization." Calling Confederate secession "black-hearted treason," he foretold that coming generations will come to regard them as "goblins damned." Recalling the prophecies of Isaiah, he asserted that "providence has already 'bathed his sword in heaven' and that 'sword shall devour and be satiate and made drunk with their blood.'" The last words of the dying Ladd were declared by the *Massachusetts Gazette* to be "treasured" and would serve as a "talisman" for other young men to "emulate the devotion to her welfare of this heroic youth." Clark called for the erection of a monument to "all that was mortal of the noble youth."[86] The souls of the youthful lad and his companions were hailed to be "marching on," and he and all of his regiment had "breasted the storm raised by the semi-barbarians."[87]

Ladd's death and his last words reverberated across literary and popular culture in poetry and song. George T. Bourse's poem "All Hail to the Stars and Stripes" declared,

> All hail the Stars and Stripes!
> The words
> Are graven now, on every heart
> A Nation's watchword—Freedom's song!
> Of every future act a part.[88]

Another poem, "Apocalypse," by Richard Realf, an abolitionist and former compatriot of John Brown, declared,

> Thus, like a king, erect in pride,
> Raising his hands to heaven, he cried,
> "All hail the Stars and Stripes!" and died.[89]

B. B. Wade, published his poem "All Hail the Stars and Stripes" in the New York literary magazine *Knickerbocker* in 1862, declaiming,

> The dying youth his flag beside,
> The death-damp from his forehead wipes,

As, throwing wide his arms, he cried,
All Hail! All Hail! The Stars and Stripes![90]

As the legend of Ladd spread, it began to take on different forms. G. Gumpert's song "The Dying Volunteer" was dedicated to Ladd, but completely mythologized his biography, portraying him as a young man with a widowed wife and a child. Gumpert also fictionalized Ladd's father, who was alive and well, as having also died for his country in an unnamed battle, and portrayed Ladd's own enlistment and death as the noble fulfillment of a childhood promise to his dead father:

My father died on freedom's field,
I promis'd on his knee,
That I would fight and never yield,
Until our land was free.
All hail to the Stars and Stripes.[91]

In this adult version, the trope of the dying volunteer continued to spread across the country. J. P. Webster composed a new version in Chicago for the volunteers of the prairie states; another new version was composed by Andrew Boyd in Boston; and by 1865 it had spread to the Confederacy, with A.E.A. Muse's composition in New Orleans in which the dying Confederate volunteer proclaimed to his mother "for stamped in my brain were the last words from thee, Though life be the forfeit be true to thy flag."[92] In this way the death of the first soldier, a boy of seventeen, came to represent not the tragedy of the death of a child but the noble sacrifices of all volunteers to the Union and Confederate causes.

Four years later, at the end of the Civil War, a monument to Ladd and Whitney was raised and dedicated the center of Lowell, Massachusetts. Once again, it was a grand patriotic moment that attracted twenty thousand people.[93] Army regiments accompanied an immense procession of citizens led by fraternal and benevolent organizations such as the Masons and Odd Fellows. Massachusetts Governor John Albion Andrew, a major force in the creation of the Fifty-Fourth Regiment, the famous black army unit led by Robert Gould Shaw, offered the dedication speech. The emphasis in the ceremony was on the sacrifice of youth, the principle of human liberty, and "the two young artisans of Lowell, who fell among the first martyrs of the great rebellion." The monument, Andrew declared, would "speak to your children, not of death, but of immortality. It shall stand here, a mute, expressive witness of the beauty and the dignity of youth and manly prime consecrated in unselfish obedience to duty."[94]

Clarence McKenzie (1849–1861)

Less than two months after the death of Ladd, another boy soldier's death again focused the nation's attention on the sacrifices of young soldiers. This was the accidental shooting in Annapolis, Maryland, of twelve-year-old drummer boy Clarence McKenzie of Brooklyn, New York. McKenzie, known as the Little Drummer Boy, was born on February 18, 1849, and enlisted in the drum corps of the Thirteenth Regiment of the New York State Militia, the National Grays, on July 9, 1860, at age eleven. He was killed by a fellow soldier in a shooting accident and died in Annapolis, Maryland, on June 11, 1861. He was twelve years, four months, and three days old. McKenzie was killed about six weeks before the Battle of Bull Run (July 21, 1861), the first major combat of the Civil War.

McKenzie was born into poverty in Brooklyn, lived in tenements with his parents and siblings, and attended the John Street Mission Sunday School. As his family moved from residence to residence, he attended other mission schools, the last of which was that of the Lawrence Street Presbyterian Church. He was widely regarded as a model student and devoted Christian, and was awarded a leather-bound Bible by the school shortly before he enlisted. His mother was opposed to his enlistment, but he was supported by his father. He is reported to have comforted his mother by telling her not to be afraid because he was such a little boy that no one would try to shoot him. McKenzie's older brother Willy also enlisted as a drummer boy in the regiment. McKenzie was widely liked in the regiment and bunked with the regiment's captain. He was thought of as a "child of the regiment."[95] On June 12, 1861, McKenzie was killed when another soldier accidentally discharged a rifle and fatally shot him in the back. He died about two hours after being shot. There were many witnesses to McKenzie's death, and all agree that in the end he forgave the soldier who shot him. His last conscious words were, "Oh my dear God, I hope you will save my soul."

Clarence McKenzie was buried on June 14, 1861, in a ceremony that attracted thousands of mourners. The coffin and funeral cortege traveled from his home on Liberty Street to Saint John's Church in downtown Brooklyn and then onward for the three-and-a-half-mile journey to Greenwood Cemetery. The more than three thousand mourners included public school and Sunday school children, and the funeral itself was described as being one of "such public demonstrations of respect and sympathy as is rarely exhibited."[96] The *Brooklyn Daily Eagle* provided a detailed account of the accident that resulted in McKenzie's death as well as the preparation and shipment of his body back to Brooklyn. McKenzie was borne to the grave by the captain of his company and the friends who were with him when he died, accompanied by a guard of honor, muffled drums, and draped colors. The *Daily Eagle* described the way the children of Public School I and the Congregational Sabbath School "bid a long farewell to the friend of their early days."[97]

At the funeral service itself, the Reverend Thomas F. Guion, the rector at Saint John's Church, declared that McKenzie's death was the "first fruit of the rebellion" and called upon the mourners to drive the traitors, the "responsible authors of this child's death" down to the Gulf of Mexico and crush the conspiracy.[98] In a speech that roused patriotic fervor, he called upon the mourners to remember the duties they owed to themselves, God, and country.[99] A second funeral sermon was delivered by the Reverend Adam McClelland, the blind preacher of the Fort Green Presbyterian Church and one of the most well-known ministers in Brooklyn.[100] McClelland specifically addressed the children with a direct religious message. He declared, "We loved this boy because of his sweet and genial disposition, for the noble patriotism that fired even his young bosom; but we loved him most of all because we believed him to have been a child chosen of his God."[101] Not long afterward, the Dutch Reform Church in New York compiled a detailed account of the events of McKenzie's life and death, directed primarily to the children and youth of Sunday schools and to soldiers in the field.[102]

After the war, McKenzie's regiment continued to honor him as a child of the regiment. The Grand Army of the Republic, the four-hundred-thousand-strong Union veterans organization, named a post in Brooklyn after him. In a memorial service in 1884 at the Fort Green Presbyterian Church, his last words were again recalled and he was saluted as one of those who marched to battle with a patriotism born of Christianity.[103] In

1886, a statue of McKenzie was erected at Brooklyn's Greenwood Cemetery, dedicated to "Our Drummer Boy." The inscription on the monument proclaims, "This young life was the first offering from King's County in the War of the Rebellion."

Joseph Darrow (1846–1861)

Joseph Darrow joined the New York State Militia at age fifteen. He enlisted as a private on April 18, 1861, at Brooklyn, New York, and was mustered into the Eighty-Fourth Infantry shortly thereafter. On July 21, 1861, he was wounded at the Battle of Bull Run. He was captured and died on September 26, 1861. He is buried at Shockoe Hill Cemetery in Richmond, Virginia.[104]

Darrow's funeral sermon was delivered by Bernard Harrison Nadel, a confidant of Abraham Lincoln and a staunch supporter of the Union.[105] Reverend Nadel reflected on the character of a boy who was gentle in nature and attractive to all who knew him. He stated, "I found it almost impossible to conceive of him in the stern work of fighting . . . as pressing fiercely in a charge, rifle in hand, shooting, cutting, thrusting with deadly purpose."[106] Nevertheless, he described Darrow's character as manly. "Joseph," he said, "was never a child, at least not like the others; but an instance of manly care and thoughtfulness in infantile habiliments."[107]

In his funeral sermon, Nadel described the social and cultural forces that gripped both the northern states and New York City at the beginning of the war. "You well remember," he said, "how the flags flew from steeple and roof and window, how drum and fife crescendoed, how pulpit and nostrum poured blasting and thunderous broadsides, and how the great warwave of excitement rolled wildly, fiercely over the whole country, and then rolled back, and back, and back again." This was a war in which "Patriotism and Christianity were at one. . . . Praying and preaching and arming and mustering and fighting seemed suddenly to become one work." But for Nadel, it was the patriotism of principle that was fighting for the Union, liberty, and the Constitution, all of which were threatened by the wickedness of human servitude and by the attempt to make slavery national. He described Joseph Darrow as one of "a number of brave and pious companions in church" who were inspired by this patriotism.[108]

Nadel also described how much Joseph's decision to join the army had been a family decision. He "never would have gone from home, ever to fight the enemies of his country, without the consent and blessing of his parents."[109] The sermon recounted the tension as both father and son felt duty-bound to serve, but the family could not spare them both. Joseph's arguments apparently prevailed, because he was already in the New York State militia and the family needed the father's income. Finally, Nadel focused on the meaning of Joseph's death. "Though to lose such a boy," he said, "was more terrible than the loss of millions of treasure, who shall say that, in the view of its results, it was on the whole any loss at all. A pure soul . . . has been in the army . . . and bequeathed to its young soldiers the heritage of as pure an example as the ages of war can furnish, and his parents and young friends have the power of his beautiful Christian life, indelibly fixed in their minds and hearts by his death."

These three funerals were all held at the beginning of the Civil War. As the war began, few people had any notion of the "harvest of death" that would follow, and these funerals reflected the shock at the deaths of northern soldiers in the early days of the war. Rather quickly, the Civil War became the bloodiest conflict ever fought by Americans. Recent estimates are that between 750,000 and 800,000 people died on both sides of the conflict.[110] Battlefield deaths and those from disease far exceed the total number of deaths from all other wars fought by Americans combined. With a few notable exceptions, the sheer enormity of the casualties soon put a bitter end to mass public funerals. Death had become far too commonplace and frequent to sustain grand rituals and public outpourings of righteous sentiment. But these public funerals show that in the war for both the preservation of the Union and the abolition of slavery, the death of soldiers was understood in the language of martyrdom and sacrifice to a great cause. It is almost impossible to overstate how deeply patriotism and Christian belief were entwined, in the experience and understanding of these unprecedented levels of slaughter. Even the deaths of the youngest of soldiers were understood and sanctified by the greater purposes for which this war was fought.

The texts that describe the deaths and funerals of these children emphasize their social and psychological maturity and their commitment to principles greater than themselves. Ladd was described as having been a brave child whose ambition was to emulate his heroes, Napoleon Bonaparte and George Washington. He was portrayed as a strong young farmer. The scenic grandeur of the mountains, rivers, and lakes of New Hampshire was said to have imparted to him a natural bravery and patriotism. His love of complex machinery and a desire to learn a trade were the reasons he followed his sisters to Lowell, where he became esteemed by everyone. His purpose in enlisting was described as "firm" and "inflexible." McKenzie was witty and apt and the kind of boy who could always look you in the eye. He was regarded as the model of the virtuous poor, who could be further transformed by a Christian life, and became an example of how Christian life could influence soldiers throughout the army.

In all of these instances the decision to enlist was seen as "family decision." Ladd's sisters and brother-in-law acquiesced to his determination. McKenzie's father was not merely willing, but actively encouraged his son's enlistment. Although McKenzie's mother was clearly opposed to his enlistment, her opposition was minimized as natural motherly fears and sentiments. Darrow's enlistment involved an extended discussion between father and son as to who could more easily be spared. All these posthumous narratives emphasize a strong unity of purpose among the individual, the family, and the state in pursuit of war. Of course we know very little about the private grief of these families. In the Civil War, no child's death could be imagined as ignoble, no matter how painful or tragic to his family and friends. For most, the language of modern-day efforts to end the use of child soldiers would have been incomprehensible. In the war to end slavery and preserve the Union, how could any enlistment, even of a child, be abusive, immoral, or criminal? The death of a child might be tragic, but the causes for which he died were transcendent. Nor were boy soldiers forgotten after the war ended; their sacrifices were once again memorialized by their former comrades in arms and by the general public, making plain that Americans continued to validate and value their service.

John "Jack" Travers Cornwell (1900–1916)

The United States was not the only country in which the death of a child in battle became a rallying cry for patriotism. In Great Britain, the most famous young military hero of World War I was John "Jack" Travers Cornwell, a boy seaman first class in the Royal Navy. He received the Victoria Cross posthumously for his service at age sixteen in the Battle of Jutland (May 31–June 1, 1916), the largest naval battle of World War I. Cornwell was a "sight setter" as part of a crew for a five-and-a-half-inch gun on the light cruiser HMS *Chester*. During the battle, the *Chester* sustained many casualties; Cornwell's entire gun crew was killed, and he himself was fatally wounded. Despite his wounds he remained at his post awaiting gun sighting orders, which never came. The wounded Cornwell was taken to Grimsby Hospital, where he died on June 2, 1916. The gun Travers never abandoned, as well as his Victoria Cross, are on display at the Imperial War Museum in London.

Cornwell was originally buried in a pauper's grave in Manor Park Cemetery in London. However, his bravery was noted by the captain of the *Chester*, who wrote of him as "standing with just his own brave heart and God's help to support him." The tale of the boy who stayed at his post achieved instant fame in England and quickly spread throughout much of the English-speaking world. His body was exhumed from its grave and interred in a military funeral at a different site in the cemetery. The military funeral for Cornwell attracted thousands of mourners and was a grand military and civic ritual. According to newspaper accounts, the great crowds included members of the armed forces, the Boy Scouts, the Boy's Naval Brigade, a navy band, a firing party, members of Parliament, and other representative of local and national government and the military. Students from the Walton Road School, which he had attended, as well as a "host of lads of all ages" joined the procession to the cemetery. The coffin was carried on a gun carriage drawn by a crew of boys from the Crystal Palace Naval Depot. Six other boys from the Chester were in the procession. Cornwall's father, who had enlisted in the home guard, was in his uniform bedecked with ribbons from his previous military service in the Zulu Wars and in Egypt. His mother, dressed in black, "wept bitterly" throughout the entire service. Cornwell was eulogized by Dr. T. J. MacNamara, a member of Parliament and parliamentary secretary to the Admiralty, a former schoolteacher and noted child welfare advocate.[111] Speaking of Cornwall in the language of sacrifice, MacNamara declared "the hope and aspirations of early youth, the expectations of vigorous manhood, the dreams of life . . . its opportunities—he laid all these on the altar of duty." He concluded, "First Class Boy John Travers will be enshrined in British hearts as long as faithful unflinching duty shall be esteemed a virtue amongst us. Think of him: seek to emulate him."[112]

In the period following Cornwell's death, his fame was celebrated in numerous ways. By October 1916 it was reported that over four million boys and girls in the British Empire had contributed to a fund in his memory for the endowment of a hospital ward for disabled sailors.[113] On November 16, 1916, his mother received the Victoria Cross from King George V at Buckingham Palace. His image was widely distributed in two series of cigarette cards that depicted "Famous Boys" and "Famous Minors" by Godfrey Phillips in London. Lord Baden-Powell, generally regarded as the founder of the worldwide scouting movement, created the Cornwell Award for Courage, which is sometimes called the Victoria Cross of Scouting. A wax model of Cornwall was exhibited at Madame Tussaud's in London. When his mother visited the exhibit, she is said to have burst into a fit of weeping when she first saw her son's likeness.[114] British child portrait painter Frank Salisbury's posthumous portrait of Cornwell standing at his post launched his career as one of the most famous portrait painters of the twentieth century. By 1926, Salisbury was being hailed as the "painter laureate of England." The Cornwall painting was exhibited in America, where the story of Jack Cornwell passed into legend, and his was compared to the then-celebrated story of Giancomo (Giocanta) Casabianca, the young son of the commander of the French ship *Orient*, who remained at his post and perished when the ship exploded during the Battle of the Nile 1798.[115]

The images of the child soldier as patriot (almost entirely boy soldiers) were not confined to military tributes. Heroic depictions of children under arms pervaded literature and poetry. There was some dissent, especially in some of the poetry of Wilfred Owen and Siegfried Sassoon, but they had limited popular impact at the time and largely gained influence in the 1930s.[116] On the whole, World War I provided an opportunity for poetry to venerate boy heroes. Katharine Tynan celebrated the nobility of youth in World War I in "The Children's War," the opening poem to her volume *Late Songs.*

This the Children's War, because
The victory's to the young and clean.
Up to the Dragon's ravening jaws
Run dear Eighteen and Seventeen.[117]

C. A. Renshaw's *England's Boys: A Woman's War Poems* offered a tribute to all of England's youth, in which it is clear that that she is referring to real and not merely metaphoric boys. For Renshaw, England's call "Stirred their child-souls to strenuous Chivalry, / And swept them into battle— from their toys!"[118] In her poem "Beatty's Boy Hero," Renshaw gives special tribute to Jack Cornwall:

> Fierce battle on the seas! The "Chester" rears
> And plunges in the shell-lashed foam. Each gun
> Booms ceaseless, till her gunners one by one
> Are stricken down. No craven doubts or fears
> He knows, this sailor-boy of sixteen years.
> Who stands, death-smitten, waiting for the word
> To bid him fall; the screaming shells unheard,
> The flames unseen,—undreamed a nation's tears.
> We all are England's, and our pride leaps high,
> Glowing through tears to know you are England's too.
> Boy-hero, strong in battle. Such a debt
> We owe you—you who showed us how to die
> Firm-lipped and fearless. . . . England's sons are true;
> The ancient Viking-blood streams redly yet![119]

Understanding the celebration of Cornwall's sacrifice in its social and historical context makes plain that it came at a time when Britain, reeling from its first experience of total war, may have been in desperate need of a hero.[120] In this context, whatever the true details of Cornwall's life, he was iconographically transformed into a symbol of democracy, the humble sailor boy who willingly sacrificed himself for his country.[121] Like all the venerated child soldiers before him, his essential qualities of youth and innocence made him the perfect patriot and hero at a time of national calamity.

Symbolic Reversals

It has been more than 150 years since the deaths of Luther Ladd, Clarence McKenzie, and Joseph Darrow, and almost a century since the death of Jack Cornwall. Yet every November 11, the world still commemorates the end of the Great War. Known as Veterans Day in the United States and Remembrance Day in the United Kingdom, Canada, and the Commonwealth of Nations, the day was originally called Armistice Day to commemorate the armistice that was signed on the eleventh hour of the eleventh day of the eleventh month of 1918.

Nowadays, it is impossible to imagine anyone offering similar tributes to child soldiers. Who today would applaud them as heroes, martyrs, and patriots? "Faithful unflinching duty" at time of war, as the Honorable T. J. MacNamara put it, is hardly an esteemed public virtue, especially for young boys, and there are few people, if any, in whose hearts Cabin Boy Travers remains enshrined. Indeed, there is little room for the public celebration of the lives and deaths of boy soldiers. Instead we have witnessed a symbolic reversal. The image of the child soldier has been turned on its head, now representing virtually everything that is wrong with war. The prevailing contemporary view is that child soldiers are the victims of adult abuse and criminality. They exist as the most transgressive form of noncombatant: children who have been forcefully and unlawfully transformed into combatants in violation of their essential qualities. Like the child laborer, child bride, or child prostitute, the child soldier is seen to be a deviant product of adult abuse, and the presupposition is that these children are dependent, exploited, and powerless. Even where a child may have committed terrible war crimes, the child's culpability is attributed to adult misuse and exploitation. We no longer appear to recognize the connection between the word "infant" and the word "infantry," both of which derive from the Latin *infantem* and clearly mark the age and inexperience of the young foot soldier. The West especially has been afflicted by a kind of historical amnesia, in which the long history of youngsters' presence in the ranks of fighting forces has been conveniently erased. Even where child soldiers are remembered, they are often seen as odd exceptions, something akin to the modest number of women in disguise who joined traditional armies and fought as men. The reality is that until the beginning of the twentieth century, youngsters were a regular part of armed conflict. Of course, they were never the majority, but their presence was an ordinary, and sometimes extraordinary, part of military life.

2

The Struggle over Child Recruitment

Despite the widespread presence of children under arms in both Great Britain and the United States, and the striking public adulation and veneration of those children as models of personal sacrifice and patriotism, there was also an ongoing public concern with the age at which children should be permitted to join the military. This concern played out among three key players—the child, the family, and the state—whose interests often differed radically from one another. The place of child soldiers in the military was continually affected by shifting dynamics of power among these players.

One central issue in the recruitment of children and youth is the distinction between voluntary enlistment and conscription. Almost invariably, youngsters have been permitted to voluntarily enlist at a younger age than that at which the state was entitled to compel their military service. An added complication was whether the voluntary enlistment of children required a parent or guardian's consent and whether voluntary enlistment in the absence of consent remained valid. Furthermore, there were questions of how rules and regulations governing enlistment or conscription were legally and practically enforced, and who among these key players bore the burden of enforcement. Finally, there was the problem of war itself, which can challenge all rules and make a mockery of laws and regulations created for a peacetime military. This chapter examines the history of these fraught issues against the backdrop of changing cultural attitudes toward childhood and war.

Family Power and Authority over Children

The struggle over recruitment was shaped by social and cultural shifts in the relative power of the family and the state over the lives of children. In the eighteenth century, children were understood to be functioning within the institutions of the family or the state, and little attention was paid to their rights or concerns as individuals. Legally and morally, family authority over children was extremely powerful, and was understood to be central to the proper moral and social organization of society. In Protestant and Puritan thinking, the authority of the family over its member was all-encompassing. The English Protestant clergyman William Gouge, in his widely followed 1622 treatise on the family titled *Of Domestical Duties*, wrote that the family was "a school wherein the first principles and grounds of government and subjection are learned."[1] Likewise, for New England Puritans the family was "little commonwealth" in which power and authority were largely wielded by the family patriarch.[2] Indeed, in England and colonial America the family remained, at least in the eyes of the law, a powerful self-governing institution, a microcosm of government where disobedience by children (and women) was regarded as treason.[3]

Although the legal and moral principle of the subordination of children was crystal clear, in actual practice there was a great deal of diversity in the organization of family life and in the practical agency and autonomy of children. Moreover, because the legal and institutional subordination of children was not intimately coupled with the idea of child protection (as became the case in later centuries), the boundaries between childhood and adulthood seem blurred. As a result, legally subordinate children had a great deal of de facto autonomy. Few, if any, eighteenth- or early nineteenth-century children could be regarded as possessing the kind of psychological autonomy prized in modern life, but their range of independent action was quite large, far greater than for contemporary children. As John Grinspan has pointed out, the eighteenth and nineteenth centuries, especially in America, was the era of the wild child. Children, especially boys, were expected to embody democratic virtues—independence, autonomy, and the rejection of authority. America was a society that prized assertiveness and risk taking and there was little or no room for ideas about childhood vulnerability.[4]

But beginning later in the nineteenth century, new ideas—perhaps best regarded as a new modern mythology about childhood—were taking root. As Janet Dolgin has described it, this idea involved a shared axiomatic conviction that the family is a sacred unit and children, purer and more innocent than adults, were to be treated as treasured objects deserving exceptional care.[5] This new view of childhood became more entrenched, so that in many areas of social life, the courts, legislators, and society as a whole began to have greater concern for the interests of children and began to articulate their own ideas about children's interests and needs. Absolute family legal authority over children slowly eroded; it came to be perceived as strongest only when family authority was consistent with the larger society's notions of "the best interests of the child." But these changes often simply substituted the authority of the state for the authority of the family. More important, at the practical level, the very concept of the best interests of the child reflected the growing belief that children did not have the fundamental liberty, right, or competence to choose for themselves how to conduct their lives.[6]

In Britain, America, and other places in the West, the cultural and social distinctions between childhood and adulthood hardened, and childhood gradually came to be regarded as a separate and distinct stage of life characterized by innocence, vulnerability, and the need for protection. Great deference was paid to the psychological autonomy of the child, but though the family's authority per se waned vis-à-vis the child, the independence of the child also lessened considerably. Childhood autonomy may have been celebrated both philosophically and conceptually, but the psychologically autonomous child was placed within a gilded cage. Of course, none of this happened overnight. Real changes took place more rapidly among the middle class than among the working class and poor, but these new sensibilities did spread quickly into law, especially family law, which was increasingly fashioned around middle-class sensibilities in both America and Britain.[7]

The growing assumption in the West that children should be protected dependents was accompanied by state intervention in family life. The modern state assumed control over many functions of family life, positioned itself as the ultimate protector of children, and assumed regulatory function over compulsory education, the regulation of child labor, and protection of children from parental cruelty. By 1866, Massachusetts law allowed courts to intervene in family life when "by reason of orphanage or of the neglect, crime, drunkenness or other vice of parents," a child was "growing up without education or salutary control, and in circumstances exposing said child to an idle and dissolute life."[8] Similar developments were taking place in Great Britain with the 1889 Act for the Prevention of Cruelty to, and Better Protection of, Children. The act provided for criminal penalties for any person "over sixteen years of age who, having the custody, control, or charge of a child . . . willfully ill-treats, neglects, abandons, or exposes such child, or causes or procures such child to be ill-treated, neglected, abandoned, or exposed, in a manner likely to cause such child unnecessary suffering, or injury to its health."[9]

Despite these shifts in the law and changing attitudes toward children, the government itself rarely directly intervened in the protection of children. Throughout the eighteenth and nineteenth centuries, most protective services for American children were provided by nongovernmental organizations such as the New York Society for the Prevention of Cruelty to Children. By the beginning of the twentieth century, direct governmental involvement began to slowly replace these nongovernmental agencies, beginning with the U.S. federal government's Children's Bureau in 1912.[10]

The growing concern about the protection of children did not automatically extend to the notion of protecting children from military service. Military service, per se, was understood to be a clear public good, and service in the military was considered to be in the best interest of the child. Put simply, childhood itself was not axiomatically understood as incompatible with or in opposition to military service. In both wartime and peacetime, the militaries of all societies continued to recruit young people into their ranks. The continuing conflict over the age at which children would be permitted to enlist or be subject to conscription was not so much about the protection of children as it was about who exercised lawful authority over children.

The Doctrine of Parental Consent

Throughout the eighteenth and nineteenth centuries, controversies over the age of voluntary enlistment reflected tensions between the interests of the child, the family, and the state. Much of this turned on the issue of parental consent, which in itself reflected the way in which the power and control of a family over its members was expressed. Today when we think of parental consent, we almost invariably imagine it as a means of ensuring the welfare of children through the provision of a protective umbrella. The contemporary idea of parental consent stresses the protective aspects of consent and is primarily based upon the presumption that children lack the capacity to make appropriate autonomous decisions. Because children are deemed to lack full adult decision-making ability, adults serve as proxies for their best interests. In this light, parental consent means protecting children (now said to lack the capacity to make proper and rational decisions) from duress, exploitation, or abuse, or merely from the consequences of their own actions. Today, a parental consent requirement for a minor to marry or to receive medical treatment is understood as a way to ensure that parents are able to advance the best interests of their child. This is a very different understanding of the role of consent than was prevalent in earlier centuries.

Formal parental consent first emerged as part of the legal regulation of marriage, which itself did not exist in pre-Reformation Europe.[11] Before then marriage was a private act, regulated solely by religious authorities, not the state. Strict systems of parental control and consent were first established throughout Europe in the sixteenth century.[12] Protestant theologians generally offered two key justifications for requiring consent, which bolstered the view that parental consent was required by the laws of God and nature, namely, that nature itself granted natural authority to parents and that the will of God was expressed in Fifth Commandment to "Honor Thy Father and Thy Mother."[13] First and foremost, parental consent to marriage was designed to give the family control over the admission of new members.[14] It was a way in which the family expressed its autonomy and power. This is not to say that consideration of the welfare of the family's offspring played no part, but the heart of the issue was the role of the parent as the authoritative gatekeeper of family life.

The concept of parental consent is distinct from the concept of the "age of consent," which refers to a person's capacity to consent (sometimes called "the age of discretion"); there was often major tension between these two ideas. Parental consent laws institutionalized parental authority over children, while the concept of the age of consent involved ideas about the mental capacity of children to make autonomous and responsible decisions. Today, the exercise of parental consent is frequently predicated upon the putative incapacity of children, but in the eighteenth and early part of the nineteenth century, this was not so. Parental consent expressed the authority of the family over older children and applied to children who were otherwise presumed capable of making autonomous decisions. It actually had far more to do with who held the power to determine a course of action, rather than with presumptions about the capacity of a child to make decisions. This distinction played out in many areas of life, not just in the question of military service.

Void and Voidable Marriages

The gap between the age at which children were presumed capable of giving consent and the age at which they were also required to obtain parental consent is expressed in the legal distinction between void and voidable marriages. Marriages contracted below the age of consent were regarded as void and treated as if the marriage had never taken place. The parties were deemed to be too young to be able to give their consent to the marriage agreement. Marriages that took place above the age of consent but still required parental consent were treated as voidable. The marriage was deemed valid, but the parents had the right to have the marriage voided or annulled.

The tension between the age of consent and the doctrine of parental consent in England was central to the very controversial Marriage Act of 1753.[15] Until 1753, the requirements for a binding marriage contract under church and canon law were quite simple: the verbal consent of the both partners, the presence of witnesses, that the parties be of sound mind, and that the male be at least age fourteen and the female age twelve.[16] The age of consent for marriage reflected the accepted understanding of the capacity of children to enter into a binding relationship. But these traditional arrangements were unsatisfactory to a combination of elite families and the state and church authorities under their influence, who wanted to be sure that it was parents, guardians, and friends, not children, who controlled the transmission of family property.[17] Accordingly, the new law not only required specific forms of public consecration of marriage, but also inserted the condition of parental consent for all persons under age

twenty-one. The 1753 law made clear that the new parental consent requirement was designed to protect property relations and, to the extent possible,
squelch the ability of young people to form relationships that would subvert
parental authority.

Even with this 1753 act, English law as a whole did not draw a single
hard line about age. Instead, it contained the legacy of earlier thinking in
which the boundaries between childhood and adulthood were not clearly
distinct, coupled with a recognition that children move gradually toward
full maturity. Accordingly, common law recognized different levels of
rights and responsibilities by both age and gender. A male could take the
oath of allegiance at age twelve (presumably required for any person enlisting in armed service); at age fourteen could marry, choose a guardian, or
make a will, and attained the age of legal discretion; at age seventeen be an
executor of an estate; and at twenty-one reached "full age." A female could
betrothed at age seven and consent or disagree to a marriage or bequeath
her personal estate age at age twelve; she was regarded as having reached
the age of legal discretion at age fourteen and reached "full age" at twenty-
one. English law also recognized the arbitrariness of the idea of "full age,"
acknowledging, for example, that in other countries such as France the
absolute right to marry did not occur until age thirty.[18] We might today
disagree with the details of the common law schema, but the legal recognition of a gradual unfolding of rights, duties, and responsibilities makes far
more sense than the growing tendency in contemporary international law
to draw a single bright-line distinction between childhood and adulthood
at age eighteen.

In the United States, the basic marriage laws of the states were laid
down long before independence. In New England, the age of consent generally followed the English common law, providing that boys above age
fourteen and girls above age twelve could consent to a marriage. But reflect-
ing the same concerns about clandestine marriages that existed in Great
Britain, the law also provided that such marriages also required parental
consent until the parties reached ages eighteen or twenty-one.[19] States differed in the way they treated underage marriages. By the last half of the
nineteenth century, South Carolina was particularly zealous in guarding
family property rights, providing for the forfeiture of inheritance for any
woman, child, or maiden between twelve and sixteen who entered into a

clandestine marriage.[20] Any man over age fourteen who contracted a secret marriage with a so-called woman-child under age sixteen was subject to a fine or imprisonment.[21] The moral component of the argument grew stronger, as middle-class reformers, notably women, also sought to raise the age of consent to having sex. Through much of the nineteenth century, the age of consent was as low as age ten, eleven, or twelve, but by the end of the century sixteen to eighteen was the legal age of consent across much of Europe and America.[22] So by the end of the nineteenth century, restrictions on marriage that had once been based largely upon family authority had evolved into state control over the marriage and sexuality of adolescents, who were increasingly thought of as dependent children in need of protection.

Parental Consent and the Military

Parental consent also played a complicated but subordinate role in recruitment into military service. Like marriage, enlistment in the military usually took place at a time of transition between childhood and adulthood. In legal terms, marriage and enlistment both involved significant changes of personal and legal status based upon a contractual agreement. In order to enter into the status of marriage, both husband and wife were required to have the capacity to consent to the agreement. The U.S. Supreme Court made clear that marriage "is something more than a mere contract. The consent of the parties is of course essential to its existence, but when the contract to marry is executed by the marriage, a relation between the parties is created that they cannot change. Other contracts may be modified, restricted, or enlarged, or entirely released upon the consent of the parties. Not so with marriage."[23]

Marriage creates a social relationship that cannot easily be undone. The rights and duties of the marital partners to one another are determined by society through law and not by the private agreement between the parties. So it is no small wonder that families worried about clandestine marriages. Marriages created bonds along with corresponding economic, financial, and social duties that could not easily be undone.

Military recruitment, like marriage, also changed the status of a child. Once the child enlisted, duties to the family were replaced by duties to the state. Whereas state regulation of marriage involved an alliance, however uneasy, between the family and state interests, parental consent to enlistment was a direct challenge the authority of the state over its citizens or subjects. Historically, parental consent was subordinate to the military requirements of the state. In England under the common law, there was no specific minimum age for enlistment, nor was parental consent required. Long before the formation of a standing national army, young people often joined or were conscripted into local militias composed of all subjects or citizens capable of bearing arms, regardless of their age.[24]

Militias have a long history in the common law going back to the Anglo-Saxon period. In England, at the time of Alfred (849–899), the obligation to serve was largely imposed upon youth at about age sixteen, but the state did not recognize any requirement for parental consent to which it was required to defer.[25] A regular standing state army emerged in England only after the English Civil War, and was in many respects still modeled on its feudal antecedents. The early English national army was composed of free landowners between the ages of sixteen and sixty; the term of service was fixed by custom at two months of the year.[26] The age requirements were very lax, however, and children found their way into the army through many different routes. Often children obtained officer's commissions in regiments their fathers had either commanded or served well in. These children, who were often as young as age twelve, were often given commissions either to help provide funds for the widows of fallen officers or as a reward for their father's service. This practice was sometimes criticized, not because it was considered to be an abuse of children, but rather because it showed undue favoritism to leading officers.[27] Age, physical ability, customary preferences, social class, the presence or absence of conflict, and modes of conscription or enlistment all had bearing on the recruitment of children, but none of these factors were definitive.

Enlisting Children: The American Revolution

Many of the essential elements of the English militia system came to America. All colonies recruited "infants," that is, persons not of full age, into colonial militias, with no requirement for parental consent. Where statutes mentioned age they invariably focused on conscription. Throughout the American colonies, all able-bodied men within prescribed age limits were subject to compulsory training and service in the colonial militias.[28] In 1757, the Virginian legislature passed a law requiring, in what it termed "this time of danger," the chief officer of the militia in each county to "list all male persons above the age of eighteen and under the age of sixty years."[29] In January 1776, on the eve of the Revolution, Massachusetts required that the militia be constituted from "all able bodied male persons therein from sixteen years old to fifty."[30] Colonial legislation focused on persons to be conscripted into military service by government; it was ambiguous or indifferent regarding the age of volunteers.

On June 14, 1775, the Continental Congress resolved to create the first companies of the Continental Army, but it made no mention of age. It called for the voluntary recruitment of officers and men, ranging from captains to privates, riflemen, trumpeters, and drummers. The oath of recruitment was brief: "I _____ have, this day, voluntarily enlisted myself, as a soldier, in the American continental army, for one year, unless sooner discharged: And I do bind myself to conform, in all instances, to such rules and regulations, as are, or shall be, established for the government of the said Army."[31]

On July 18, 1775, the Continental Congress resolved "that it be recommended to the inhabitants of all the united English Colonies in North America that all able bodied effective men, between sixteen and fifty years of age in each colony, immediately form themselves into regular companies of Militia."[32] The Congress gave no deference to parental authority. The local response was varied. For example, on January 10, 1776, the Continental Congress resolved that New Jersey raise a third battalion of soldiers. In response, the Provincial Congress of New Jersey in February 6, 1776, resolved that the "recruiting officer inlist [sic] none but healthy, sound, and able bodied freemen, not under sixteen years of age."[33] New Jersey actually provided a stringent consent requirement for apprentices of any age, who were required to obtain their master's or mistress's consent in writing before enlisting. But New Jersey gave less deference to parents, providing only that anyone under age twenty-one who had "enlisted himself" could "obtain his discharge" within twenty-four hours of the time that his parents or guardians received notice.[34] Obtaining a discharge was the youngster's right, not the parent's right, but the resolution did at least implicitly recognize a parent's right to influence a child and a child's right to act on that influence. But absent the youngster's decision, the enlistment was neither void under law nor voidable by the parents, who had no veto power over enlistment.

The New Jersey approach suggests that obtaining parental consent to enlistment was often understood as a moral obligation to family rather than a formal legal requirement. That this was a widespread sentiment is borne out by the narrative of Joseph Plumb Martin, who joined the Connecticut state forces in June 1775, when he was age fifteen. In his autobiography *Private Yankee Doodle*, Martin describes his urge to enlist and how he frequented the "rendezvous" where many of his "young associates" would join up. Of his decision to enlist, he said, "I had obtained my heart's desire."

Martin lived with his own parents (his father was a Congregationalist minister) until he was seven years old, when he went to live with his wealthier maternal grandparents. Prior to enlisting, Martin reflected on the issue of consent, wondering what "plan to form" to get the consent of his parents and grandparents to procure the "bewitching name of soldier." He worried about how his decision might "hurt their feelings" and, for a while, hoped that some kind of personal confrontation might arise among them that would provide the pretext to justify his abandoning them for military service without their "consent, leave or approbation." What is crucial here is that Martin's concerns about consent reflect a moral duty he felt toward the family that he loved and that supported and cared for him, but very much needed his labor on the farm. No legal or technical issues of formal consent were involved. Indeed, once Martin finally did enlist, at age fifteen, he did so without their consent, and although he realized that his grandparents were hurt by his decision, it was, he says, "too late to repent."[35]

These patterns of recruitment persisted throughout the Revolutionary War. Once peace and victory were secured, Congress turned its attention to the composition of recruitment into the newly established regular army, and the targeted age of enlistment began to rise. Congress passed military regulations providing that both noncommissioned officers and privates be limited to able-bodied men between the ages of eighteen and forty-six.[36] This regulation did not affect the recruitment of younger boys as musicians, a frequent route for the enlistment of younger boys.[37] In 1802, Congress further tightened its restriction on enlistment in the peacetime U.S. Army by requiring any recruit between eighteen and twenty-one to have the consent of a parent guardian or master.[38] But the peacetime army was minuscule. In 1783, at the end of the Revolution, virtually the entire Continental Army was disbanded, with the exception of one company assigned to protect the U.S. military stores at West Point and Fort Pitt. A year later, Congress created the U.S. Army, but in 1798 it remained tiny—comprising merely twenty-one hundred soldiers.[39]

After the dissolution of the Continental Army, Congress began to expand its authority over state militias, and raised the age of peace-time conscription for these armed forces. On May 2, 1792, Congress passed the Uniform Militia Act, which gave the president the right to mobilize state militia.[40] Shortly thereafter, Congress passed the Calling Forth Act, which mandated virtually universal conscription into state militias, providing "that each and every free able-bodied white male citizen of the respective states, resident therein, who is or shall be of the age of eighteen years and under the age of forty five years . . . shall severally and respectively [be] enrolled in the militia."[41] These two acts called for mandatory enrollment in the militia, not volunteers, but Congress was, in fact, never able to fully implement universal conscription in accordance with the standards set forth in the legislation.

Enlisting Children: The War of 1812

Just a few months before the outbreak of the War of 1812, Congress sought to raise additional military forces for the U.S. Army. Still clinging to peacetime restrictions on recruitment, Congress required written consent by parents, guardians, or masters for recruits who were between eighteen and twenty-one. As had been the case during the Revolution, musicians were exempted from these age requirements.[42] These age restrictions were repeated again in the legislation passed in 1813.[43] But by the middle of the war, Congress revoked the written consent requirements because of growing manpower shortages in the army. The new law allowed any person "under full age," but between ages eighteen and twenty-one, to enlist of his own free will. However, for those recruits who were under full age, it did allow a four-day grace period for them to reconsider and withdraw without penalty.[44] During the War of 1812 the recruitment picture was, therefore, quite complex. Though enlistment and conscription into the U.S. Army was officially restricted to those eighteen years of age and above, when the army required manpower, Congress appeared ready and willing to reject the idea that parents should be gatekeepers to the recruitment of eighteen- to twenty-one-year-olds. In military matters, national interests overrode considerations of parental consent. At the same time, however, the law gave credence to the idea that individuals of less than full age might need more time to make a considered decision. Once the grace period was over, a youngster's enlistment was as binding as that of a person of full age. The new law seemed also to create independent decision-making power for older teenagers, but it may in fact have been little more than a fig leaf to cover the already widespread practice of recruitment in this age category.

Although Congress addressed the issue of recruitment, its actions had little or no impact upon the age of voluntary enlistees. For example, on July 24, 1812, Lieutenant Uriah Allison came to the town of Kingston, Tennessee, along with his fifers and a drummer boy, to recruit for the U.S. infantry. The 1812 war against Great Britain had been declared only a month earlier, and he was looking for volunteers. People gathered before the courthouse, and emulating the long tradition of the British army whereby taking the king's shilling meant agreeing to serve, Allison laid shiny new U.S. dollars across the head of the drum. Anyone who picked up a dollar was a volunteer. On that day, Allison recruited thirty volunteers. Among these were the three Buchanan brothers—sixteen-year-old Horeulas, fourteen-year-old Moses, and twelve-year-old Jeremiah, who joined along with their father. Aaron Bledsoe and Elijah Pruet, who were both fifteen, and seventeen-year-old Henry Miller also joined up. On that one day in Tennessee, 20 percent of the volunteers were under age eighteen.[45] Acts of Congress had little or no impact on recruitment into state militias, which made up the bulk of the armed forces in wartime and where recruitment of even younger soldiers was widespread. The regular army of the United States consisted of about 7,000 soldiers at the beginning of the war and grew to about 35,000 by the end. At the beginning of the war, this force was supplemented by 80,000 volunteers and militia.

By the end of the war, 450,000 soldiers—the great bulk of the American fighting forces—were from state militias, where all males between sixteen and sixty were subject to conscription but volunteerism was the norm.[46] In fact, throughout the first half of the nineteenth century, a combination of Jacksonian democratic sentiment and hostility to professional armies meant that, as a practical matter, states nullified the rules of national conscription. Throughout the new republic, as states and local communities continued to raise volunteer forces of men and boys, the ages and composition of those fighting forces were based upon local custom and practice.

Parental Consent: The Courts Weigh In

The conflict over parental consent and the age of recruitment reached U.S. courts in 1816 in the case of *United States v. Bainbridge*, the first major legal challenge to the enlistment of youngsters.[47] *Bainbridge* directly dealt with the issue of enlisting boys into the navy without parental consent. At the time the case was decided, enlistment unto the navy was governed by the act of June 30, 1798, which allowed boys to be employed on frigates and other the vessels of the U.S. Navy according to the exigencies of the public service. The statute specified no minimum age and made no mention of parental consent.[48] For most of the early nineteenth century, Congress continued to reauthorize the enlistment of boys without reference to age or consent.[49]

The facts of *Bainbridge* were straightforward. Robert Treadwell, a sailor, enlisted in the navy at about age twenty and later deserted. He was court-martialed and sentenced to serve two years in the navy and to forfeit all wages due him. Following his conviction and sentencing, his father filed a habeas corpus petition demanding that his son be released on the grounds that he was a legal "infant" when he enlisted in the navy and had enlisted without his father's consent. Absent a parent's consent, he argued, the enlistment was void and the navy had no right to court-martial his son. Although Treadwell was twenty years old, the decision by the court addressed the recruitment of all "infants," which in nineteenth-century legal terms meant anyone under twenty-one. The case was heard by Supreme Court Justice Joseph Story, serving in his capacity as the justice of the U.S. Circuit Court for Massachusetts. Story is most well known for his famous judicial opinion in the case of the slave ship *Amistad*, where the Supreme Court held that the slaves onboard had been illegally kidnapped.

The heart of Treadwell's claim was that Congress had no power to authorize the enlistment of minors without parental consent, and that enlisting minors without parental consent was a violation of the common law rights governing parent and child relationships. Under the common law, Treadwell asserted, the father is the natural guardian of the son, and has a right to control his person and dispose his services and labor. Moreover, Treadwell argued, because the general common law required a father's consent to create a valid contract with an infant, absent this consent his son had not entered into a binding contract with the navy.[50] Since his son had never lawfully enlisted, he could not be charged with desertion or made subject to court-martial proceedings. In sum, Treadwell argued, the enlistment was void and the son should be discharged from the navy and returned to his father's custody. Note that the father's legal assertions said nothing about the protection of his child, although it may well have been an underlying concern. But as a matter of law, the claim could have been based only upon the old common law notion that parents had rights in their children for their services and labor.

In his decision, however, Justice Story rejected the father's claim that the common law right of parents to the custody and services of their children superseded legislative action. He made plain that enlistment regulations are determined by the laws of the state, and that these can be altered as law and policy dictate unless there is a constitutional prohibition. He asserted that the Constitution delegated to Congress the power "to raise and support armies" and "to provide and maintain a navy" and that this included the power "to make all laws, which shall be necessary and proper for carrying into effect the foregoing powers." Justice Story held that it was central for the navy to enlist minors and made it clear that although the particular decision in *Bainbridge* affected a twenty-year-old minor, the principle involved applied to far younger recruits. For the navy in particular, he asserted, the employment of minors was almost indispensable. "Nautical skill," he stated, "cannot be acquired, but by constant discipline and practice for years in the sea service; and unless this be obtained in the ardor and flexibility of youth, it is rarely, at a later period, the distinguishing characteristic of a seaman. It is notorious that the officers of the navy generally enter the service as midshipmen as early as the age of puberty; and that they can never receive promotion to a higher rank, until they have learned, by a long continuance in this station, the duties and the labors of naval warfare." Congress's power trumped private rights, and the loss of such right was one of the sacrifices that society exacts from its members for the furtherance of the public welfare.[51]

In dismissing Treadwell's common law claims, Story held that it was within congressional or other legislative power to declare that a minor was at full age and capable of acting for himself at age fourteen, or even to decide to emancipate a child completely from its parents. He went on to affirm that Congress could constitutionally authorize the enlistment into the naval service of any minors, independent of the private consent of their parents. This power, he argued, was hardly novel to the United States, pointing out that minors not only could be enlisted into the British navy without the consent of their parents, but also could be forcibly impressed into service against their own will. Story stressed that in wartime the state may establish and maintain an army and navy for its defense and stated that it would be a "strange and startling doctrine, that the whole youth of the state might, unless the consent of their parents could be previously obtained, be withheld from the public service, whatever might be the pressure of the public dangers or necessities."[52] *Bainbridge* makes clear that the military needs of the state trump any common law considerations of consent.

Interestingly, though *Bainbridge* vindicated the rights of the state over those of the family, it also contained the germ of a powerful shift in legal thinking, suggesting that even without congressional action, common law notions of absolute paternal authority were more and more limited. Instead of parents having absolute authority over their child, *Bainbridge* implies that there are three overlapping spheres of interest: the state, the family, and the child. A child's rights were no longer subsumed under the rights of the father; rather, a father's authority over a child was strongest where it was consistent with the interests and needs of the child. Although it did not affect the outcome of the case, the legal calculus of *Bainbridge* hinted at a future transformation of consent from an expression of parental *rights* over the child to an expression of parental *duty* to protect and nurture the child. But perhaps more important for child recruitment, the court did not see childhood and military service as incompatible. Indeed, Story concluded that any statute authorizing minors to enter public service was by definition "for their benefit" as well as "for the public benefit."[53] In sum, in military matters at least, Congress could substitute its definition of what was beneficial for a child over that of the parents.

Following *Bainbridge*, Congress continued to authorize the recruitment of boys into the navy without restrictions as to minimum age and without requiring the consent of parents or guardians.[54] Yet as the country moved toward midcentury, the issue of consent also emerged as a factor for both the navy and the marines. In 1835, Congress considered a bill permitting boys between thirteen and eighteen who were "sons of citizens" of the United States to enlist in the navy, but only "with the consent of their parents or guardians, expressed in writing, and acknowledged before a justice of the peace, who shall certify to the same not being under thirteen nor over eighteen years of age."[55] Congress was clearly considering more formal legal regulation of the consent process, but by the time the bill was passed these formal consent requirements were stripped. Instead, in 1837 Congress enacted "an act to provide for the enlistment of boys for the naval service and to extend the term of the enlistment for seaman," which declared that "it shall be lawful to enlist boys for the navy, with the consent of their parents or guardians, not being under thirteen nor over eighteen years of age, to serve until they shall arrive at the age of twenty-one years; and it shall be lawful to enlist other persons for the navy, to serve for a period not exceeding five years, unless sooner discharged by direction of the president of the United States."[56] By 1858, similar restrictions were applied to the U.S. Marine Corps; marines could enlist boys between ages eleven and seventeen with the consent of their parents or guardians.[57]

In sum, while the consent of parents to the enlistment of a child was not a strikingly important issue during the period of the Revolution, it emerged as an issue of greater consequence in the period following independence. The disbanding of the Continental Army heralded more restrictive age and consent requirements for the much smaller peacetime U.S. Army. These restrictions were partially suspended during the War of 1812 and, in any event, did not apply to the state militias, which constituted the bulk of the fighting forces. Moreover, they did not apply to the navy or the marines, which continued to recruit very young children into their ranks. Moreover, under the decision in *Bainbridge* it became clear that Congress had absolute discretion to legislate rules of enlistment without regard to parental interests.

Void and Voidable Enlistments

This legal conversation, as we shall shortly see, was interrupted by the practical exigencies of war. With the outbreak of the Civil War, the immediate need for soldiers sidelined the more theoretical debate about the appropriate age of enlistment and the requirement for consent. But the shift in requirements for consent points to a trend by Congress to try to strike a balance between the needs of society and the rights of parents, specifically between the armed services' need for very young recruits who could serve lengthy terms of military apprenticeship and the rights of parents to make decisions for their children. After the Civil War ended, the legal conversation continued, and by the end of the nineteenth century, the principles involved in balancing the interests of parents and the state became settled in the legal distinction between void and voidable enlistments. As with marriage, age became the determinant as to whether or not enlistments are void or voidable. A void enlistment is a nullity (that is, it is simply not valid on its face), while a voidable enlistment remains valid until it is challenged. The leading U.S. Supreme Court case on this issue is *In re Morrissey* (1890).[58] At the time *Morrissey* was decided, federal law prohibited anyone under age twenty-one from enlisting or being mustered into the U.S. military without the written consent of his parents or guardians. The one exception was emancipated minors who had no parents or guardians entitled to the custody and control of the minor.[59] For those minors who obtained parental consent, Congress set the minimum age of enlistment at sixteen. Morrissey fraudulently enlisted by claiming to be over age twenty-one, when he was in fact just seventeen. Had he enlisted at age fifteen, his enlistment would have been void. Because he was above age sixteen, however, his enlistment was only voidable. The question before the court was who had the right and the obligation to challenge voidable enlistments. The court squarely sided with the parents or guardians. The parental consent provision, the court declared, "is for the benefit of the parent or guardian. It means simply that the government will not disturb the control of parent or guardian over his or her child without consent. It gives the right to such parent or guardian to invoke the aid of the court and secure the restoration of a minor to his or her control; but it gives no privilege to the minor." As in *Bainbridge*, the court interpreted the issue of parental consent not as designed for the protection of a minor, but rather as a function of the statutory right of parents to exert their power and control over their child. Neither the minor nor the military had the right or the duty to release from military service a minor between ages sixteen and twenty-one who had fraudulently enlisted. Interestingly, *Morrissey* itself was major shift in the direction of parental rights in contrast to the British common law tradition, which gave neither the minor nor the parent the right to challenge an underage enlistment. British judges were sometimes undecided as to whether the enlistment of a minor was itself an act of self-emancipation from parental control, but in the end determined that the enlisted minor was not emancipated by enlisting but rather that the British crown's authority over an enlisted child superseded that of the parents.[60] Even with the decision in *Morrissey* in place, there remained more flexible backdoor mechanisms for youngsters who wanted to enlist, since not every U.S. state modeled its rules on Congress. New York, for example, held that absent any New York State statutory requirement of parental consent, youngsters could enroll in the New York militia at age sixteen without parental consent.[61]

The Civil War and the Recruitment of the Young

The evolving peacetime legal consensus about parental consent was upended by the tidal wave of conflict that engulfed Americans during the Civil War (1861–1865). At the beginning of the Civil War the U.S. Army was made up of about sixteen thousand volunteers. Its recruitment standards were those of the previous peacetime generation, which allowed the recruitment of eighteen- to twenty-one-year-olds upon parental consent. In the prewar years, prohibitions on the recruitment of minors were clearly in place. In fact, by 1850 Congress had also addressed a related problem of dealing with minors who had somehow managed to evade the consent requirements. That legislation required the secretary of war to order the discharge of any minor under the age of twenty-one upon evidence produced to him that the enlistment was without the consent of a parent or guardian. While the statute did not impose a duty on the army to seek out minors within its ranks, it imposed a duty upon the army to discharge a minor upon presentation of adequate evidence.[62]

The Civil War completely altered this picture. The first major changes to army enlistment came in 1862, after President Lincoln, frustrated by delays in mobilizing military forces against the Confederacy, issued General War Order No. 1, which required U.S. Army forces to combat the southern insurgency. Shortly afterward, Congress repealed the provision of the 1850 law requiring the discharge of minors enlisted without the consent of their parents or guardians. Instead, new legislation ostensibly set a minimum age of enlistment by declaring that no person under the age of eighteen shall be mustered into the U.S. service. But as a practical matter, this legislation actually opened the door to underage enlistment, by providing that the age sworn to by an enlistee at the time the oath of enlistment would be accepted as conclusive.[63] This meant that whatever age the recruit swore to at the time of enlistment, his so-called declared age, would be the final determinant of his age, regardless of actual age, and none of these recruits would be subject to mandatory discharge even if their actual age was ultimately revealed. This situation was exacerbated by the fact that, as in previous generations, states and local communities raised volunteer units for the war, and enlisted men and boys and commissioned officers to lead them, all in accordance with local customs and standards. So once a youngster enlisted, he would remain in service regardless of the circumstances surrounding the recruitment.

Enlistment in the navy remained open to even younger recruits. By August 1861, shortly after the Battle of Bull Run, Congress authorized the expansion of naval enlistment to increase the number of able seamen, ordinary seamen, and boys, as the secretary of the navy judged necessary and proper.[64] Somewhat later, Congress allowed the president the right to annually select three of these boys for appointment as midshipmen in the Naval Academy so long as they had not reached the age of eighteen and also had at least one previous year in service, at least six months of which were at sea.[65] These actions continued the long tradition of the navy of recruiting young boys for service.

Conscription and Bounties during the Civil War

As the war went on, even these relaxed recruitment standards could not fill the army's need for soldiers. The Enrollment Act of 1863 introduced conscription for men between ages twenty and forty-five, but the act did not create a system of universal conscription. Unlike the national systems of conscription that would later be established in both Great Britain and the United States during World War I, the real purpose of the Enrollment Act was to coerce or stimulate voluntary enlistment, but not to replace it.[66] Under the Enrollment Act, military conscription was based upon quotas assigned by congressional district. Conscription served to supplement the number of enrollees not otherwise filled by volunteers and members of the state militias.[67] The act also allowed those drafted to arrange for substitutes. As a result, of the 2,213,363 men who served in the Union Army during the Civil War, only 168,649 were obtained via the draft, and of these 117,986 were substitutes. Thus only 50,663 people were actually conscripted, and only 46,347 of these literally entered the ranks of the army; so only about 2 percent of the actual Union fighting forces were draftees.[68]

The threat of conscription was only one side of the carrot-and-stick mechanism that generated recruits. The central means for securing enlistments was the payment of cash incentives, so-called bounties, to enlistees. The federal payment of bounties was spread out across the whole period of a soldier's service, and sums varied. At the beginning of the war, one hundred dollars was paid, with twenty-five dollars at the time of mustering in and the remainder at discharge. By 1864, sums of up to three hundred dollars were being paid, with one-third at the time of mustering in. Local communities also paid bounties, in addition to those paid by the federal government, and because of local communities' needs to meet their enlistment quotas, these bounties were often larger and almost always paid in advance.[69]

The sums paid out as bounties were enormous. Total bounties, federal and local, that were paid out during the war exceeded 586 million dollars—the equivalent of more than seven billion dollars in 2013.[70] The bounty system also facilitated the recruitment of underage soldiers. The payment of money for enlistments created an entire class of entrepreneurs, often criminals, called bounty brokers, who advertised for recruits, and arranged for substitutes, frequently drawn from new immigrants to the United States.[71] As the war dragged on, voluntary recruitment lagged and the pressure to fulfill local enlistment quotas intensified. Many congressional districts began to rely almost entirely upon contracts with brokers to fill their quotas.

Corruption permeated the system, as bounty brokers, U.S. provost marshals, and other recruiting officers either negligently enforced enlistment laws or intentionally conspired to evade them.[72] The system was simple: the broker and a prospective recruit agreed upon a fee to be paid to the recruit upon enlistment. The fee set was less than the actual bounty to be paid by the government. When the recruit was brought to enlist before the provost marshal, the military office supervising conscription and recruitment, the broker pocketed the difference between the bounty actually paid and the arranged fee.

Bounty brokers were often experts at forging recruitment papers and drugging and kidnapping new recruits. In March 1865, a broker allegedly abducted two boys of sixteen in Brooklyn and sent them off for enlistment in Boston. In December 1864, two teenage boys who had immigrated to New York were enlisted as substitutes for five hundred dollars. The broker kept the money for "safekeeping," and the boys never saw it again.[73] Fifteen-year-old Edward Wheeler, from Vermont, was kidnapped and, in the language of the time, sold as a recruit. His kidnappers were arrested and a warrant was issued for other persons involved. According Wheeler's statement, one of the kidnappers gave him liquor until he became intoxicated. He was then taken to Albany and later to Poughkeepsie, where the kidnappers tried to make him swear that he was eighteen. When he refused, he was the taken to Troy, where he was held for days and taken by the kidnappers to the provost marshal's office, where he was enlisted as a substitute. The brokers received a sum of six hundred dollars.[74]

Many brokers made large fortunes through these activities, although some were caught and either jailed or fined. A broker who persuaded two Albany, New York, boys to enlist in 1863 was forced to pay the full bounties to their parents, since the boys were already away in the army.[75] Twenty-seven bounty brokers were arrested in February 1865, including Arthur Carron, who conspired with several U.S. Army sergeants on Governors Island to enlist "old deserters, invalids, youths of fifteen, and cripples" into the army and also to arrange for the desertion of others. Carron used the profits to buy a farm in New Jersey.[76] Immigrants were easy targets for bounty brokers. In fact, almost a quarter of the Union Army was made up of immigrants who were scattered throughout the army.[77] The abduction of recruits became so brazen that it contributed to diplomatic tensions between the United States and Great Britain, when two boys of fifteen, British subjects, were kidnapped and fraudulently enlisted. One was an Asian Indian servant who spoke no English who was drugged and enlisted in New Hampshire; the other was snatched while on an errand for his father and was then drugged and enlisted into the Sixty-Seventh Regiment of New York Volunteers.[78]

A common device for recruiting underage enlistees was the "fictitious mother," a woman who worked with the broker in the kidnapping and enlisting boys; she would testify before the provost marshal that she was the boy's mother and consented to the enlistment.[79] Henry Isaacs, a bounty broker, was sentenced to prison for creating a fraudulent consent of Amelia Wolff for her seventeen-year-old son. The consent, dated September 26, 1864, read, "I, Amelia Wolff, do certify that I am the mother of Joseph Wolff; that the said Joseph Wolff is seventeen years of age; and I do hereby freely give my consent to his volunteering as a soldier in the army of the United States for three years." At the time Amelia Wolff had been dead for sixteen years.[80] In addition, brokers were alleged to have applied to the surrogates courts for guardianship over young boys in order to facilitate enlistment.[81] The funneling of underage youth from New York City to the front lines was so pervasive that the *New York Times* later declaimed that "in nearly every street in New York parents lamented the enlistment of their hapless sons, between fourteen and seventeen years of age, who had been made drunk and then enlisted and robbed of every dollar of their bounty."[82]

The Enrollment Act, targeting the conscription of twenty- to forty-five-year-olds, made no mention of minors.[83] But a year later, in response to widespread concern about underage soldiers, an amendment to the Enrollment Act gave the secretary of war the right to order the discharge of all persons in the military service who were under the age of eighteen years at the time of application for their discharge. However, the procedural hurdles in the law were clearly designed to make the discharge process cumbersome. First, the law did not actually require the secretary of war to discharge minors. Second, it required proof to be provided that those under age eighteen were in the service without the consent, either expressed or implied, of their parents or guardians. Finally, it required that "the soldiers, their parents or guardians, shall first repay to the government and to the state and local authorities all bounties and advance-pay which may have been paid to them."[84] Clearly these requirements were designed to ensure that few, if any, minors would be released from service. The act was further amended in July 1864, making clear that the real target of the law was recruits under sixteen years of age. The amendment, enacted nine months before Lee's surrender at the Appomattox Court House, provided for the immediate discharge of any person under the age of sixteen years, even if the individual enlisted with the consent of his parent or guardian; it also required the repayment of all bounties received prior to discharge. But for the first time, the law also provided some penalties for recruiters, albeit these were instituted only in the final months of the war. Recruiting officers who knowingly enlisted anyone who was under sixteen years of age were subject to dismissal from the army.[85]

Juvenile Delinquents on the Front Lines

Until now, we have primarily considered the factors affecting the enlistment of individual youngsters. But there is an even a darker side to this story, which involves institutional compulsion and duress. The children of the poor and minorities who found themselves in state custody were particularly vulnerable to being pressured into military service without their parents' consent and, indeed, over the clear objections of parents. Children in reform schools who were designated juvenile offenders could easily be sent to the front lines, because these institutions functioned *in loco parentis* and could legally substitute their consent for that of the children's parents. From Michigan to Rhode Island to Massachusetts, this became standard practice in reform schools, as state officials sought to reduce costs, deal with discipline problems, and garner recruiting fees from the military.[86] During the course of the war, 162 boys of the Massachusetts Nautical Reform, about 22 percent of its population, enlisted in the army or navy.[87]

Michigan established a reform school in 1856, which even before the war was drastically underfunded by the legislature. The situation became worse when war broke out and the state government was required to enlist and equip regiments of volunteers. As men responded to the call to arms, many children were left fatherless and the ensuing widespread family dislocation led to a rapid increase in the number of reformatory inmates.[88] To ameliorate the overcrowded conditions and underfunding, school authorities developed an early release program for inmates who enlisted in Michigan units. The school was spurred on by the patriotic fervor of the boys and the fact that many previously discharged boys had enlisted.

In March 1861, the state of Michigan passed legislation that allowed for the enlistment of minors, without specifying age, with the written consent of parents or guardians. Moreover, if a boy had no parents or guardians, consent could be given by a justice of the peace where the boy resided.[89] Available records show that it was quite easy to get boys to enlist, and about ninety-five were granted early release. It appears that the majority of boys were seventeen or eighteen years of age, but some were between fourteen and sixteen. Boys who were disciplinary problems were encouraged to enlist regardless of their age. For example, five of the ten most frequently punished boys were sent into the military. These included Startling Farley (age sixteen), William Parker (age fifteen), David Moss (age fourteen), Charlie Points (age fourteen), and Charles Crockett (age seventeen or eighteen).[90] The board apparently found it quite easy to obtain parental consent, since state bounties provided a cash incentive of two hundred dollars. Much of the money went to parents and stepparents, although it is clear that the school held on to some bounties. Another incentive for minors was the Homestead Act of 1862, which promoted Western settlement by providing land grants to Union war veterans. It specifically allowed minors who served in Union forces to be treated as adults for the purpose of perfecting land claims.[91]

In Rhode Island, the role of bounties in channeling children into the military came under scrutiny by a committee of the state senate, which investigated the relationship between the Providence Reform School and U.S. Army recruiters. Providence was an industrial city both before and during the Civil War, and attracted large numbers of Irish immigrants and free blacks. It was also a hot bed of nativism and a regional center for the Know Nothing Party, with its avowed hatred of Irish immigrants. In Rhode Island, the Providence Reform School was established by the state in 1850 to deal with the children of the urban underclass. As officially stated, the school was created for the "confinement, instruction, and reformation of juvenile offenders and of young persons of idle, vile, or vicious habits."[92] During the Civil War, the school routinely organized the movement of boys between sixteen and eighteen, and perhaps younger, into the armed forces. The Providence Reform School had a clear monetary incentive to promote enlistment. They received "head money" directly from the army for each boy recruited. In addition, the school took control, as "trustees," of the enlistment bounty.

In 1864, the school's practice came under investigation following a letter of complaint sent to the governor of Rhode Island by Mary Dexter, whose sixteen-year-old son George had enlisted in the army without her consent. He was one of eleven boys, some Irish, some so-called colored boys, and others who were recruited at the school at the same time. George had been sent to the reform school in July of 1863 in lieu of a three-month jail sentence for receiving three dollars in stolen cash from a friend who has stolen it from his mother.[93] Had these children been adults, they would have served short prison sentences, but as minors they were subject to long-term confinement until age twenty-one in a juvenile reform facility. The open-ended length of their sentences and the fact that their release was a matter of school discretion provided both the incentive and the pressure to enlist.

The boys were under significant duress to enlist even if their parents objected. George enlisted, he told his mother, because he "wanted his liberty." His mother was adamant that she would rather her son serve time in prison than in the army. But the school pushed enlistment as the only option, and the practice was to encourage boys to enlist for the longest period possible at the time—three years. James M. Talcott, the school superintendent, described the process in testimony before a Rhode Island Senate Commission that investigated the issue. Talcott reported that the enlistment issue was discussed at the semimonthly board meeting of the school, where, Talcott told the board, boys under eighteen who were large and strong would be taken in to the army if presented to the recruiters. Talcott's testimony before the senate commission made clear that arrangements for recruitments were made between the school and local provost marshal of the army. The recruits went to a single location where they enlisted and where the head monies and bounties were handed over to the school.[94]

In response to questioning by the commission about the enlistment of George Smith, Talcott testified that there were no problems in enlisting younger soldiers and that he did not have to hide their ages.

Q. You had to call them over eighteen, didn't you?

A. We handed the Provost Marshal the names and ages as on our records. We handed him the exact record of their births according to our record. The Provost Marshal had them before him when he took them.

Q. Were you present when they were sworn?

A. I was present when one or two of them was sworn.

Q. Were they not required to swear that they were eighteen?

A. Not those that I saw. They didn't make any oath that they were eighteen years old. The Provost Marshal says: "I can't take any under sixteen, (16) and all who have leave of parent or guardians, between that and eighteen, (18) I can take them. Over eighteen, (18) he didn't want any leave of anybody."

Q. Did you tell him that their parents and guardians were willing that they should enlist?

A. We claimed to be his guardian, and told the Provost Marshal so.

In response to pointed questioning about the enlistment of another boy, John Thomas Sykes, Talcott reaffirmed that age was not an issue.

Q. Did you enlist into the service of the United States, John Thomas Sykes?

A. No, sir; I did not enlist him. I allowed him to enlist himself.

Q. Did you receive from the State the head-money?

A. I received it. I presented him for enlistment.

Q. What notice did you send to the parents?

A. I sent no direct notice to the parents at this particular time. I had said before, to Mrs. Sykes,—as I always supposed was her name,—it is about eighteen months since I began to tell her that the boy had been in the Reform School quite as long as we usually kept boys, and asked her what we should do with him; and said that we should be obliged to place him in the navy or somewhere else. And Mr. Whitney has talked with her also, about his enlisting into the navy.

Q. Did you give her any notice at all, that you intended to enlist her son into the United States army?

A. I told her, as much as three times, that I intended to send him whaling or enlist him into the army or navy.

Q. What did she say?

A. She objected every time.

Q. Did the boy swear that he was eighteen?

A. I did not hear him.

Q. You knew that he was obliged to before he could enlist.

A. I did not. I presume he did not.

Q. Didn't you know that a recruit, when he enlists, is obliged to swear that he is eighteen?

A. He is not obliged to.

Q. Do they enlist boys under eighteen?

A. Yes. They enlist them from sixteen. The Provost Marshal said to him, in my presence, "No boy under sixteen must present himself at all. After sixteen, I can receive him."

Asked whether he felt at liberty to enlist any minor against a minor's will, he stated, "It has been done."[95]

Theodore F. Lord, who witnessed the monetary transaction between reform school officials and the U.S. Army, also testified at the hearing. He stated that several boys told him they didn't want to leave the money with Talcott, but that they all made an agreement to leave it with him, except for fifteen dollars. According to Lord, when the army paymaster appeared, a Mr. Carpenter (another reform school official) sat on one side of a table and the paymaster on the other. The recruit was brought in, and as his name was called the money was handed to him. Lord testified that there "there were two colored boys. I suppose Sykes was one. They took the money to go back. Mr. Carpenter stretched out his hand, across the table, and said, 'Give me that money.' They did so; both of these colored boys." Other boys resisted. One boy, whom Lord described as Irish, said that he wanted the money to go to his mother. But Carpenter refused, saying that it was "not according to the agreement." The investigatory committee concluded that the practices of the reform school and the army were "justified by no law" and were "a perversion of the objects of the institution."[96] In fact, the commission recommended changes to curb these practices, but by the time the commission issued its report in March 1865, the war was nearly over, and the commission's recommendations were never passed into law.

At war's end, it was clear that thousands upon thousands of underage boys had enlisted. The crisis of war, the power of patriotic sentiment, the desire of youth for adventure, the inherent corruptions in the bounty system, and the ease with which institutions of juvenile reform saw early enlistment as a resolution to many of their fiscal and social control problems made certain than a steady stream of young boys filled the ranks of the Union Army.

The Recruitment of Boys in Great Britain

The United States was not alone is creating a link between reform schools and the military. In Great Britain, such schools were also used as sources for recruits. Until conscription began in World War I, the British Army was completely composed of volunteers and was constantly concerned with how to expand recruitment. The army considered boys to be the best candidates for the army, especially if they had received prior skilled training; these boys were seen to be the best source of noncommissioned officers and artificers (highly skilled mechanics and technicians). In 1857, the Industrial School Act allowed magistrates to send homeless children to industrial schools; the act was later expanded to allow them to send any child found begging or receiving charity or who had committed an imprisonable offense or was not able to be controlled by his parents. The primary targets of the industrial schools were impoverished children, while the reform schools dealt with more serious juvenile offenders. All these types of schools were filled with the children of the urban poor.

In 1877, a commission established by the British government examined the entire matter of the enlistment of boys and the role that schools could play in expanding recruitment.[97] At that time, youngsters age sixteen and above could enlist in the army without parental consent, and those fourteen and fifteen could enlist only with parental consent. The nineteenth century was the peak of British imperial power, and British forces fought in numerous colonial wars, including the Indian Mutiny or Rebellion (1857), the Anglo-Zulu War (1879), the Boer Wars (1880–1881; 1899–1902), the First and Second Opium Wars (1839–1842; 1856–1869), the First and Second Anglo Afghan Wars (1839–1842; 1878–1880), as well as the Crimean War (1853–1856). All these wars were fought with an all-volunteer army. The army was very interested in recruiting boys, who could be recruited beginning at age fourteen. The boys would be enlisted and trained, but would ordinarily not "join the ranks" of the fighting men until they were older. In the meantime, they were employed in a variety of support roles. Regulations limited the number of boys to about 2 percent of the total corps. For example, in 1875 there were 3,031 boys in the army. Of these, 2,475 represented the 1 percent of boys allowed under the existing regulations at the time for training as musicians, 0.5 percent were apprentice tailors, and the remaining 0.5 percent were drummers and trumpeters.[98] It is also clear, however, that the boys were utilized in a variety of other work roles within the army. Of the fifty-nine boys enlisted in Royal Artillery from Industrial Schools as of November 16, 1876, the majority came from industrial schools in Ireland and enlisted between the ages of fourteen and fifteen. Only two were sixteen and one was seventeen at the time of their enlistment. The majority of the boys were employed as shoemakers, tailors, and carpenters, although there was also a bricklayer, a clerk, an engineer for the smith, a painter, a printer, a saddler, and a telegraphist. One shoemaker was also a harness maker. Many of the boys doubled as musicians, playing the horn, cornet, trombone, and other instruments.[99] It is by no means clear that these were the only boys in the Royal Artillery, since the data only illustrate the quality of those boys directly recruited from industrial schools.

The military believed that the best sources of soldiers were the royal military schools such as the Royal Military Asylum in Chelsea and the Royal Hiberium School in Dublin, which were military schools established primarily for the orphaned children of regular soldiers. The boys in these schools were believed to have a "hereditary predilection" for the army. But the military also strongly believed that industrial schools, reformatories, and schools established under the British Poor Laws were an important source of recruits. The army also saw that these young boys, who could be recruited out of school between ages fourteen and seventeen, would require less training than those who directly joined, because they had gained valuable skills in the schools. Boys would officially join the ranks at age seventeen. One witness before the commission, an inspector of the Industrial and Reformatory Schools in the United Kingdom, made plain that boys from reformatory schools were excellent candidates for military service. "Large number of these boys," he stated, "are only nominally criminals, who have been committed rather as a preventive measure than for any other reason. After 3 years' training their characters are usually fair, and eventually a certain number enter the Army; I believe they might be found conducting themselves well in every branch of the service."[100] However, another advantage to recruiting these boys was that because the schools acted *in loco parentis*, they could enlist without obtaining parental consent. Any boy could enlist in the army at age sixteen without parental consent in the United Kingdom, and boys between fourteen and sixteen could enlist with parental consent; but, as in the United States, boys in UK reformatories or industrial schools could enlist with the consent of their school.

Orphanages also played an important role in channeling boys into the military. In London, the Foundling Hospital created by Thomas Coram in 1741 had strong links to the military. The Foundling Hospital had many well-known benefactors and directors, including the artist William Hogarth and the composer George Frideric Handel. Established in 1847, a boy's hospital band was of singular importance to hospital life and resulted in scores of boys being sent into military bands at age fifteen during the nineteenth and early twentieth centuries.[101] By 1853 boys were being sent out to join ship bands in the navy. By 1856 the Coldstream Guards were also recruiting boys out of the hospital.[102] Hospital administrators did not usually keep track of the boys after enlistment, but occasional notations in the records suggest that being in the band did not protect boys from the dangers of military life. Augustus Brown joined the Thirty-Eighth Regiment of Foot in 1853 at age sixteen, and died at age seventeen in Sevastopol during the Crimean War in January 1855. John Rabnett, age fifteen, who enlisted with Brown, drowned in the Ganges River in 1857. James Howard, sixteen, and Charles Rutland, fifteen, both enlisted in the Second Battalion of the Royal Fusiliers in 1857. Both died in Mauritius a few years later. Edward Norton, who enlisted in the Fourteenth Hussars at age fourteen in 1874, committed suicide in Zululand in 1882.[103] As in the United States, there were multiple avenues into the military for boys. Britain's vast empire provided continuous military challenges, although nothing in the nineteenth century came close to the mass warfare that marked the second decade of the twentieth century.

British Child Soldiers in World War I

With the outbreak of World War I, national conscription was introduced in both Great Britain and the United States. This had a profound impact upon the recruitment of child soldiers, in that it brought a virtual halt to the systematic enlistment of underage soldiers. Enterprising youngsters with the will to enroll could always disguise their true ages and evade enlistment regulations, but national conscription eliminated institutional incentives to enroll the young. The entire logic of recruitment changed with conscription, which enabled the mass mobilization of the entire male population and eliminated the need for incentives to recruitment. The challenges of recruitment were replaced by the bureaucratic challenges of placing and training soldiers and weeding out the unfit; there simply was no longer any need to recruit young boys.

In Great Britain conscription was not instituted at the beginning of World War I (1914–1918). In fact at the outbreak of hostilities in August 1914, the British Army was the same army of volunteers that had served the country quite well in the nineteenth century. In 1914, the army consisted of approximately four hundred thousand soldiers, including the regular army and part-time and reserve forces. Army regulations governing recruitment provided that volunteers had to be at least eighteen years old and that only those over nineteen could be sent overseas to fight.

At the start of the war, Field Marshal Horatio Herbert Kitchener, Lord Kitchener, was appointed secretary of state for war. Correctly foreseeing a long war, Kitchener initiated a nationwide recruitment campaign. The army was flooded with recruits, as Great Britain became engulfed by a wave of patriotic and anti-German sentiment. Most of the trade unions, which had originally opposed war against Germany, lined up behind the government and the war. Public dissenters such as Bertrand Russell were few in number and widely reviled. Conscientious objectors were imprisoned. But the patriotic outburst for what many believed would be a short war was not long-lived. The summertime recruits did not march home victorious for Christmas, and enthusiasm for war and for Kitchener's army waned. By 1915, conscription was in the air and Britain instituted a national system requiring the registration of all males between fifteen and sixty-five. By 1916, Britain's volunteer army was abandoned, as Parliament introduced national conscription.

But during the first two years of the war, volunteerism was the norm, and the army was filled with boy soldiers, as boys from all over the country sought to enlist—in violation of army regulations. In the great rush to enlist, scant attention was paid any serious method of determining age. The army, hungry for soldiers, was a reluctant enforcer of its own regulations. A popular cartoon in *Punch* magazine told the tale: A recruiting officer asks an obviously underage applicant for enlistment, "Do you know where boys go who tell lies?" The boy answers, "To the front, sir."[104] George Coppard, who enlisted in 1914 in the Royal West Surrey Regiment at age sixteen, described himself as an "ordinary boy of elementary education and slender prospects" who was "as if drawn by a magnet" to the recruiting office. When he told the recruiting sergeant his true age, the sergeant said, "Clear off son. Come back tomorrow and see if you're nineteen, eh." He was back the very next day to accept the king's shilling as a new recruit.[105] Victor Silvester, the famous British dancer and orchestra leader, enlisted in November 1914 at the headquarters of the London Scottish Regiment at the Buckingham Palace Gate. He was fourteen years and nine months old. When asked his age, he said eighteen and nine months. He was examined by the medical officer, determined fit, and quickly sworn in. He returned home to inform his parents.[106]

During the course of the war some 8.7 million individuals served and 956,703 died from wounds, injury, or disease. By conservative estimates some 250,000 soldiers were underage, and about 55 percent of these were killed or wounded during the war.[107] Thus in World War I, Great Britain alone recruited as many child soldiers as are estimated to exist in the world today. Underage enlistment was at its highest in the beginning of the war, representing between 10 and 15 percent of recruits.[108] Young people could enlist without providing any documentation of age, so boys between the ages of fourteen and eighteen joined the steady stream into the ranks and formed a substantial portion of the overseas fighting forces.[109] Ultimately, the national registration system and the subsequent conscription substantially reduced the flow of those under eighteen into army, but boys who managed to enlist while underage largely remained in the service.

The White Feather Campaign

The public hunger for war reverberated through culture and society across the United Kingdom, and women and girls were quickly brought into the recruiting process. The most dramatic and controversial instance of women's involvement in recruiting was the activities of the White Feather Brigade, a strident and near paramilitary group of young women and girls that embarked on a recruitment campaign that used sexual shame to coerce boys and young men into service.[110] This group publically humiliated men and boys who were not yet in the army by handing out white feathers, traditional symbols of cowardice, to boys and men wearing civilian clothes whom they perceived to be fit for military service. The brigade was organized by Admiral Charles Penrose Fitzgerald in the summer of 1914, and its activities attracted the support of the British Baroness Emma Orczy, the novelist and playwright whose play The Scarlet Pimpernel had brought her international acclaim and success. Many of the targets of the White Feather Brigade were boys. James Lovegrove, who was sixteen when he joined the army, stated, "On my way to work one morning a group of women surrounded me. They started shouting and yelling at me, calling me all sorts of names for not being a soldier! Do you know what they did? They stuck a white feather in my coat, meaning I was a coward. Oh, I did feel dreadful, so ashamed."[111] Another fifteen-year-old who had lied about his age to get into the army in 1914 participated in the Battle of the Marne and the First Battle of Ypres, and when he subsequently contracted a fever, was discharged and sent home. He described a group of four girls who gave him white feathers. "I explained to them that I had been in the army and been discharged, and I was still only sixteen. Several people had collected around the girls and there was giggling, and I felt most uncomfortable and . . . very humiliated." He immediately rejoined the army.[112] Rifleman Norman Demuth of the London Rifles Brigade described being given a white feather just after he left school at age sixteen. But he also described another method of humiliation. "You would see a girl come toward you with a delightful smile," he said, "when she got to about five or six paces from you she would suddenly freeze up and walk past you with a look of utter contempt and scorn as if she could have spat."[113] Private S. C. Lang reported that he was walking down Camden High Street when two young ladies approached him and pushed a white feather up his nose. He soon found himself at the recruiting station.[114] These scenes were repeated in novels for children and youth published during the war such as Tom Bevan's *Doing His "Bit,"* in which the hero, Harry, describes his public humiliation and outrage at being handed a white feather in a London novelty shop.[115]

Exactly how widespread or effective the White Feather Brigade campaign was has been a subject of controversy. The novelist Virginia Woolf observed at the time that she did not believe it was very widespread. Nevertheless, she viewed these episodes as being as publicly damaging and degrading to men as a charge of unchastity was for women.[116] More recently, David Sibley, echoing her opinion, claimed that the description of the White Feather Brigade's actions have the air of myth.[117] But Nicoletta Gullace's recent systemic review of the archival data at the Imperial War Museum paints a picture of the brigade as engaging in a widespread and systematic campaign of public shaming and harassment that stampeded men and boys into the military, especially in London and the port cities of Britain.[118] To be sure, there was also some public backlash to the aggressive behavior of displayed by the brigade. But the White Feather Brigade was part of a broader movement that emerged at the onset of the war, in which women, girls, and a variety of patriotic, charitable, and humanitarian institutions joined forces to spur recruitment. The brigade's promoter, Baroness Orczy, also organized the Active Services League, whose goal was to have a hundred thousand women pledge "to persuade every man I know to offer his services to his country."[119] Other organizations such as the Mother's Union (a Christian charity that provided support and training for motherhood), the Red Cross, and the YMCA all participated in positioning women, symbolic and real, as central to recruitment efforts.[120] The key elements of persuasion were shame and pride: the shaming of those who did not voluntary serve and public displays of pride in the service, death, sacrifice, and martyrdom of those who did.[121] There is little doubt that there was widespread complicity by individuals and organizations from all segments of society—the political elite, the army, the church, the arts, civil society, the parents of the boys, and the boys themselves—to evade age restrictions.

Growing Resistance to Recruiting Children

Despite the strident patriotism of the early war years, resistance to recruiting boys emerged in some political circles. The Liberal Party, which prior to the war had been very much involved in socially progressive activities, including the creation of a national insurance system and the regulation of working hours, was a source of some dissent. The party had been the governing party when World War I began, but it split over its need to embrace a coalition government with conservatives during the war. Some opposition to recruiting youngsters came from antiwar and pacifist circles in both the Labour and Liberal Parties. Moreover, some members of Parliament, while not directly opposed to war in its entirety, were critical of specific policy issues, such as national conscription, the recruitment of underage soldiers, or the wide-ranging powers of control given the government at the onset of the war by the 1914 Defense of the Realm Act.

Among the Liberal Party leaders who opposed the recruitment of boys was Sir Arthur Markham, a member of a family of mine owners who was actively involved in developing coalfields and who served as a member of Parliament for Nottinghamshire. Beginning in October 1915, Markham and other members of Parliament, such as James Hogge, Patrick Meegan, Robert Outhwaite, James Thomas, and Henry Watt, began to challenge the government over the recruitment of underage boys who were voluntarily enlisting despite age limitations in military regulations. Given the large numbers of boys who were enlisting, he asked whether the War Office had given confidential instructions to the military to ignore age limitations.[122] Markham also attacked the military for failing to discharge boys it discovered were underage, even when parents had provided proof. He cited numerous cases, including that of John William Flint of the Eleventh Battalion of the Sherwood Foresters, who enlisted in November 1914 at the age of sixteen, and whose father and mother presented his birth certificate to the military authorities asking for his discharge. Almost a year later, their son was still overseas and not discharged from the army. He raised the case of Private G. Jones of the Eleventh Devonshire Regiment, who was sent to France on his fourteenth birthday, and asked what steps the secretary of war would take to prevent thirteen-year-olds from enlisting against the wishes of their parents.[123]

In a similar vein, Markham attacked the harassment of young men by military recruiters, claiming that they insulted boys of age fifteen who had not enlisted—labeling them "rotters" and "slackers." He asked that recruiting sergeants in Nottingham be ordered to desist from insulting and intimidating persons. He likewise protested against threats of boycotts against storeowners who refused to grant permission for their younger sons to enlist.[124]

In these and other instances the response of the government, usually delivered by Undersecretary of War Harold Tennant, was that no underage boys were enlisted with the knowledge of the War Office and that if any underage boys had enlisted it was their fault for having made false declarations.[125] As in the American Civil War, nearly insurmountable procedural and cultural obstacles blocked the way of parents who sought the discharge of their underage children. The British government refused to acknowledge the depth of the problem or to fully accept any duty to remedy the situation of underage soldiers in the ranks. As to any claims and proofs offered by parents about their underage recruits, Tennant answered that "underage soldiers serving with the Expeditionary Force will, if under eighteen years of age, be sent home *if willing* [my italics] and posted to a Reserve unit."[126] It is hard to imagine many young men, whose patriotism was already being exploited by the military, as Markham argued, would take up this offer and willingly leave their comrades on the front line.[127] Pressed by Labour Party MP James Thomas to ensure that no boy under age eighteen would be sent to the front, Tennant made clear that chronological age would not be the determining factor when he stated that "boys who have enlisted being under the minimum age are not sent abroad unless they are found to have physical qualifications of a youth of eighteen and a half."[128] In other words, anyone who looked old enough would go to the front.

Punishment and Execution of Boy Soldiers

Markham also raised the issue of the treatment of underage recruits, particularly when they were subject to adult discipline and punishment. He pointed to the charges of desertion leveled at three recruits, fifteen-year-old John Meakin, sixteen-year-old Alexander Guntripp, and seventeen-year-old William Haslewood. All had enlisted in July 1915, had deserted, and were found and taken into custody by the police while playing in a field. The justice before whom they were charged described them as children, asserting that no one could possibly have believed they were nineteen.[129]

The public was particularly outraged by the execution of boys charged with desertion or cowardice. During World War I, the British Army executed about three hundred soldiers from Great Britain and the Commonwealth. Soldiers were being executed at the rate of one soldier for each week of the war. Among these were several young soldiers, including Herbert Morris, a volunteer from Jamaica who enlisted in the British West Indies Regiment at age sixteen and was executed at age seventeen on September 20, 1917; Jamie Crozier from Belfast, Ireland, who enlisted in the Royal Irish Rifles when he was seventeen, but was eighteen at the time he was executed for desertion in February 27, 1916; Herbert Burden, of the First Battalion Northumberland Fusiliers, who was executed in Ypres in 1915 at age seventeen; and Aby Bevistein (aka Abraham Harris) of the Eleventh Battalion of the Middlesex Regiment, executed at age seventeen on March 20, 1916.

These executions had a profound effect on boy soldiers, one of whom, George Coppard, recalled that not long after he had arrived in France he was paraded into a field outside of the town of Meteren on the Belgian border. Told that his unit would be going into the trenches, he listened as the names of soldiers recently executed for desertion were read out to the troops. He described himself as "stupefied" by the experience.[130] Shortly before his death, Victor Silvester, who later in life became one of most famous bandleaders in Britain, revealed his participation in an execution squad in Staple, France, in 1917. Silvester himself was still an underage soldier, as may have been the soldier whom he shot.

> The victim was brought out from a shed and led struggling to a chair to which he was then bound and a white handkerchief placed over his heart as our target area. He was said to have fled in the face of the enemy. Mortified by the sight of the poor wretch tugging at his bonds, twelve of us, on the order raised our rifles unsteadily. . . . The tears were rolling down my cheeks as he went on attempting to free himself from the ropes attaching him to the chair. I aimed blindly and when the gun smoke had cleared away we were further horrified to see that, although wounded, the intended victim was

still alive. Still blindfolded, he was attempting to make a run for it still strapped to the chair. The blood was running freely from a chest wound. An officer in charge stepped forward to put the finishing touch with a revolver held to the poor man's temple. He had only once cried out and that was when he shouted the one word "mother." He could not have been much older than me.[131]

One case, that of Aby Bevistein, gained particular attention in Parliament because Bevistein had been seriously wounded and hospitalized and was probably suffering from shell shock at the time he was executed.[132] On May 4, 1916, F. W. Jowett of the Independent Labour Party, Labour Party MP Phillip Snowden, and Robert Outhwaite, a Liberal Party MP, raised the issue of Bevistein's execution. Bevistein was a Polish Jewish immigrant from London's East End who enlisted at age sixteen under the false name of Abraham Harris, giving his age as nineteen. On December 29, 1915, he was seriously wounded in a mine explosion that killed and wounded several fellow soldiers. He was hospitalized, suffering from wounds and shock. By February he was back for his eighteenth tour in the trenches on the front lines and was shaken up and deafened by the explosion of rifle grenades. Despite this, he was declared fit for duty once again, and was sent to the front lines; he fled from the front lines and shortly afterward was arrested and charged with desertion. He was brought before a court-martial, summarily tried, sentenced to death, and executed on March 20, 1916. After his death, his case was debated in Parliament. Robert Outhwaite castigated Harold Tennant, demanding, "Is the right hon. Gentleman aware that the sentence of death was passed within a month of this boy leaving hospital, where he had been for a nervous breakdown caused through wounds due to a mine explosion, and is it customary to shoot boys in such circumstances?"[133]

The execution of youngsters did not appear to have raised many moral issues within the army itself at the time. Frank Crozier, for example, the commanding officer of Jamie Crozier (no relation), wrote that at the time he fully approved of these harsh sentences, because of the impact that desertion would have upon the ability of the army to hold the line against the Germans, this despite the fact that Cozier described himself as a "silent witness" to what he knew was the false statement of age offered up by Jamie Crozier in his attestation papers at the time of his recruitment. In 1937, at the end of his life, Crozier reflected on the heady days at the beginning of the war outside the recruiting station: "England at War!! And outside eager youth, reckless and also glad; and flags and bands and clergy triumphant, and patriotic speeches."[134] As to Jamie Crozier, he wrote, "He was no rotter deserving to die like that. He was merely fragile. He had volunteered to fight for his country . . . at the dictates of his own young heart. He failed. And for that failure he was condemned to die—and he did at the hands of his friends, his brothers, with the approval of his church."[135]

Conscription and the End of Boy Soldiers

The British volunteer army that entered World War I in August 1914 was modeled on the army that had long been used to police the empire and suppress anticolonial revolts in the nineteenth century. The force of regular enlisted men was led by a socially elite officer corps, secure in the belief that the war would be short and victorious, and that the volunteer army would more than meet Britain's needs. As with the American Civil War, the public and the new recruits were promised a short war, an easy victory, and personal glory. The troops, it was widely proclaimed, would be "home before Christmas." Over a million men and boys volunteered to serve during the first months of the war.

War fever gripped nearly every segment of society, drawing volunteers from men and boys from all social classes. The children of the wealthy and well-educated joined skilled laborers, craftsmen, and workers from every industry in the unregulated volunteerism of the early days of the war. The recruitment of underage soldiers was an open secret. C.E.B. Russell, the chief inspector of reformatory and industrial schools, believed that 15 percent of the enlistees in the army were boys below age eighteen. Newspaper obituaries of young soldiers, such as that of Howard Tuck of the Royal Sussex Regiment, killed at age fifteen at Gallipoli in 1915, made plain the cost of the war to the young.[136] Accounts of fourteen-year-olds enlisting circulated in the *Daily Mail* and other newspapers in articles titled "Bantam Battalion of the Royal Scots—Youthful Soldiers," "The Fighting Spirit: Dauntless Youth Who Wants to Join the Army," "15 Year Old Soldiers," "Soldier of 14," "6 More Soldiers of 14," were widely published and read by the public. But there was also open dissent in letters to the editors that described what was sometimes termed the "growing evil" of child recruitment.[137]

The sudden flood of men and boys moving from the factory floor to the front lines negatively affected war production. The so-called Shell Scandal of 1915, the widespread belief that the shortage of shells led to British military failure, erupted into a political crisis that brought about the fall of the Liberal government. Moreover, as the war dragged on, casualties reached grotesque numbers and voluntary enlistments began to plummet. It was clear that the chaotic boom-and-bust character of voluntary recruitment was not sufficient for this type of mass warfare, which demanded a more efficient bureaucratic system of organizing men and allocating labor between the shop floor and the trenches. Long before the war, supporters of mandatory national service had advocated national conscription, but Great Britain was finally moved to embrace the concept by the inability of the volunteer army to meet the combined needs of both full-scale national mobilization and efficient wartime production. In July 1915, as a prelude to conscription, Parliament passed the National Registration Act, which required all persons between the ages of fifteen and sixty-five who were not members of the armed forces to register. This wartime census provided the British authorities with detailed age and manpower statistics and allowed the military to distinguish between persons to be called up for military service and those who would remain employed in the national interest in areas such as agriculture, coal mining, munitions, and shipbuilding and repair. In January 1916, Parliament passed the Military Service Act, which created a system of national service for first time in British history, that made all men from ages eighteen to forty-one subject to conscription.[138] With virtually the entire adult male population of Great Britain registered, classified, and subject to conscription, there was no longer any need to recruit boy soldiers. Doubtless some boys continued to evade regulations and enlist in the military, but the incentives for actively recruiting young boys rapidly disappeared. There would always be significant resistance to the draft, driven in part by the enormous numbers of soldiers who were killed or wounded on the front lines. Nonetheless, the combination of voluntary recruitment and conscription resulted in the enlistment of five million soldiers by the end of the war in November 1918.[139]

The issue of boy soldiers provided added moral weight to the arguments for national service, as advocates of conscription asserted that the recruitment of underage boys had a pernicious effect upon the army. In particular, they argued, the sight of wounded boys evoked both compassion and mothering among the adult troops, which interfered with their duties. They also pointed out that the killing and wounding of boys undermined the war effort by giving ammunition to pacifists and other so-called "peace at any price" advocates. They argued that the open lying and deceit involved in recruiting underage boys undermined the faith of the British people in the army and other institutions. But the arguments for eliminating child soldiers came not just from the pro-conscription camp; even many of those opposed to conscription saw the recruitment of youngsters as an evil. Some argued that compulsory military service constituted a new form of tyranny against a free-born people and reflected a growing militarism in the state. In this light the recruitment of underage boys was another sign that democracy had succumbed to militarism. Despite criticism of child recruitment from both sides, the War Office itself rejected all attempts at modifying its recruitment policies. It spurned the idea that enlistees be required to provide birth certificates, on the grounds of administrative efficiency and the overwork and confusion in governmental offices that would be required to produce these records. It rebuffed the view that young recruits be accepted provisionally until actual birth certificates were obtained.[140] It was national service alone that rang the death knell for the recruitment of boy soldiers. Generally, boys who had been recruited before national conscription were not released from service, but the flow of youngsters into the military came to a sudden and decisive end.

Conscription in America

The American experience with recruitment in World War I was quite different from that of the British. The United States entered the war in April 6, 1917, almost three years after the war began, and its involvement persisted until November 11, 1918, a period of about seventeen months. While President Woodrow Wilson originally hoped to create a volunteer army, this idea was quickly abandoned and Congress passed the Selective Service Act of 1917. Between 1917 and the end of the war, the United States drafted nearly 2.8 million men. The total number of soldiers was about 4.1 million, including voluntary enlistments and those who were part of the prewar military.[141] The vast majority of American troops were conscripts; the new Selective Service System created a national system of registration in which all U.S. male citizens and persons who declared their intention to become citizens between the ages of twenty-one and thirty-five were required to register for the draft. The age bar for conscription was set at twenty-one. The age for voluntary enlistment was set at eighteen, and by 1918 the Selective Service Act itself had been amended to require regis-tration of eighteen-year-olds. Selective Service was a national system that mobilized millions of soldiers for war. In contrast to the situation during the Civil War, volunteerism was no longer at the heart of national military conscription, and recruiters were no longer in search of volunteers to meet the demands of war. Selective Service did not completely eliminate under-age soldiers in the United States, however. Some youngsters continued to lie their way into military service, but Selective Service did allow for mass military mobilization with little need to search for recruits among younger age groups. It was no longer necessary to turn a blind eye to the presence of boys in the military.

In contrast to Great Britain, America was overtly hostile to volun-teerism as it organized its system of military conscription. American military recruitment embraced Taylorism and scientific management, and argued that voluntary recruitment disturbed the "scientific admin-istration of the task" and "impaired the efficiency" of the entire Selective Service enterprise. In this view, voluntary enlistment failed to distinguish between those persons whose labor might be indispensable for industrial production and those who were deemed "industrially worthless." Volun-teerism in the age of mass warfare and mass mobilization was inefficient in distributing manpower between military and industrial needs. By the end of the war, on November 11, 1918, more than 2.8 million men had been con-scripted. Voluntary enlistment was discontinued in the army on Decem-ber 15, 1917, and slowly came to an end in the other armed services by the end of the war.[142] The American view was that each registrant must await his time and perform his military obligations only in an orderly process.

World War I made plain the sheer horror of modern warfare. During the war 8,904,467 people were mobilized in the British Empire; of these 908,371 died from battle death, disease, and accidents, 2,090,212 were wounded, and 191,652 went missing or were taken prisoner. Total casualties numbered 3,190,235. In the United States, 4,355,000 were mobilized, 116,516 died from battle deaths and other causes, 204,002 were wounded, 4,500 went missing or were taken prisoner. Total casualties were 323,018 people. It is an ironic note that in the West the recruitment of child soldiers came to an end with the advent of mass war and the implementation of the bureaucratic and highly organized method of mobilizing the populace for war. Whatever the changing sentiments about children and war may have been, and however heartfelt the idea that childhood was incompatible with war, it was the bureaucratic management of recruitment that halted the recruitment of child soldiers in the United States and Great Britain. This vast record-keeping bureaucracy could match every person in society with the virtually unquenchable need for manpower required by mass warfare. The very system that kept children off the battlefield sent hundreds of thousands of adults to their deaths.

3

Child Soldiers in World War II

The systematic recruitment of child soldiers in Great Britain and the United States came to an end with World War I. But the end of war in 1918 did not bring about an era of peace. Though touted by U.S. president Woodrow Wilson as "the war to end all wars," World War I was only a prelude to countless horrific conflicts that spread across the globe in the twentieth century. World War II began only twenty-one years later, with the Nazi invasion of Poland on September 1, 1939. By then the landscape for child recruitment had changed dramatically, for with the notable exception of Nazi Germany the Western European powers no longer systematically recruited children. This did not mean, however, that there were no child soldiers involved in the conflict. Instead, civil wars, insurgencies, and rebellions of every type continued to draw in the young.

Child soldiers were certainly involved in the conflicts in Spain, where the rise of fascism and the Spanish Civil War (1936–1939) have come to be widely understood as a "dress rehearsal" for the World War II. Child soldiers were a constant presence in Spain during these years, although numbers are uncertain. Julian Laplaza Perez, who was fifteen when he joined the fascist Nationalist army in Spain, noted that boys his age came from all over Spain to fight.[1] In his war memoir *Homage to Catalonia*, George Orwell—who fought on the Republican side and was wounded in the conflict—described the presence of child soldiers as young as eleven in the Republican ranks, although he generally thought that there were few soldiers below age fifteen on the front lines. Orwell also thought that younger soldiers did not make very good fighters. In his view, they needed too much sleep and the youngest were so undisciplined as to constitute a "public menace."[2] Anna Starinov, who was sent to Spain by the Soviet Union to organize Republican guerillas behind the lines of Franco's rebel forces, had to contend with the presence of children in the Republican forces, and found them to be more of a nuisance than an asset.[3]

Child Soldiers in Nazi Germany

The most well-known systematic state-directed recruitment of children during World War II was carried out by the combat organizations of Germany's Nazi Party. As Nazism emerged in Germany, it involved a striking and radical mobilization of youth. Virtually all German youth—both boys and girls—were recruited into the Hitler Jugund or Hitler Youth, a highly militaristic organization that worshipped militarism and the Nazi cause. Nazi Germany was a youth-centered society; the Nazi Party itself celebrated the young, and youth was very much a key element of its vitality and strength.[4] The party publicly scorned the older generation, blaming it for Germany's defeat in World War I. Hitler himself was obsessed with the idea of youth as a potent political force. Military service for youth was widely propagated as an ideal in popular culture, including in documentaries and feature films.[5] Nonetheless, despite their militant ideological roots and widespread small arms practice, the young people of the Hitler Youth actually received little practical military training.[6]

The recruitment of child soldiers in Nazi Germany resulted from the powerful organizational relationship—a virtual generational alliance—between the Hitler Youth and the SS, an organization the Hitler Youth idealized and emulated.[7] The SS (Schutzstaffel or Protective Force) was the Nazi Party's elite paramilitary force. It was also one of the most criminal elements of the Nazi regime, infamous for its brutality and its enthusiastic participation in the wholesale murder of civilians, especially Jews. The SS was first organized to provide protection and support for Nazi Party actions and meetings, but it evolved into an actual combat force, the Waffen SS, a full-fledged army with thirty-eight divisions under the direct control of the Nazi Party. In all, about 82 percent of German young people joined the Hitler Youth, and the group's leaders were significant actors in spreading anti-Semitic propaganda and systematically stirring up hatred across Germany.[8] Hitler Youth played a key role during Kristallnacht (Night of Broken Glass), the infamous Nazi-orchestrated national pogrom against Jews in Germany on November 9, 1938. They were instrumental in the devastation and violence, including burning about a thousand synagogues, smashing Jewish shop windows, destroying and looting homes, hospitals, and schools, and murdering innocent civilians.[9] After the invasion and occupation of Poland, Hitler Youth actively supported the activities of the SS and were involved in making decisions to expel civilians and to deport and/or murder Jews and Poles.[10] Thus, by passion, ideology, design, and circumstance the Hitler Youth served as a junior SS.[11]

By 1935, military conscription was mandatory in Nazi Germany. But despite the militarization of youth by the Nazi Party, the regular German armed forces, the Wehrmacht, did not normally conscript children. This remained generally true through much of World War II, with some important and glaring exceptions toward the end. Instead, it was the Waffen SS that became a prime recruiter of child soldiers. Major recruitment into the SS began in the wake of the stunning defeat of the German army at Stalingrad in February 1943. The defeat at Stalingrad was a reversal of fortune for German armed forces, which had, from the beginning of the war in 1939, achieved near total victory in their conquest and occupation of Europe. A devastating number of German soldiers—three-quarters of a million—were killed, missing, or wounded at Stalingrad, and the defeat quashed German dreams of unchallenged conquest.[12] In response, Hitler began to dig deeper into the German population for soldiers and ordered the creation of a Waffen SS panzer (armored tank) division that recruited boys between sixteen and a half and seventeen years of age, born in 1926, from the older members of the Hitler Youth. An initial pool of some thirty thousand boys was drawn upon to form the division, which was ultimately deployed against the Allies in the Normandy invasion in June 1944. By 1943, the Waffen SS was recruiting widely from the Hitler Youth. In some parts of Germany they recruited 80 to 92 percent of sixteen-year-olds, and by 1945 youngsters as young as fourteen and fifteen were pulled into SS units.[13] Recruitment of youth increased in other areas as well. By 1943, youth began to be recruited as Flakhelferin (auxiliaries) to man aircraft batteries and assist in other activities. The American anthropologist Karl Schlesier was a fifteen-year-old high school student in Germany when he and eleven of his schoolmates became part of the two hundred thousand boys between ages fifteen and sixteen who were called up in 1943.[14] The Flakhelferin were part of the Flieger HJ, the air division of the Hitler Youth. Many died at the flak guns during air raids, others engaged in ground combat during the Allied invasion of Germany, and many were killed or captured.[15]

Children at the Endgame of War

Germany radically increased its recruitment of children in the months preceding its military defeat in 1945. The Allies demanded Germany's unconditional surrender, but the Nazi regime was determined to fight to the end. By the time Soviet troops were poised to invade Germany in 1945, child recruitment was a central element of the Germany's last-ditch attempt to save the Nazi regime. By 1945, even the Wehrmacht began to conscript children age fifteen or even younger. As part of the endgame, the Nazi Party also organized the Volkssturm, a national militia that conscripted virtually anyone between the ages of sixteen and sixty who was not otherwise serving. When the Volkssturm was first formed, the Hitler Youth offered to enroll up to three hundred thousand youngsters in the militia, but were dismayed by the intention of the Volkssturm to use the oldest children first and leave the fifteen-, sixteen-, and seventeen-year-olds as a backup force. As a result, the Hitler Youth functioned semiautonomously, and used the Volkssturm as a cover for Hitler Youth combat troops.[16] The Soviet Army referred to these mixtures of children and the elderly as "totals," seeing them as a product of the total mobilization of the civilian population; the Wehrmacht, the regular army, referred to them more casually as "casserole."[17]

Children and youth played a chilling and macabre role in the last days of the Nazi regime. As Ian Kershaw has made plain, Nazi Germany's immovable refusal to capitulate to the Allies and the Soviets was unprecedented in human history.[18] Hitler and the Nazi political and military elite had rejected surrender and were determined to fight on.[19] Although there were many complex and contradictory reasons that Germans continued to fight, even as their country was laid to ruin, this last battle was fought by adult men and women, children, and even the elderly, many though by no means all of whom remained committed to Hitler. As the Soviet Army crossed into Germany and began the drive to Berlin and the final conquest and occupation of Germany, thousands of children went to their deaths in a desperate attempt to save the Nazi regime. In the endgame, the true logic of Nazi fanaticism prevailed, as barely trained children battled experienced soldiers to the death. Even in these final moments, the national leader of the Hitler Youth, Arthur Axman, raised a Hitler Youth division and compared this final German battle to the heroism of Sparta, rallying the youngsters and urging them on to total victory or defeat.[20] In the concluding days of the war a battalion of one thousand Hitler Youth aged fifteen and sixteen fought in the Battle of Wannsee Bridge.[21] Five thousand Hitler Youth saw action in the Battle of Berlin; only five hundred survived.[22] Even as the defense of Berlin collapsed, Hitler Youth and SS systematically killed anyone trying to surrender, and fired at any house that displayed a white flag.[23] When the Berlin Philharmonic gave its last performance on the evening of April 12, 1945, the audience was filled with the Nazi military and political elite. As the concert concluded with the finale of Richard Wagner's *Götterdämmerung* (Twilight of the Gods), uniformed Hitler Youth distributed baskets of cyanide capsules among the audience.[24] Many Hitler Youth demonstrated near-apocalyptic fanaticism, but the final days of battle also involved large numbers of youngsters who had been press-ganged into the slaughter by the SS.[25]

In the closing days of the war, children and youth also participated in the final atrocities visited upon Jews and others who were still held captive in German concentration camps. Between January and March 1945, as the Red Army closed upon Germany, the Germans began to evacuate concentration camps in western Poland and eastern Germany and force-marched their captives into Germany beyond Allied reach. Between March 1945 and the end of the war, these marches ceased to have any purpose and had become simply death marches; prisoners were marched aimlessly through the countryside and died of wounds, exhaustion, disease, starvation, and massacre. Even in the last hours of the war, German children threw stones at dying and starving Jews. A survivor of the death march from the Dora-Mittelbau concentration camp (a subcamp of the Buchenwald camp at Weimar, Germany) described how on April 13, 1945, the marchers were attacked by a combination of young people from the Hitler Youth and local police, and chased en masse into a large barn that was then set ablaze, burning thousands of people alive. One day later, while the bodies were still burning, the area was liberated by Allied troops.[26]

The Werewolves: Children as Terrorists

Some children continued in their combatant roles after the formal surrender of the Nazi regime. During the final days of the war, the SS recruited Hitler Youth into the so-called Werewolves, a last-ditch effort to create a Nazi guerrilla movement behind Allied lines. Werewolf guerillas were deployed to penetrate enemy lines, obtain information about Allied troop locations and movements, assassinate German officials cooperating with Allied forces, and engage in murder and sabotage of every kind. The SS saw the Werewolves as the core of any future Nazi guerrilla movement that might emerge after surrender. But the Werewolf forces were quickly overwhelmed. Werewolf activity reached its peak in the spring of 1945, but their attacks, although vicious and fanatical, remained small scale, and most of the youngsters involved came to a bad end.[27] Many Werewolf units, including a group of heavily armed twelve-year-olds, were virtually wiped out. Others seem to have been captured, disappeared, or summarily executed.[28] Some captured Werewolves were subject to formal military tribunals. Two youngsters, Heinz Petry and Josef Schorner, ages sixteen and seventeen, were captured and tried for espionage by the U.S. military. Their youth did not save them. While the military court condemned German army leaders for assigning boys to be spies, it determined to make an example of the boys by imposing the death penalty. The court told them, "You will pay the supreme penalty for your offenses so that the German people will know that we intend to use whatever force is necessary to eradicate completely the blight of German militarism and the Nazi ideology from the face of the earth."[29] They were executed by an American firing squad in June 1945, just a few weeks after the war in Europe had ceased.[30] Karl Panzeler, another captured youth, was luckier; his death sentence was commuted because of his age.[31]

Child Prisoners of War

Many thousands of German boy soldiers were captured by the Allies and placed in POW camps. The U.S. Army established the Attichy-Compiegne-Croutoy POW camp, known as the Central Continental Prisoners of War

Enclosure #15, on a Luftwaffe airfield, and held about seven thousand child soldiers between twelve and seventeen who had been drafted into the Wehrmacht in the final months of the war. All were held as prisoners in the so-called Baby Cage, a separate enclosure for younger prisoners of war.[32] Although this POW camp had serious food shortages and many of the prisoners suffered from hunger, the younger soldiers were given both better food rations and an opportunity for education.[33]

Boy soldiers who fell into the hands of the Red Army could not count on surviving. The Soviet Army was poised for revenge, and the Red Army probably executed many of the German boy soldiers it captured, especially if they had been part of the hated SS or Hitler Youth units. Gabriel Sedlis, a well-known New York architect, was a Jewish teenage partisan under the authority of the Red Army in Poland; he described the fate of a teenage SS volunteer captured and turned over to the army when the German garrison in Vilna was overrun. Sedlis was attached to headquarters and was fluent in German; he spent the night speaking informally to the boy captive and in that conversation assured the boy that he would be treated as a prisoner of war. He described the moment as a conversation between two teenagers who were talking about their futures now that the war was almost over. However, the very next morning Sedlis was ordered to shoot the boy; though he refused, someone else carried out the sentence. Sedlis did, however, follow orders to bury him.[34]

The role of child soldiers in Nazi Germany is notable because of the levels of commitment and fanatic devotion many children retained for the Nazi cause, but in this respect the children were not very dissimilar to adults. The Nazi movement was always a radical populist movement that held the German people in thrall. The mass of ordinary Germans, adult and child, who were Hitler's "willing executioners" were also his willing soldiers. Hitler's passion and charisma shaped and drove the Nazi agenda, but it was youngsters, often fanatical youngsters, who largely provided the Nazi movement's cultural resonance.

In the contemporary discourse about child soldiers, the assertion is usually made that child soldiers are the result of adults exploiting children. Were German child soldiers victims? Clearly some were the victims of pressure or exploitation in Nazi Germany, but what is more striking is the collective participation of the German people—children, youth, and adults—in the mad spectacle of power and violence that characterized Nazi Germany during peace and war. The Nazification of children and adults began as a peacetime project between 1933 and 1939, and the early Nazi conquests and victories in war only cemented popular support and devotion to Hitler. Only as Germany began to lose the war and Germans began to pay the price for a decade of Nazi rule did Hitler's star begin to fade. Tagging German children as "victims" may be an interesting legal notion, but it distorts the role of children and youth in the collective expression of power and violence in Nazi Germany, and equally important, does a supreme injustice to the real victims of Nazi terror. By relinquishing the modern lens of child soldier as "victim" in this instance, and looking at the actual circumstances of children's participation in the Nazi agenda, we are left with a sense of both fascination and repulsion at the virtually unparalleled embrace of collective violence by children and youth in modern history.

The Child Partisans of World War II

The child soldiers of Nazi Germany stand out as an example of the mobilization of children and youth for war and terror. But the vast majority of the child soldiers of World War II were not among the ranks of the Nazis but rather among their victims. All across Europe—from France to Italy, Spain, Yugoslavia, Poland, and the Soviet Union—youngsters joined in guerrilla actions to battle the German invasion and conquest.

Such guerrilla resistance was exceptionally dangerous and risky. Partisan fighters, even children, were not protected by the laws of war, and when captured they were not deemed prisoners of war. They were generally regarded as *francs-tireurs* or "free shooters," that is, civilians who had taken up arms against the enemy. Under the laws of war, partisans were considered unlawful combatants or unlawful belligerents and could be summarily executed upon capture. Indeed, this is exactly how Germans dealt with captured partisans, regardless of their age.

That this ruthless approach toward captured partisans had the imprimatur of international law was made plain in the so-called Hostages Trials, where General Siegmund Wilhelm Walther von List and others were tried before the U.S. Military Tribunal at Nuremberg. In the trial, held from

July 8, 1947, to February 19, 1948, List and others were tried for the German policy of seizing and executing civilian hostages as well as for the routine execution of captured partisans. List commanded the German army in Yugoslavia and Greece following the surrender of the Yugoslavian and Greek armies.

In the court's view, after the regular armies of Yugoslavia and Greece capitulated, both countries were deemed occupied by Germany within the meaning of international law. In both countries armed groups of partisans emerged to fight the German occupation. These partisan armed groups battled the German occupation by damaging transportation and communication lines and engaging in surprise attacks on German soldiers, after which they retreated and concealed themselves among the civilian population. The partisans' ambushes of German troops became a common practice, and they often tortured and killed captured German soldiers.[35] For their part, the Germans executed not only all captured partisans and resisters, but also thousands of innocent civilians in reprisal. At trial, List and others were found guilty of war crimes for the reprisal executions, but were acquitted as a matter of law for the routine summary execution of captured partisans, including children.

During World War II the treatment of captured partisans was governed by Article I of the Hague Convention of 1907, which defined the kinds of captured combatants entitled to be treated as prisoners of war. Captured combatants who were deemed prisoners of war could not presumptively be treated as criminals by their captors. Under the Hague Treaty, combatants who qualified for prisoner of war status were required to operate under the following conditions: They had to (1) be commanded by a person responsible for his subordinates, (2) have a fixed, distinctive emblem recognizable at a distance, (3) have carried arms openly, and (4) have conducted their operations in accordance with the laws and customs of war. Typically, those combatants qualifying for prisoner of war status were members of the official armed forces of a nation. In contrast, civilians, including former soldiers, who took up arms against an occupying power were not entitled to prisoner of war status upon capture. These persons, sometimes called unlawful belligerents or unlawful combatants, could be treated by their captors as war criminals and summarily executed. The military tribunal at the Hostage Trials determined that under the Hague

Convention the guerrilla forces participating in the incidents noted at trial were not entitled to be classed as lawful combatants, and were therefore not entitled to prisoner of war status upon capture.[36] Accordingly, for their sheer survival, the vast majority of partisan and guerrilla forces fighting against Nazi Germany relied on their ability to disguise themselves and blend in with the civilian population. The military tribunal made plain that although such guerrillas may have rendered a great and heroic service to their country, when they were captured by the enemy, they could lawfully be treated as war criminals.[37] For this reason, the court found the Yugoslavian and Greek guerrillas to be *francs-tireurs* who could be put to death when captured. General List therefore bore no criminal responsibility for the execution of captured partisans in Yugoslavia and Greece while he was the German commander in the region.[38]

The basic rules of the Hague Convention remained in force following World War II and were incorporated into the Geneva Conventions of 1949. The Hague Convention made no exception for the treatment of children who were unlawful combatants. Of course, in many respects, consideration of age was largely irrelevant to German forces, who routinely executed children under a wide variety of pretexts. During the Hostages trials, evidence of the German execution of children included the cases of a fourteen-year-old boy who was executed as a hostage and a young partisan who was publically tortured, beaten, shot, and thrown on a refuse heap.[39]

The fate of many child partisans was sealed when they were captured. Among the more notorious killings of youngsters was the hanging on October 26, 1941, of two child partisans—Maria "Masha" Bruskina, age seventeen, and Volodia Sherbateyvich, age sixteen—together with Kiril Trus, a World War I veteran. These are believed to have been the first public executions during the Nazi occupation of Soviet territory.[40] All were members of the Minsk Resistance in Belorussia (now Belarus). The executions were spectacles of terror. The condemned were paraded through the streets of Minsk. Bruskina was a Jewish volunteer nurse who helped wounded members of the Red Army escape.[41] She was forced to wear a placard proclaiming in Russian and in German, "We are partisans and we have shot at German soldiers," although she had shot at no one. Carried out one at a time in front of a yeast factory, the hangings were designed so that the victims would slowly strangle to death at the end of the rope;

their bodies were left hanging for three days. But the brave composure of the partisans as they faced a cruel death, especially that of Bruskina, resulted in their being widely recognized as heroes of the resistance in postwar Soviet Union. Many other public executions of partisans by the Germans involved girls and women, no doubt with the idea that the executions of these youngsters would be particularly terrifying to local populations. Among these was seventeen-year-old Lepa Svetozara Radić, who was posthumously awarded the Order of the People's Hero of Yugoslavia.[42]

Children in the Resistance

Many children risked their lives in the struggle against German occupation and Nazism, despite the high risk of severe retribution or death. Danielle Mitterrand, the wife of former French president François Mitterrand, became actively involved in the French Resistance at age seventeen. Guy Môquet, another member of the French Resistance, was only seventeen when he was executed by the Germans in retaliation for the killing of a German officer. One of the youngest members of the French Resistance during World War II, Elisabeth Sevier, joined at sixteen.[43] In Yugoslavia, as the novelist Howard Fast described it, men, women, and children rose up against the invader.[44]

The 1943 *Life* magazine photo-essay "The Battlefield of Naples" dramatically captured the participation of children and youth in the Italian Resistance. German control of Naples was collapsing, and partisan attacks broke out everywhere. One partisan, Sandro Aurisicchio De Val, photographed three of his young comrades in arms, including a nine-year-old sniper. In the photograph the children look weary, defiant, and proud. One boy was wounded in an arm and a leg. A cigarette juts out of the mouth of the nine-year-old, who is armed and barefoot. In another photograph, a nine-year-old with a side arm declares that he would not take any Germans or Italian fascists alive. He was said to have been admired by his fellow soldiers for his ruthless seriousness. In Curia, a high school teacher named Antonio Tasia led his young students, ages fourteen to twenty, against German positions; twenty students were killed in the action. *Life* war photographer Robert Capa captured the anguish of the women of Naples over the deaths of their young sons in his iconic photograph *Funeral of 20 Teenage Partisans.*[45]

Children in Central and Eastern Europe played perhaps an even greater role than those in the West. Partisan groups arose in virtually every country from Poland to Belarus in response to the German conquests of Eastern Europe. In her recent study of Soviet children during World War II, Olga Kucherenko shows that up to three hundred thousand children were in Soviet-affiliated partisan groups, primarily connected to the Red Army. Many received military honors for their actions. The majority of children were not direct combatants, although the German invasion of the Soviet Union obliterated any meaningful distinction between civilians and combatants as everyone—adult or child, male or female—was drawn into warfare. Though Kucherenko points out that there were no special units in the Red Army that consisted solely of underage soldiers, she mentions that war veterans refer to so-called *patsaniach'i divizii* (lads' divisions) or *detskie sady* (kindergartens), where the majority of men were ages sixteen or seventeen. Kucherenko makes clear, however, that the majority of children who joined the war-related struggles fought on their own volition.[46]

Jewish Children

Jewish children played a key role in Jewish resistance during World War II and the Holocaust. In the era between World War I and II, Jewish youth groups flowered all over Europe, especially in the Eastern European countries of Poland, Lithuania, Belorussia, and Ukraine. The most prominent of these groups brought together largely secular Jewish youth for social and cultural activities, and relied upon a scouting model for their basic organization. All tended to recruit children from about thirteen to eighteen into their activities and sometimes even created additional groups for younger children.

Many youth groups were tied to political movements. The socialist Jewish Labor Bund, a left-wing political party tied to the trade union movement, and its youth wing, Tsukunft (officially Yugnt Bund Tsukunft or Youth Bund—the Future), are prominent among these. The Bund promoted the activities of Jewish adults and youth, promoted Yiddish as the language of the Jewish working class, and spread socialism throughout Poland and Eastern Europe. The Bund also had a paramilitary militia, composed of the toughest members of its largely working-class constituency. In contrast to the Bund, Zionist youth groups combined socialism with the more ancient

Jewish tradition of return to the land of Israel. The primary goal of these groups was to promote the immigration of youth to Palestine and create socialist communal and collective settlements (*kibbutz*, plural *kibbutzim*) in which Jews would neither be exploited nor exploit others. These groups' underlying belief was that life as socialist farmers in the land of Israel would be the solution to anti-Semitism and the oppression of Jews in Europe. The most important of these groups were Dror (Freedom), which was tied to the Zionist Workers Party in Poland and the United Kibbutz (Kibbutz Meuchad) movement in Israel, and HaShomer Hatzair (the Young Guard), which was linked to the National Kibbutz (Kibbutz Artzi) movement in Israel. There were some significant differences between these groups. Dror tended to draw its membership from working-class youth, had a less dogmatic and more liberal view of socialism, and was skeptical of the Soviet Union. HaShomer Hatzair's membership came from better educated and wealthier Jews, but the organization was far more Marxist and tied to the policies of the Soviet Union. HaShomer also actively promoted scouting activities that brought it into contact with non-Jewish scouting organizations in Poland, contacts that would serve it well when the war broke out. A wide range of other youth organizations also played a role in the resistance, such as Gordonia, named after A. D. Gordon, an intellectual follower of the Russian novelist and utopian socialist Leo Tolstoy, and Akiva, named after a rabbi and scholar of the Talmudic era, which, despite its name, was nonreligious but respectful of Jewish traditions. Akiva was Zionist in orientation but also nonsocialist. Other groups, like Hanoar Hatzioni (Zionist Youth), were generally nonpolitical and humanist in their orientation, while others, such as Betar, were right-wing Jewish nationalists. Just prior to the outbreak of World War II, the main Zionist groups had almost sixty-seven thousand members spread over more than nine hundred branches in Poland alone.[47] If the non-Zionist youth wings of the socialist and communist parties are included, organized youth movements had a membership of about a hundred thousand just prior to the outbreak of the war, and of these, some two thousand youth were active members of the ghetto-fighting organizations in Poland.[48]

In the 1930s in Europe, Jews were the targets of individual and collective anti-Semitic attacks. With the rapid spread of anti-Semitism, youth groups became more concerned with self-defense. The idea of organized self-defense was not unique to the youth groups. Many European political parties had paramilitary units that protected their members from attack, but the concern was especially acute in Poland, the center of the Jewish youth movements. The increasing intensity of anti-Semitism in Poland paralleled developments in Germany, and by 1935 at least one girl had been shot and killed by unknown attackers at a youth movement lecture.[49] By 1939, shortly before the outbreak of the war, some five hundred youth group members had received some self-defense training,[50] but these training sessions were seriously constrained because it was almost impossible for Jews to obtain arms for training. Moreover, until the actual outbreak of the war in 1939, the youth groups remained primarily focused on encouraging immigration to Palestine. The outbreak of war radically transformed these groups into fighting units.

The actual outbreak of the war surprised many of the most prominent members of the youth organizations. As German bombs were dropping on Bialystok, Poland, nineteen-year-old Chaika Grossman was meeting with the fifteen- and sixteen-year-old members of her HaShomer Hatzair group and was concerned that they could not grasp the dangers of war.[51] But despite the sudden onset of war and initial organizational disarray, it was not long before the youth movements responded to the danger. The house owned by the Dror movement in Warsaw was quickly transformed into a center of communal living, clandestine education, and underground activity. Disguised as a center for refugees, the house became a residence for Dror and other youth movement leaders and members, where they met to develop a response to the German occupation, prepared and distributed papers and publications of the underground, and reestablished Jewish educational programs that had been suppressed by the Germans. As food became increasingly scarce, members began to move in together to share resources. Activity within the house intensified when the Warsaw Ghetto was created and sealed.[52] An article in the underground newspaper *Dror*, published in Warsaw in August 1940, speaks the need to forge a "cadre of Jewish youth that is prepared for battle."[53]

As the occupation deepened, more and more youth groups evolved into underground resistance organizations. At first, resistance was nonviolent and centered on creating an underground press, disseminating anti-Nazi materials, and developing a courier network to keep the youth movements informed about the activities of members of their own groups and communities and those of the Jewish community in other regions and cities. Participating in any form of resistance, even nonviolent resistance (especially the underground press), was punishable by death. To make the point clear, on April 18, 1942, the Germans publicly executed a group of printers and distributors of underground papers.

Zionist youth groups figured prominently role in armed resistance. Of course they were not the only organizations that resisted the Germans: the Jewish Labor Bund, the communists, and other groups were involved in the resistance, and in some ghettos may even have had a dominant role. But as a whole, Zionist youth groups were the leaders of armed Jewish resistance to the Germans.[54] Long before the war, youth groups had functioned as surrogate forms of family and kinship for their members, and the relationships between many members were strengthened during the occupation. In addition, the occupation generated a move toward communal living, as young people left their families and lived with friends in the movement. Because of the intimacy and trust built among the members over many years, local chapters could be converted into clandestine cells of resistance that utilized movement resources such as meeting places and mimeograph machines to publish underground papers.[55] Another reason the youth movements were so effective in the resistance was that their leadership system remained intact after the occupation, and youth group leaders were committed to not abandoning their groups. This was significantly different from the situation faced by most of the Jewish political parties in Poland, whose leadership fled to the safety of the Soviet umbrella, leaving the rank and file with less experienced and less able leaders who could not agree upon a decisive course of resistance.[56] In stark contrast, at the very beginning of 1940 many of the most important youth activists from HaShomer Hatzair and Dror returned from the relative safety of Soviet-occupied Poland back into German-occupied territory to ensure the continuity of the youth movements.[57] So the youth groups had a leadership cadre with both the discipline and the courage to mount an armed resistance.

Finally, the situation of Jewish child partisans was distinctly different from that of non-Jews, in that all Jewish children were marked for death, whether or not they joined the resistance: There were no zones of safety for Jewish children. They could not save themselves by remaining noncombatants. One and a half million Jewish children—90 percent of the Jewish children of Europe—were murdered by the Germans and their allies during the Holocaust. The challenge for Jewish child partisans was one of identity as much as of survival. In the face of near certain death, they wanted to die with their dignity—and their identity—intact.

Contested Legacies: Child Soldiers and the Politics of Memory

Both during and after World War II, the child soldier emerged as a key symbol of national sacrifice, suffering, and valor. In 2007, newly elected French president Nicolas Sarkozy's first official act was to order that the final letter of Guy Môquet, written to his parents right before his execution by the Germans, be read annually in French schools.[58] In April 2013, the Italian child partisan Ugo Forno was posthumously awarded the Gold Medal for Civic Merit in Rome. Forno, a twelve-year-old student, led an attack on German positions on June 5, 1944, and was killed in action.[59] The attack took place as German armies were retreating from Rome and blowing up bridges to cover their retreat. Forno, said to have been a lively, intelligent, restless, and above all patriotic boy, was armed with light weapons, and organized a group to attack a band of soldiers who were attempting to destroy a railway bridge over the Aniene River.[60] Forno's death has been commemorated with a number of public events. At a memorial service to Forno, a plaque was placed near the old railway bridge and a certificate delivered to his former school. There are plans to build a monument to him and five other youngsters who fought alongside him that day.[61]

Zoya Kosmodemyanskaya: The Joan of Arc of the Soviet Union

Many of the most interesting and powerful stories of the sacrifices of child soldiers are those that also have the most contested and problematic legacies. The most famous is that of Zoya Kosmodemyanskaya, widely regarded as the Joan of Arc of the former Soviet Union. Zoya was a teenage school girl when she joined a Soviet partisan unit in October 1941. The Germans captured her and executed her on November 29, 1941, which led to her elevation as a Soviet martyr. She was the first female to be awarded the title Hero of the Soviet Union during World War II. Her exact age is unclear:

some sources report her birth date as January 21, 1924, others September 8 or September 13, 1923,[62] so she was either seventeen or eighteen when she joined a partisan unit in October 1941.

Zoya began to participate in partisan activities after the Germans invaded Eastern Europe in June 1941. By November 1941, the German army seemed unstoppable, and Germany had seized control of Latvia, Lithuania, Estonia, Belarus, Ukraine, and western Russia. By October 1941, the Battle of Moscow was under way and Soviet troops fought a bitter and bloody campaign to halt German advances on its capital city. As the Soviet Union desperately organized its armed forces in defense of the capital, it also deployed partisan units to infiltrate German lines in German-occupied territories of the Soviet Union to disrupt German communications and wherever possible to destroy resources in the villages and towns that had fallen under German occupation. Zoya was one of these partisans.

After being trained in sabotage and reconnaissance, Zoya crossed the German lines about seventy kilometers southwest of Moscow. The partisans were under orders to burn and destroy Russian settlements behind the German lines, including the village of Petrishchevo. On November 27, Zoya and two other partisans, Boris Kraynev and Vasily Klubkov, set out to torch houses in Petrishchevo, where German soldiers were quartered. Kraynev is said to have quickly fled alone after the action and Klubkov was captured. Zoya decided to return to Petrishchevo the next day, and was captured by the Germans as she tried to burn down a barn. There is no doubt that she was brutally tortured. *Time* magazine reported that her German captors flogged her with a leather belt, punched her with their fists, held lighted matches to her chin, scraped a saw across her back, and walked her for hours through the snow at bayonet point, barefoot.[63] The next morning, November 29, 1941, she was publicly hanged in the village.

Zoya's fate was consistent with German policy toward partisans or anyone else who resisted the German conquest and occupation of Eastern Europe. The Germans ordered that all captured partisans were to be hanged—without exception.[64] Women and girl partisans were particularly vilified. On October 10, 1941, General Walter von Reichenau issued a secret order to troops operating in the eastern territories that reiterated that female partisans, whom he termed "unnatural women," should never be treated as prisoners and should be executed.[65]

Little was known of Zoya's terrible fate until Petrishchevo was recaptured by Soviet forces in January 1942, more than a month after her execution. Pyotr Lidov, a journalist for the Soviet newspaper *Pravda*, heard about Zoya's execution and traveled to the village to gather the grim details from village residents. He published a detailed account in *Pravda* on January 27, 1942, that contained photographs taken from captured Germans of Zoya's execution. One showed her being publicly paraded through the village to the gallows, with a sign around her neck labeling her a *Brandstifter*, or arsonist. Another photograph showed her hanging by the neck from the gibbet that had been hastily erected by the Germans. A third even more horrible picture also circulated: after her hanging Zoya's body was left exposed on the gibbet for a month before she was buried in a shallow grave. During that time her body was mutilated by German soldiers, who bayoneted the body and cut off her left breast. When the Soviet troops recaptured the village, Zoya's body was exhumed, and a photograph by Sergety Strunnikov of her mutilated body—lying in the snow, the hangman's rope still around her neck, and her left breast severed—was made public.

The accounts of her death that Lidov collected gave evidence that she met her death bravely. As in the case of many heroes, her last words were deemed powerfully important. Zoya was said to have been defiant to the end, calling out to the assembled villagers watching her execution, "Comrades! Why are you so gloomy? I am not afraid to die! I am happy to die for my people!" Then to the Germans she shouted, "You'll hang me now, but I am not alone. There are two hundred million of us. You can't hang us all."[66]

Following the publication of the *Pravda* article, Zoya's death and martyrdom rapidly became a national obsession. Zoya was canonized as a partisan heroine and a key symbol in struggle against German fascism. For Stalin, she was the people's heroine and was transformed into a secular saint, the Soviet Joan of Arc. No doubt Zoya's veneration had significant utilitarian and propaganda value for the Soviets. The British novelist Martin Amis posits that Stalin knew that the Russian people would not fight for him but would fight for Zoya.[67] Whether that notion is accurate or not, it is certain that Zoya's story rang true to the Soviet people who were fighting a war in which millions of men, women, and children were dying and in which family losses were catastrophic. Margarita Aliger's 1943 poem "Zoya" received the Stalin Prize. Later Aliger turned the poem into a play, *Tale of Truth*, which then evolved into an opera by Aram Khachaturyan and Nina Markova.[68] By 1944 the story of Zoya was adapted into a film, *Zoya*, directed by Lev Arnshtam with a musical score by Dmitri Shostakovich, that was seen by more than twenty-two million people in the Soviet Union.[69] The film was even shown in the United States, with a narration written by the American novelist Howard Fast.[70]

Masha Bruskina: Heroism Denied

There is strong evidence that the image of Zoya was carefully cultivated because she could easily represent the people of the Soviet Union. But Zoya was not the first child subject to Nazi cruelty. Recall that in Minsk, Belarus, the partisans Maria "Masha" Bruskina, seventeen, and Volodia Sherbateyv-ich, sixteen, were executed on October 26, 1941, more than a month before Zoya was killed. Bruskina was the first partisan girl in the Soviet Union to be publicly executed by the Germans. As with Zoya, there was ample testimony of the bravery exhibited by her and her companions as they faced the anguish of asphyxiation by hanging. As with Zoya, their executions were designed to terrify and to intimidate the Belarus population. Unlike the case of Zoya, however, the horrifying photographs of Bruskina's execution did not emerge until after the war, when photographs of executions carried out by Lithuanian soldiers collaborating with the Germans were made public. The man and the boy executed alongside Bruskina were immediately identified as Kiril Trus and Vlodia Sherbateyvich. Trus, and Sherbateyvich's mother Olga, were actually organizers of their partisan group; the Nazis hanged Olga elsewhere in Minsk on the very same day. Soviet and Belarusian authorities claimed that Masha could not be identified, and she was memorialized as an "unknown" partisan.

The case of Masha Bruskina's identity was extensively reviewed by Nehama Tec and Daniel Weiss.[71] In 1968 Lev Arkadiev, a Russian film-maker, and Ada Dikhtiar, a journalist, began an investigation to determine the identity of the hanged girl. The investigators interviewed eyewitnesses to the events and those who knew Bruskina well, and proved beyond any doubt that the girl was Bruskina. When the investigators published their findings, Soviet authorities demoted Dikhtiar in her job. Belarusian authorities and academics continue to deny her identity and place in history—offering up the names of different women, but without providing any substantial corroborating evidence. It has become increasingly clear that because Bruskina was Jewish and because she displayed extraordinary heroism in facing death, her identity was suppressed by Soviet and Belarus officials as well as by the academic establishment in Belarus. Few states have attempted to control collective memory to the degree shown by the Soviet Union, which asserted its constant authority over what was to be remembered.[72] Indeed, the entire history of Jewish partisan resistance as well as the fact that Jews had been the main victims of the war were suppressed in the Soviet Union.[73] It seems clear that in a society with a long history of anti-Semitism, no one wanted a Jewish girl as a hero, with its potential to undermine Zoya's legacy as the central icon of child martyrdom. But there have been some recent changes. In 2009, the memorial plaque at the execution site was changed. Where it once identified Bruskina as "unknown," it now states, "Here on October 26, 1941 the Fascists executed the Soviet patriots K. I. Trus, V. I. Sherbateyvich, and M. B. Bruskina."

Rethinking the Zoya Legacy

After the war, the story of Zoya became a foundational narrative for the rebirth of the Soviet Union under Stalin. Maria Tumarkin, who was a schoolchild forty years after Kosmodemyanskaya's death, tells us, "We read about Kosmodemyanskaya, sang about Kosmodemyanskaya, attended schools named after her, laid flowers at her statues, [and] wrote countless school assignments about her undying legacy."[74] Tumarkin lived her own postwar childhood in the shadow of Kosmodemyanskaya's death, constantly worrying whether she could live up to the standards of bravery, duty, and self-sacrifice of this child martyr. Tumarkin describes the narrative of the death of Kosmodemyanskaya as a "necropedagogy," referring to the way the Soviet Union used the narrative of the death of the martyr to imbue its concept of the child with particular subjectivities and emotional attachments.

In Tumarkin's view, the national veneration of Kosmodemyanskaya was tied to the state's agenda of creating children who would see their prime duty as serving the state through labor or through defense. For Tumarkin, Kosmodemyanskaya's story was part of the militarization of childhood, which also involved erasing the boundaries between childhood, adolescence, and adulthood. Children were not to be understood as persons who were incomplete or unfinished, but rather, despite their age, as real citizens. Accompanying this were attempts to diminish the boundaries between the public and the private spheres, and between family life and the state. Children's energies, loyalties, and commitments were directed to state-sponsored children's and youth organizations, including the Little Octoberists (ages seven to nine), the Young Pioneers (ages ten to fourteen), and the Komosomol or the Communist Youth League (ages fourteen to twenty-four). Kosmodemyanskaya was the perfect cultural vehicle for creating this new childhood. The commemoration of her death, which symbolized the sacrifice of all those whose participated in and suffered through the Great Patriotic War, validated not only the experience of the Soviet people, but the existence of the entire social order created in the Soviet Union.

After the collapse of the Soviet state, officially sanctioned historical narratives began to unravel. The nation's end cleared the way for the emergence of antipodal and corrosive counternarratives of the Zoya story, all of which served to alter Zoya's image from that of a heroic patriot and martyr into an abused victim of the Soviet state. Numerous charges began to circulate on the Internet. Some stated that Zoya's grandfather, an Orthodox priest, had been executed in the Stalinist terror of the 1930s and that Zoya's mother had pushed her into military service in order to bolster and solidify the image of their family loyalty to the communist state. Others argued that she had a history of mental illness and had suicidal tendencies or that all partisan missions at that time were de facto suicide missions that sacrificed Soviet youth for little or no purpose. The details of the mission itself raised many problems, as Zoya was ordered to burn down peasant houses in the village, which left peasants homeless. One of these villagers reported the partisans to the Germans. Another villager directly participated in Zoya's abuse—pouring a pot of kitchen slops over her after she was captured and even beating her with an iron bar as she was about to be executed. Others argued that Zoya was betrayed to the Germans by local peasants who were angry that she was burning down their homes, although later it became clear that she was in fact betrayed by a fellow partisan.[75] Still others argued that it was another partisan who was actually hanged, not Zoya. None of these charges, some of which rely on flimsy or nonexistent evidence, have ever fully undermined the dominant Zoya narrative, but they have served to unyoke the story from the propaganda of the Soviet regime.

In many respects there were at least two Zoyas celebrated in the Soviet Union. The first Zoya was clearly the child soldier who went bravely to her death. This image of Zoya was sometime exemplified by statues and other public iconography that celebrated her military bearing and stoic heroism. The second Zoya was the vulnerable girl who was brutally killed by the Nazis. It is this second Zoya who increasingly takes pride of place in Russian memory, even to the degree that there have been attempts to canonize her as a Russian saint within the traditions of sainthood and martyrdom of the Orthodox Church. The secular Soviet saint was a child soldier; the Russian Orthodox girl was a martyred and vulnerable child.[76]

The transformation of Zoya is hardly complete. The memory of Zoya is still a contested site. Whether she is cast as child soldier or vulnerable child, she remains first and foremost a victim of Nazi Germany, and attempts to rebrand her as a victim of her own society—the Soviet Union—have borne only partial fruit. Clearly, for those in Russia who choked under communism there is a great temptation to dismiss much of the Soviet heroic iconography as propaganda, but many from an older generation still cling to Zoya as the symbol of their suffering and accomplishments. It makes perfect sense that the cruel death of Zoya, a teenage girl standing on the cusp between childhood and adulthood, invited multiple interpretations. It was her very polysemic utility that allowed her to serve as an icon for every child, girl, woman, warrior, martyr, and victim. But it is no longer possible to absolutely dismiss the view that Zoya was not simply a Soviet patriot who was the victim of Nazi tormentors, but also a victim of her own society's exploitation of its children. In that sense, the story of Zoya, despite its deep connection to the Soviet experience, is being reinterpreted and reconstructed around the modern idiom of the child soldier.

The Little Insurgent: The Warsaw Uprising, 1944

Another powerful example of contested memory comes from the Warsaw Uprising of 1944 (different from the Warsaw Ghetto Uprising of 1943), part of a major attempt by the Polish nationalist Home Army (Armia Krajowa) and the Polish Underground State with which it was aligned to end the

Nazi occupation of Warsaw. The anti-Soviet Home Army was the main resistance organization in Poland during World War II, although the smaller Soviet-aligned Polish People's Army (Armia Ludowa) remained an important resistance movement throughout the war. The Home Army had two goals in organizing the Warsaw Uprising—liberating Warsaw from Nazi control and preventing the Soviet Union from seizing complete control of Poland. Central to the Home Army's concerns was the 1939 Hitler-Stalin Pact, which divided occupied Poland between Germany and the Soviet Union. But the Soviet Union lost control of its occupied Poland territories when Hitler launched the German attack on the Soviet Union in June 1941. The Home Army hoped to oust the Germans from Warsaw and Poland, and prevent the complete takeover of Poland by the Soviet Union. The uprising was an assertion of Polish nationalism and a rejection of sovereignty by either Germany or the Soviet Union.

The uprising lasted two months before it was crushed by the Germans. As was true elsewhere in Europe, many children were involved in resistance activities in Warsaw and in other areas of Poland. The Warsaw Uprising included active participation by boy scouts, girl scouts, and many other youngsters, who served in a wide range of roles, ranging from postal couriers to combatants. The song "We, Warsaw Children," composed before beginning of the uprising, became emblematic of the entire uprising:

> We Warsaw children shall fight a battle,
> For every stone of yours, the Capital, we shall spill our blood!
> We Warsaw children shall fight a battle,
> When you give the order, we shall carry our wrath to our enemies![77]

The most famous of the Polish child partisans was Witold Modelski. He was born on November 11, 1932, and killed in action on September 20, 1944, at age eleven as part of the Gozdawa combat unit that fought in Warsaw's Old Town.[78] Other celebrated children include Jerzy Bartnik, a fourteen-year-old Polish boy scout who became one of the most highly decorated combat veterans of the Warsaw Uprising. Bartnik survived the war, and later lived in both the United Kingdom and the United States, where he died in 2011. He was still alive and active when President Barack Obama made an official trip to Poland and placed a wreath at the Tomb of the Unknown Soldier. Bartnik, the former child soldier, was on the receiving line as one of the heroes of the Warsaw Uprising, and was greeted by and spoke briefly with the president.[79] Another of the many Polish child soldiers was Wieslaw Chrzanowski, who at age seventeen was reputed to be the youngest officer among the insurgents.

Many Poles believe that the Soviet Union, whose forces were deployed at the very edge of Warsaw, deliberately allowed Germany to crush the uprising to ensure that there would be little internal opposition to its own planned reconquest of Poland. Indeed, at the end of World War II, the Soviet Union annexed the bulk of the Polish territory it had held in 1939. The remaining areas of Poland, those previously under Nazi domination, became part of the communist-controlled country of Poland, which by treaty with the Soviet Union ratified the transfer of territory from eastern Poland to the Soviet Union. Whatever the truth of these allegations against the Soviet Union, it is clear that the celebration of the Warsaw Uprising in Poland remained controversial in the period from 1945 to 1989 when Poland was under communist domination, because the uprising was perceived to be anti-Soviet and anticommunist. After communist control ended in 1989 and the Third Republic of Poland emerged, there was a surge in the public recognition and celebration of the Warsaw Uprising.

Elżbieta Wiącek points out that from the end of World War II until 1956, official Polish propaganda sought to erase or distort the memory of the uprising by treating the Home Army as fascist collaborators with Nazi Germany. Mention of the Home Army in film and literature was frequently censored, and the anniversary of the uprising was not celebrated. After the death of Stalin in 1956, communist authorities relaxed censorship efforts, and allowed public mention of ordinary heroic soldiers during the uprising. They still prohibited the erection of statues commemorating the uprising. Despite this prohibition, every year on August 1, large numbers of Poles came to Powązki Cemetery to visit the insurgents' graves.[80]

Young insurgents such as Witold Modelski and Jerzy Barnik were the inspiration for one of the most powerful memorials to the Warsaw Uprising, the statue of the *Little Insurgent*. Sculpted by Jerzy Jarnuszkiewicz, the statue in Warsaw's Old Town depicts a child partisan wearing oversized boots, a German Wehrmacht helmet, carrying a gun that is obviously too small to be real.[81] Jarnuszkiewicz designed the sculpture in 1946, but its resonance with Polish nationalism made it impossible to erect at that time.

Despite this prohibition, the statue rapidly became a popular icon; small-scale models of the *Little Insurgent* spread throughout Warsaw and could be found in the homes of many city residents, surrounded by pictures and flowers. By the early 1980s, as celebration of the Warsaw Uprising became more politically acceptable, statues of the *Little Insurgent* also began to show up on Warsaw streets. By 1983, when the full-sized statue was finally erected, the *Little Insurgent* had reemerged in exactly as the way Polish communist officials had feared—a child soldier who was a symbol of Polish patriotism and served as a popular anti-Nazi and anti-Soviet national icon.[82] Boy and girl scouts raised the fund to erect the statue, which is routinely visited by groups of children and visiting political delegations. The monument was unveiled by a former boy scout, Jerzy Swiderski, who was a fourteen-year-old insurgent during the uprising. The statue of the *Little Insurgent* and other similar monuments helped revitalize Polish nationalism by injecting children's agency and heroism into the narrative of Polish history.[83] To this day, on the anniversary of the Warsaw Uprising, the statue is decorated with flowers and candles. Scarves and wreaths are laid at its feet in ways that clearly mark it as a site of pilgrimage and martyrdom.

The *Little Insurgent* was part of Polish nationalists' attempts to seize control of the narrative of nationalist aspirations; the patriotic child soldier resonates powerfully with these aspirations to this day. But as in the case of Zoya, it is virtually impossible for Poles to remain unaffected by the emerging modern counternarrative of the child soldier as victim. The statue was conceived at the end of World War II, when many Poles knew children who had fought and sacrificed their lives to end the Nazi occupation of Poland. In that context, if child soldiers were deemed victims of war, it was because they were victims of the Nazi occupation and not because of their participation in the Polish resistance.

Seventy years have now passed since the Warsaw Uprising. Poland is a prosperous country with a free-market economy. Polish child soldiers are a distant memory, and contemporary child soldiers largely populate the conflict zones of Africa and the developing world. Not surprisingly, some Poles now question Poland's pride in its child soldiers and ask how the resistance could have permitted children to wage war against a powerful German army. Indeed, despite its popularity, the statue is placed in a somewhat far-flung spot, unlike that of the main Warsaw Uprising

Monument, which was unveiled in 1989 and depicts adult partisans. There have also been attempts to soften the image of the role of children during the uprising by suggesting that they served as couriers or nurses, but none of this can detract from the fact that many children served in face-to-face combat with the German army. Children's rights activists have also entered the fray. On Children's Day in Warsaw, the statue has sometimes been festooned with balloons and passersby have distributed postcards with the silhouette of the *Little Insurgent* holding balloons. Activists speak of the need to "restore childhood" to the *Little Insurgent*, reframing the Warsaw Uprising not as a war between Poland and Germany but as an "adult war" in which children should be seen as victims and not volunteers. It would be an exaggeration to suggest that the site of the *Little Insurgent* has been transformed from a site of pilgrimage to a contested zone of children's rights—it remains, first and foremost, a symbol of Polish patriotism and the bravery of children—but activities and conversation around the statue make plain that contemporary humanitarian narratives about child soldiers may ultimately have a profound effect on collective memory. It is too soon to know whether these children will ultimately be remembered as patriots or as victims.

4

The Child Soldier in Popular Culture

Outside of international politics and law, humanitarian discourse about childhood and child soldiers has had a profound effect upon contemporary popular culture—especially literature and film. At first blush, it might seem that humanitarian accounts and literary accounts would narrate the experience of childhood in antithetical ways. In traditional literature, fully developed characters drive narratives about children. Literary conventions set children into roles as active players and participants in society. The development of modern literature and the development of character go hand and hand, and most modern literary forms, including the novel, focus on individuals and their engagement with surrounding psychological or social forces. In contrast, humanitarian rhetoric sidesteps character and creates essentialist categories with universal applicability. Humanitarian and human rights reports tend to be breathtakingly superficial and thin, and bear scant relationship to the experience of children at war traditionally found in literature, anthropology, or history. Many human rights reports appear to depend upon highly repetitive and near-ritualized templates and tropes.

Child Soldiers in Literature

Humanitarian rhetoric seems to have seeped into and reshaped the literary images of child soldiers, upending many of the images of children under arms that pervaded nineteenth- and twentieth-century literature.

The transformation is startling: the heroic child fighters like Gavroche in Victor Hugo's *Les Misérables* or the boy spy Kim in Kipling's eponymous novel have been replaced by Ago, the battered victim of a nameless war in Uzodinma Iweala's *Beasts of No Nation*. This is not to suggest that there were no dissenting views in the past. As early as 1861, Herman Melville raised his skeptical voice against the chorus of hosannas surrounding young boys marching off to the Civil War. In his poem "The March into Virginia Ending in the First Manassas," he writes, "All wars are boyish, and are fought by boys, the champions and enthusiasts of the state."[1] But Melville was in the minority, and it took more than one hundred years before his lone voice was joined by the noisy chorus of humanitarian critique.

How did the heroic child soldier of an earlier era come to be replaced by the abused and exploited child who is both killer and victim? What alterations in literary conventions and moral attitudes were required in order to transform the child soldier into its modern literary construction? Clearly these changes are part of other major historic trends in thinking about war in general. Martin van Creveld has shown that before the eighteenth and nineteenth centuries, much of the commemoration of war in popular culture involved the celebration of victory over the enemy, often depicted as captured, defeated, or killed. But by the time of the U.S. Civil War and World War I, much of this had disappeared and the focus of popular culture became the commemoration of the dead and heroic sacrifice and suffering.[2] As shown earlier in this book, the commemoration of the death and sacrifice of child soldiers was particularly embedded in funerary rituals of communal and national grief. In that very important sense the death of the child soldier symbolized the death and sacrifice of all soldiers.

World War I provided an important opening to the reversal of these images in popular understanding of war. While the bulk of popular literature supported the war, there were important literary dissenters such as the British poets Siegfried Sassoon, Wilfred Owen, and Isaac Rosenberg. Owen's poem "Anthem for Doomed Youth" skewers the possibility that funerals for the young can have any meaning, asking, "what passing-bells for these who die as cattle?"[3] Postwar novels and films broadened the critique. The 1929 novel *All Quiet on the Western Front* by Erich Maria Remarque details the physical and psychological cost of the war and became a best seller after the war. The book tells the story of German schoolboys harassed and shamed into enlisting by their teacher and who are all killed in the war.[4] In the book the boys are ages eighteen and nineteen, but in the 1930 Hollywood film of the same name, directed by Lewis Milestone, they appear to be somewhat younger high school boys.[5] Nonetheless, these and numerous other films and books set forth an important, if nascent, critique of war and gave rise to the idea that warfare could also involve the cynical and meaningless sacrifice of the young. Much of the criticism focused on the tragedy of war and the corruption, hubris, and vanity of military and political leadership. A classic example was Herbert Cobb's 1935 novel *Paths of Glory* (the source of the 1957 Stanley Kubrick film of the same name), focused on the true story of four French corporals randomly and cynically selected for execution as scapegoats for military folly and failure. But despite such portraits of immorality and borderline criminality by wartime commanders, war, per se, was not generally treated as a criminal enterprise.[6] One possible exception was the 1927 Soviet film *The End of St. Petersburg*, directed by Vsevolod Pudovkin, in which the horrors of World War I are directly attributed to the criminal greed of capitalists.[7] But the impact of these critical works was felt mostly in the post–World War I period and was soon set aside by the rise of Nazism in the 1930s.

Portraits of war as a criminal enterprise began to emerge more fully in contemporary literature and are especially prominent in literature that focuses on African conflicts. While children have been recruited as child soldiers in wars all over the world—Columbia, Kurdistan, Laos, Mexico, New Guinea, Pakistan, Palestine, Peru, the Philippines, Sri Lanka, and New Guinea come immediately to mind—the contemporary literary gaze remains firmly fixed on Africa. Exactly why is unclear. Certainly some contemporary examples of the use of child soldiers in Africa, such as the Revolutionary United Front in Sierra Leone and the Lord's Resistance Army in Uganda, have provided chilling examples of the abuse of children. But these extraordinary cases have also come to serve as the archetype of children's experiences in both Africa and elsewhere. Literary treatments of African children at war, almost all geared to Western audiences, magnify this perspective by the lingering tendency to see Africa with Conradian eyes, seeing only the heart of darkness. In fact the general Western discourse about war in Africa, whether precolonial, colonial, or postcolonial, has remained remarkably consistent since the middle of the nineteenth century. In this discourse, warfare in Africa—in contrast to that in the West—is invariably cast as irrational, meaningless, and criminal.[8]

The Child Soldier as Hero

The classic nineteenth-century literary representation of the child at war is the character of the street urchin Gavroche in Victor Hugo's *Les Misérables*. The character is at least partly based on an existing icon of the child soldier found in Eugène Delacroix's nineteenth-century painting *Liberty Leading the People*.[9] The painting depicts a scene at the barricades during the July Revolution of 1830. At the center of the painting is Liberty in the form of a woman leading the charge over the barricades while clasping the flag of the French Revolution in one hand and a musket in the other. To her immediate left is an equally powerful portrait of a child, a young boy brandishing a musket in each hand. The child under arms was often thought to serve symbolically as a personification of class struggle. Armed children represented the lofty goals of popular insurrection that drew people from all walks of life into the battle against monarchy and entrenched privilege.[10]

Les Misérables was written some thirty-two years after these events. A key moment in Hugo's novel is the Paris student uprising of June 1832, where many of those who die are students involved in a short but violent antimonarchist revolt. As with Delacroix, the main action is on the barricades, and focuses on the orphan boy Gavroche, a street urchin who joins with the students rebels, pistol in hand. During the battle he crosses over the barricades into the line of fire in order to gather unspent cartridges from among the dead. He is killed while singing.

In Hugo's novel, Gavroche's heroic actions are marvels. Margaret Mead once opined that adults view children as "pygmies among giants";[11] Hugo turns this image on its head, describing the diminutive Gavroche as a giant concealed in a pygmy body and comparing him to Antaeus, the great mythical Libyan giant defeated by Hercules. As Hugo put it, "The rebels watched with breathless anxiety. The barricade trembled, and he sang. He was neither child nor man but puckish sprite, a dwarf, it seemed, invulnerable in battle. The bullets pursued him but he was more agile than they.

The urchin played his game of hide and seek with death, and . . . tweaked its nose."[12] Gavroche does not survive, but when he is finally brought down by a bullet, Hugo tells us that "his gallant soul had fled."[13] For Hugo and for others, the child fighter very much represented the people in their struggle for democracy; in this sense, the child served as a collective representation of all that was good, striking to break out of an encrusted social order.

Hugo's story of the death of Gavroche must be placed in the context of his understanding of the violence of war. *Les Misérables* combines both narrative and social commentary, and is marked by Hugo's observations on revolution, which he understood as inevitably flowing from the conditions of social inequality. Hugo likened revolt to the releasing of a spring, or even more powerfully, to a whirlwind whose destructive force smashes those whom it carries away as well as those whom it seeks to destroy.[14]

Hugo carefully distinguished his judgments about the morality of collective violence from the particular makeup of the participants. The latter, he recognized, could be a rather motley stew of combatants. Hugo was well aware that violence could take a negative turn, but citing Lafayette, Hugo argued that true insurrection, as form of expression of collective and universal sovereignty guided by truth, was a sacred duty.[15]

For Hugo, Gavroche's participation in the insurrection is part of the rights and duties of all citizens, men, women, and children, to resist oppression. Given the oppressive nature of childhood for children of his class background, Gavroche's best interests are served by participating in insurrection. In no sense could it be said of Gavroche that war "robbed him of his childhood," to use a modern humanitarian cliché. Instead, insurrection is the harbinger of a new moral order designed to eliminate the immorality of the social order that framed the ordinary life of a street child in nineteenth-century Paris.

Hugo sees a moral order in revolutionary violence. Indeed, because insurrection is a noble striving, revolutionaries must not act like criminals.[16] This view is made clear in an incident involving the murder of an elderly man, a doorkeeper who refuses entrance to a home by a group of fighters. What seems clear is that Hugo is tracking the customary laws of war, which criminalize the intentional killing of noncombatants. Revolutions must follow moral codes, even in the context of organized violence. It is clear that Hugo does not imagine that this would bar children from joining in class struggle. In fact, the character and personality of Gavroche came to symbolize all French soldiers, children and adults.[17]

The veneration of child soldiers in the nineteenth century was not confined to adult literature. I have previously discussed some aspects of popular culture during the American Civil War, but it bears repeating here that novels for children and young readers published in the United States during and after the Civil War (1861–1865) celebrated the heroic role of the child soldier. Among these was Harry Castlemon's *Frank on a Gun-Boat*, written in 1864.[18] Castlemon was the pen name of Charles Austin Fosdick, who served in the Union Navy during the Civil War and later became one of the most popular authors of adventure tales for boys in the nineteenth century. Even more popular were the adventure novels of Oliver Optic, the pen name of William Taylor Adams, perhaps the most popular and success-ful writers of fiction for children and youth in the nineteenth century. He was, in many respects, the J. K. Rowling of the late nineteenth century. By the time he died in 1897, he was rich and famous and had sold some two million copies of his books, more than any other author living in his time.[19] He wrote six novels in his Soldier Boy and Sailor Boy series and did not shy away from or whitewash the horrors of war.

In Optic's 1864 novel *The Soldier Boy; or, Tom Somers in the Army*, sixteen-year-old Tom Somers finds himself in the midst of battle:

Tom looked upon the fearful scene. The roar of the artillery and the crash of the small arms were absolutely stunning. He saw men fall, and lie motionless on the ground, where they were trampled upon by the horses, and crushed beneath the wheels of cannon and caisson. But the cry was that the army of the Union had won the field, and it inspired him with new zeal and new courage. . . . Tom soon found himself in the thickest of the fight. Shot and shell were flying in every direction, and the bullets hissed like hailstones around him. In spite of all his preparations for this awful scene, his heart rose up into his throat. His eyes were blinded by the vol-umes of rolling smoke, and his mind confused by the rapid succes-sion of incidents that were transpiring around him. The pictures he had painted were sunlight and golden compared with the dread reality. Dead and dying men strewed the ground in every direction. Wounded horses were careering on a mad course of destruction, trampling the wounded and the dead beneath their feet. The hoarse shouts of the officers were heard above the roar of battle. The scene mocked all the attempts which the soldier boy had made to imagine its horrors.[20]

But Tom does fight and finds both his courage and his patriotism:

As soon as the regiment reached its position, the order was given to fire. Tom found this a happy relief; and when he had discharged his musket a few times, all thoughts of the horrors of the scene forsook him. He no longer saw the dead and the dying; he no longer heard the appalling roar of battle. He had become a part of the scene, instead of an idle spectator. He was sending the bolt of death into the midst of the enemies of his country.

"Bravo! Good boy, Tom," said old Hapgood, who seemed to be as much at ease as when he had counseled patience and resignation in the quiet of the tent. "Don't fire too high, Tom."

"I've got the idea," replied the soldier boy. "I begin to feel quite at home."[21]

By the end of this tale, Tom's patriotism and courage are fully rewarded. He is promoted to lieutenant and stands to win the hand of the girl of his dreams. Like much of nineteenth-century literature for boys, these war novels tied the proper development of boys to their meeting and overcoming important trials and tribulations. His experience of war, despite its horrors, is portrayed as a period of personal and moral development. Tom's future life, the narrator tells us, "if not always as fortunate as that portion which we have recorded, was unstained by cowardice or vice."[22]

Despite the critique of war that began to emerge during and after World War I, the same spirit of revolution, sacrifice, and personal growth and development that informed nineteenth-century novels about boy soldiers is also found in patriotic literature that was published during World War II. A prime example is *Johnny Tremain*, one of the best-selling American novels for youngsters in U.S. history. Written in 1943 in the middle of World War II, it focuses on the saga of its eponymous hero as he grows and develops from a self-centered and arrogant child into a young soldier who takes up arms on behalf of the American Revolution. Johnny is fourteen when the novel opens in 1773 and just sixteen when it ends in the aftermath of the battles at Lexington and Concord, two of the most iconic events of the revolutionary era.

The arc of Johnny's development and growing maturity tracks the arc of his emergence as a revolutionary activist. At the outset of the novel, Johnny is an apprentice to a silversmith in Boston, and his main concerns focus on developing his abilities in a skilled trade. The novel adeptly recognizes that the American Revolution was very much a civil war that pitted those who were loyal to Britain (Tories) against the rebels (Whigs or Patriots). Boston is a city divided between these groups, with many individuals holding feelings in between. Johnny himself is divided in his sentiments, as well as in his conflicting love interests in both Priscilla the Patriot and the Lavinia the Tory.

Johnny's transformation takes place after a prank by another apprentice results in his hand being severely burned, which makes it impossible for him to continue as an apprentice silversmith. Unable to find other skilled work, he is befriended by the sixteen-year-old Rab, whose family publishes and distributes a Whig newspaper. They hire Johnny to distribute the newspaper to its subscribers by horse throughout Boston and the surrounding areas. This brings Johnny into contact with various rebel leaders and groups, which together with his self-education in the library, turns him into a Patriot. As the rebel movement grows and the British military occupation deepens, Johnny is drawn into the violence of the growing rebellion. Several key events mark the transition to open revolt, including a powerful patriotic speech by the Patriot Otis; a British officer's cruel injury of Rab when he catches Rab trying to examine the locket of a musket; the execution of Pumpkin, a young British deserter who has given Rab his musket; and finally the death of the heroic Rab, who is fatally wounded at Lexington and gives Johnny his musket just before he dies. Most important, it is discovered that Johnny's burned hand can be made usable by a simple surgery, and that while he may never be a silversmith, he will be able to fire a musket in battle. In the last lines of the novel, Johnny recalls Otis's speech and says, "Hundreds would die but not the thing they died for."[23]

The novel's construction of Johnny's development shows the way political and revolutionary activity, including revolutionary violence, contributed to Johnny's development as a mature and responsible person. There is very little depiction in the novel of those things that are deleterious about war. Likewise, there is no mourning of the loss of Johnny's childhood. His life as a young teen is portrayed as constricted and confined by the narrow and dull system of apprenticeship. In this novel, revolution and the idea of fighting for an ideal are seen as enhancing the individual and bringing the person from the narrow confines of childhood into the open vistas of adulthood. The novel presents an understanding of the relationship between war, revolution, and the growth from childhood to responsible adulthood that was the cultural norm in the West until recent decades.

Finally, images of the heroic child soldier continued to live on in films produced in the Soviet Union. Andrei Tarkovsky's 1962 film *Ivan's Childhood* is set on the eastern front during World War II as Soviet forces try to repel the Nazi invasion.[24] Ivan is a twelve-year-old boy who works as a spy for the army because he is able to cross into German lines without attracting suspicion. Because of his age, Soviet soldiers take great care of him and are reluctant to make use of him, but Ivan, who had been part of a partisan group and who is desperate to revenge the murder of his family by German soldiers, proves both unstoppable and useful. In the end, Ivan is captured and killed by the Germans. But Ivan's story is framed clearly as a tragedy. War is hardly glorified, but the blame for Ivan's death is clearly laid at the hands of German aggressors and not the Soviet soldiers who recruited him and let him serve in their ranks. More recently, Elem Klimov's 1985 film *Come and See* opens with two young boys searching for guns so as to be able to join the partisans fighting the Nazis in Belorussia.[25] The screenplay for the film was written with Ales Adamovich, who himself was a teenage partisan during World War II. The film, widely regarded as one of the best and most realistic films ever made about the war, focuses on the tragedy of war and the lives ruined in its wake. It makes clear that responsibility for the horrors of war lies with the Nazi invaders and not on the people of Belorussia, whose population—including children and youth—joined in the partisan efforts to defeat them.

The Child Soldier as Victim

The heroic child soldier of the earlier era is virtually nonexistent in contemporary adult fiction. Novels such as *Song for Night* by Chris Abani, *Beasts of No Nation* by Uzodinma Iweala, *Moses, Citizen and Me* by Delia Jarrett-Macauley, and finally *Johnny Mad Dog* by Emmanuel Dongala exemplify this trend.[26] In all of these works, the role of the child soldier is at best a terrible tragedy and more profoundly a threat to any sense of morality and social justice. Indeed the contemporary child soldier appears to subvert not just the social order but the natural order as well.

All these novels were published for the Western market. They are among the few works in fiction that foreground the actions of children under arms.[27] In Chris Abani's novella *Song for Night*, a story seemingly set during the war in Biafra, twelve-year-old My Luck is recruited into a mine-defusing unit. After training, his vocal chords and those of all the other boy sappers are surgically cut to render the boys voiceless, so that if a mine blows up, they will not scare the others with their death screams.

Beasts of No Nation is written as a comic nightmare allegory. As the title implies, it functions as the antithesis of a war novel. It is not about the human soldiers of a particular nation-state, but rather of "beasts" who have no national identification. Iweala was born in Nigeria, but was educated in the United States, and was named by *Granta* in 2007 as one of the twenty best American novelists. It is tempting to imagine that this story is set in Nigeria, although the narrative does not follow any known conflict in Nigeria. Rather, it is a symbolic tale of modern warfare.

The book tells a horrifying story of the forced recruitment of Agu, a child soldier, through his initiation into the most brutal forms violence: his participation in the gruesome murders of both captured soldiers and civilians, which are portrayed in graphic detail, his drug-infused killing frenzies, and his routine rape and sodomization by the commander of his unit.

The book is set in a kind of dream time, although in this instance the dream is a nightmare. From the beginning, Iweala uses the conventions of comic books. For instance, the Commandant, the nefarious nameless leader of the nameless force that kidnaps Ague and murders his family, has all the attributes of a comic supervillain. Like the Joker in the Batman comics, he has no ideology. He is not interested in power, money, or land. He kills for the sake of killing, and for his own lust and amusement. Like other supervillains, he has his servile minions, Luftenant and Rambo, as well as his army of soldiers who laugh when he laughs and seek to imitate his walk and his every gesture.

The terrible action scenes of the text are garnished with the classic devices of the comic book narrative. In conventional comics, uppercase words such as ZAP, WHAM, BANG, and especially KAPOW mark the scenes of violence. In this book, Iweala converts and expands the classic KAPOW into a new faux-African action comic vocabulary of evil: KPAWA marks the beating of Agu as he is dragged before the Commandant,[28] KPWISHA as the Commandant dashes cold water over him, KPWUDA as the machete-wielding Agu chops a captured enemy soldier into pieces, KPWUD as he stomps a young girl to death, KPWAMA as soldiers kick down a door. KEHI KEHI marks the raucous laughter of soldiers as innocents are mutilated and murdered, AYEEEIII! scream the murdered villagers as they die.

All this is dramatically effective, and none of it is funny in any way, but it has the immediate effect of stripping the story of any social and cultural context. The story unfolds both nowhere and everywhere. There is no history and no meaning to anything that is going on. Strongly paralleling the humanitarian understanding of war, it portrays people simply dying for nothing. Unlike the classic comic, there is no superhero to save the day.

Placing the action of the novel outside of any temporal, historical, or societal context gives the horror it describes an elusive transcendence. The action stands outside of history, and is the proxy for "Every War" or at least every African war. In this respect, at least, there is little difference between this novel's understanding of Africa and that found Joseph Conrad's *Heart of Darkness*. Conrad took Africans out of history and suspended them between the human and the animal. Here, the narrator Marlow describes his journey up Congo River:

> The pre-historic man was cursing us, praying to us, welcoming us—who could tell? We were cut off from the comprehension of our surroundings. . . . We could not understand because we were too far and could not remember because we were traveling in the night of first ages, of those ages that are gone, leaving hardly a sign—and

no memories. . . . No, they were not inhuman. . . . They howled and leaped, and spun, and made horrid faces; but what thrilled you was just the thought of their humanity—like yours—the thought of your remote kinship with this wild and passionate uproar.[29]

And here is Agu, more than one hundred years later, on his way to the killing fields:

> We are walking down into the valley and down into the bush so I am feeling like an animal going back to his home. . . . I am hearing water and I am thirsty and wanting to drink. . . . Everybody is looking like one kind of animal, no more human. Everything is just looking like one kind of animal. . . . I am liking how the gun is shooting and the knife is chopping. I am liking to see people running from me and people screaming for me when I am killing them and taking their blood. I am liking to kill.[30]

Like Conrad, Iweala's characters hover between the human and the inhuman, but their battlefield is no longer merely metaphysical. Nonetheless the metaphysical struggle continues. Iweala may well have a larger purpose in stripping his characters of their humanity, because in doing so he also immunizes them from their culpability in murder, a central theme in the humanitarian efforts to "protect" children under arms.

Moses, Citizen and Me was written by Delia Jarrett-Macauley, who was born and resides in England but is of Sierra Leonean descent. The setting of the novel is the civil war in Sierra Leone. The novel's protagonist, Julia, living in London, is summoned back to Sierra Leone after a twenty-year absence. She returns to the home of her beloved Uncle Moses and Auntie Adele in Freetown, where she encounters their grandchild, Citizen, an ex-child soldier who murdered Adele—his own grandmother—during the civil war. Eight-year-old Citizen is living with Uncle Moses after having been released from Doria, a rehabilitation camp for former child soldiers. Uncle Moses is torn between his grief for his murdered wife and his duty toward his grandson. The questions of the story are basic. Is Citizen ruined? Is he redeemable? Who can redeem him and how?

At first wanting to understand who Citizen is and later wanting to build a connection to him, Julia visits Camp Doria, where she has her first encounter with an ex-child soldier. The soldier, a boy nicknamed Corporal Kalashnikov, has just been rehabilitated from his regular habit of drinking tea laced with gunpowder and marijuana. Julia perceives him as a caricature of a soldier who could otherwise be leading a carnival parade. Nonetheless, the encounter with Corporal Kalashnikov serves as personal rite of passage, which enables her to begin to understand the plight of child soldiers.[31]

All of Julia's future contacts with child soldiers take place not in reality, but in a magical dream-like state, while her hair is being plaited by Uncle Moses's next-door neighbor Anita. As Anita plaits her hair, Julia begins a magical journey into the forest, where she encounters a unit of child soldiers that includes twelve-year-old Abu, his older brother Masa, Citizen himself, and their vicious commander, the twenty-year-old Lieutenant Ibrahim, who is the leader of the "number-one-burn-house-unit."[32] The scene is starkly brutal and violent. Ibrahim carries a knife that he has stolen from a corpse, one of many in the trail of corpses he has created in his campaign of extermination. The unit is about to attack a village of the "enemy," although it is clear that it is merely a rural village. Under the influence of drugs, the child soldiers join in the spree of chaos and murder, where they see the dying and fleeing inhabitants as just so many insects. But despite their participation in murder, the novel presents the children as being completely under the murderous control of Ibrahim, whose calculated terrorism and violence propels them into combat. Ibrahim cruelly beats Abu for crying for his mother, lashes Citizen fifty times for his "failure" to beat a fellow child soldier to death, murders the helpless Musa who has come down with malaria, and forces the children to dance in order to keep them from comforting one another over the Musa's murder. Despite this, and despite how broken the children are, in the world of this novel, the children retain their "innocence" and their humanity in this war.

For the rest of the novel, Julia magically tacks back and forth between Freetown and "the bush," where this unit of child soldiers finds its redemption, deep in the Gola forest on the borderlands between Sierra Leone and Liberia. The war is now over and the children are cared for by Bemba G, an elderly shaman-like character with magical powers. Bemba G's plan is to redeem and rehabilitate the child soldiers through staging of the Shakespeare's play *Julius Caesar*, in which all the children will play a part. Citizen is to play Lucius the boy servant of Brutus, who in Shakespeare's play is implicitly with Brutus when he dies on the plains of Phillipi, and whom the novel casts as a boy soldier of ancient times. Lucius is sleeping in Brutus's tent when he encounters the ghost of Caesar, who foretells his death. In Shakespeare's play, Lucius cries out in his sleep, clearly disturbed by the presence of Caesar's ghost, but does not see him. In the novel, while acting out his part, Citizen/Lucius has an unscripted dream where the ghost is not that of Caesar but of his murdered Aunt Adele. The encounter is transformative. Lucius sees the ghost and "the glory of her voice, those assessing eyes, naked brown arms with flesh gently drooping. He thinks of tenderness and love—and joining hands. The Ghost turns, revealing a back torn with wounds from a cruel death."[33] But in contrast to Brutus, Citizen's encounter with the ghost foreshadows not his doom but rather his reconciliation with both his family and society.

To its credit, Jarrett-Macauley's novel seeks to redeem child soldiers not by members of the so-called helping professions—social workers and psychologists—but rather by reconnecting these child soldiers, who have been artificially isolated and brutalized by war, back into the global culture they have always inhabited. But though the novel clearly demonstrates the intellectual richness of Sierra Leone society, its portraits of children at arms remain remarkably thin; Jarrett-Macauley reduces them to the stereotypes of human rights reporting. Indeed as the author admits, she has never met a child soldier and relied almost entirely upon her own interviews with personnel from agencies that deal with child soldiers. This is not to argue that a novelist must be constrained by reality, but rather that the novelist's imagination, even in this otherwise wonderfully drawn story, has been constrained by the rhetoric of advocacy. This is a rather surprising result since Brutus's kindness and gentility toward Lucius on the eve of his death suggest that Lucius and Citizen, despite their both being called child soldiers, actually have very little in common. Brutus may have betrayed Caesar, but he is no Lieutenant Ibrahim. Indeed, in the novel we never get a child soldier who departs from the stereotype. We never get the child soldiers who believed, even if wrongly, that they were fighting for a cause, or those child soldiers who fought to protect their homes and villages from rebel deprivations.[34]

Johnny Mad Dog, by Emmanuel Dongala, is the story of a civil war in an unnamed country in Africa. It is partly based on the personal experiences of Dongala, who was a director of academic affairs at the University of Brazzaville. He fled the Congo at the onset of the civil war in 1997. *Johnny Mad Dog* is the story of two teenagers, sixteen years old, Laokolo, a young girl on the run from the conflict who wheels her crippled mother around in a wheelbarrow, and Johnny Mad Dog, a leader of a unit of a militia group called the Mata Mata, or Death Dealers. Johnny lives in a world of falsehood and deception. "'Looting,' he says, 'was the main reason we were fighting. To line our pockets. To become adults. To have all the women we wanted. To wield the power of a gun. To be rulers of the world. . . . But our leaders and our president ordered us . . . [to say] that we were fighting for freedom and democracy.'"[35]

Johnny Mad Dog's world is also one of total self-deception. He imagines that he brings sexual pleasure to the women he rapes, regards himself as an intellectual even though he has only finished the second grade, and has endless justifications for wanton murder. If this were a novel about a single individual, Johnny would clearly be a criminal sociopath. He is dangerous, glib, and grandiose, has absolutely no conception of the rights of others, and shows no guilt, shame, or remorse. The essence of a sociopathic personality disorder is a disregard for cultural and social norms or rules, but in this novel it is Johnny's world itself that is devoid of meaningful social and political categories. The novel uses patently absurd and inauthentic social and political categories to convey the meaningless cruelty of war. There are no authentic rules to break, which renders both Johnny and warfare ultimately unintelligible. For example, the two ethnic groups at war are the Dogo-Mayi and the Mayi-Dogo, patently fictional ethnic categories that have blossomed out of squabbles between postcolonial political leaders with little prewar intergroup salience. The warring political parties formed around these ethnic categories are the equally contrived MFTLP (Movement for the Total Liberation of the People) and the MFDLP (Movement for the Democratic Liberation of the People). The categories of the allies of the opposition are all a jumble; Johnny and his militiamen imagine they are also hunting down fantasy "Chechens" and "Israelis," all of whom turn out to be innocent African civilians who are casually murdered by Johnny and his unit. Some of this madness is balanced by the story of Laokolo, a courageous young woman of uncommon intelligence who tries to survive in an insane world. But, in the end, in an almost

Orwellian way, both Johnny and Loakolo are manipulated by forces outside of their control, with adults serving as stand-ins for Orwell's Big Brother.

In the literature, folklore, and songs about war, the very common name "Johnny" has frequently been used been used as a proxy name for the ordinary soldier. Over the last two or three centuries, there have been many Johnnys. Johnny Reb was the slang term for the common soldier of the Confederacy in the U.S. Civil War. In the same war, soldiers of both the North and South sang and marched to Patrick Gilmour's "When Johnny Comes Marching Home Again."[36] In World War I, Americans sang George M. Cohan's "Over There," the first verse of which begins with "Johnny get your gun, get your gun, get your gun." And in World War II, U.S. audiences listened to the patriotic sounds of the Andrews Sisters singing Don Raye and Gene De Paul's "Johnny Get Your Gun, Again" in the 1942 film *Private Buckaroo*.[37] In all of these wars, especially the U.S. Civil War, there were large numbers of children under arms, and "Johnny" easily stands for any soldier, whether adult or child. Certainly Johnny Tremain, the eighteenth-century Johnny who was clearly a child soldier, fits easily into the genre of a patriotic soldier fighting for a just a cause.

Of course, literature provides us not just with patriotic Johnnies. One of the most powerful portraits of a "Johnny" in modern literature is the anti-war novel *Johnny Got His Gun* by Dalton Trumbo. The tale depicts Joe Bonham, a young American soldier of World War I who, after being hit by an artillery shell, has lost his eyes and all his limbs. Lying in hospital, Bonham is unable to communicate except by using his head to bang out Morse Code.[38] At first blush, *Johnny Got His Gun* seems to speak of the unjustness of any war and to reject all attempts to justify war or to distinguish between just and unjust wars. The sheer horror of Bonham's situation implies that war is meaningless. Bonham has little use for any of the myths of war and rejects all of the so-called reasons for fighting—liberty, freedom, decency, democracy, or independence. His thoughts on the American Revolution subvert every sentiment found in *Johnny Tremain*: "America fought a war for liberty in 1776. Lots of guys died. And in the end does America have any more liberty than Canada or Australia who didn't fight at all? . . . Can you look at a guy and say he's an American who fought for his liberty and anybody can see he's a very different guy from a Canadian who didn't? No by god you can't and that's that. So maybe a lot of guys with wives and kids died in 1776 when they didn't need to die at all."[39] By the end of the novel, however, we are less certain that Joe's position implies a complete rejection of war, because the novel's critique of war is tied to a broader critique of class-based societies that locates the meaninglessness of war in an economic system that exploits the vulnerable. Although Bonham's acute suffering leads him to an antiwar position, it is not clear that Trumbo meant the novel to imply that there was no possibility of a just war. Indeed, Trumbo delayed the 1939 release of his book, apparently because he feared it might unfavorably distort the efforts to defeat fascism in Europe. So even this most powerful of Western antiwar novels retains at least a residue of the idea that both prowar and antiwar sentiments must be grounded in politics.[40]

The current pattern of Africanizing the child soldier issue can be seen in contemporary cinema. Prime examples are films such as *Blood Diamond* and *Johnny Mad Dog*.[41] *Blood Diamond* is set in Sierra Leone, but it almost makes no difference where the story is set: African contexts are fungible. The film *Johnny Mad Dog* is based on the novel by Emmanuel Dongala; although no specific country is named in the novel, the setting is apparently Congolese. The film, by contrast, is set in Liberia. Even stories about child soldiers that did not originally take place in Africa become Africanized for dramatic effect. The recent award-winning film *War Witch*, for example, is set in a nameless African country, though it is based on a story that originated in Burma.[42] In keeping with the Africanization of the child soldier, the Canadian filmmaker Kim Nguyen relocated the story from Burma to Africa. *War Witch* was filmed in the Democratic Republic of the Congo but set in an unnamed but familiarly generic Africa country. In this film, we are again shown a rebel attack on a defenseless village that takes place for no comprehensible reason by rebels who commit senseless war crimes. Komona, the main character in the story, is first forced to kill her parents and then abducted into the rebel army as a child soldier and made the virtual property of the rebel leader, Great Tiger, who believes that Komona has the magical power to foresee coming attacks by the enemy, so she is designated his "war witch."

Not all of the accounts of child soldiers reflect this simplified ahistorical iconography of extremes and moral panics. There are both personal accounts and novels that tell far more complicated tales. Emmanuel Jal's

memoir *War Child: A Child Soldier's Story* relates how he and his family fled
from the rampages of the Arab soldiers of the Sudan, many of whom seem
similar to the murderous racist Sudanese militias of Darfur that Woli Soyinka likened to an African version of the Ku Klux Klan.[43] Jal finds himself
taken into the Sudan People's Liberation Army, where he had many harsh
and shockingly brutal experiences during his recruitment, training, and
deployment. There is little doubt that members of the SPLA also committed war crimes, but it is also clear that Jal's commanders in the SPLA were
not gratuitous abusers and murderers of civilians or of their own troops.
In fact, Jal himself witnessed the execution of fellow soldiers for the rape
of women.[44] But he is also very troubled by the fact that in an attack on
Juba, now the capital and largest city of the Republic of South Sudan,
he mercilessly killed soldiers who were trying to surrender and whom he
knew he should have taken prisoner.[45] These events, however, are hardly
unique either to warfare or to child soldiers. Killing surrendering soldiers
in the heat of battle has not been uncommon even in the well-disciplined
armies of the West.[46] And as Jal himself asserts, he never killed anyone in
cold blood.[47] Despite his youth and the fears, passions, and terrors of war,
Jal's experiences as a child soldier are akin to those of an ordinary soldier,
whether child or adult.

There are also examples in popular culture that provide a more nuanced
view of child soldiers. Biyi Bandele's *Burma Boy* depicts the fourteen-year-
old Nigerian child soldier Ali Banana as he is fighting the Japanese in Orde
Wingate's British army in Burma.[48] It is a picaresque novel filled with terror
and with humor, and Banana ends up having to kill his mortally wounded
comrade to save him from torture and mutilation by the Japanese. The
novel is both a coming-of-age story and a tale of the madness of war, but
it employs virtually none of the tropes of terror, exploitation, abuse, and
criminality that characterize most contemporary novels about child soldiers. Similarly, Ken Saro-Wiwa's *Sozaboy*, a lyrical, funny, and terrifying
novel written in the wake of the war in Biafra, was clearly written before
the set-piece tropes of the child soldier novel coalesced.[49] Finally, the
tone of some francophone novels such as Amadou Kourouma's *Allah Is
Not Obliged* have retained this picaresque quality.[50] As in the humanitarian
and human rights literature, there is clearly a North-South dimension to
much of the understanding of child soldiers. But there has also been some

pushback from the South against the dominant tropes of this literature. Catarina Martins argues that a clear shift of tone is more likely where African writers and filmmakers control the narrative. These latter stories often place war and the children who fight them in historical context and contain elements of children's responsibility, voice, agency, tragedy, adventure, and a strong diversity of life stories.[51] Moreover, some African writers are also able to voice unforgiving anger toward children who wantonly kill in ways that leave little room for Western notions of innocence. In Sierra Leone writer Aminatta Forna's novel *The Memory of Love*, Kai, a physician, attempts to pick up the body of a rebel commander killed by desperate and oppressed Freetown residents at the close of a brutal occupation: "[She] was a young girl, lying upon the road, angled in death. Fourteen, sixteen at most. Someone had tried to remove her clothing. She lay in the street in a scarlet bra and panties, doubtless at one time looted from an upmarket boutique. The people who lived there refused Kai and his team leave to touch the body. She'd been the commanding officer in charge of the attack. They would deny her the dignity of burial. The teenage commander, in stolen, silken underwear."[52]

The 2007 feature film *Ezra*, by the Nigerian director Newton I. Aduaka, provides another example of at least a tentative nod toward complexity.[53] It, too, is located in an unnamed country in West Africa, but one that is remarkably similar to Sierra Leone. One strength of the film is that some attention is paid to the daily life of child soldiers in a way that blurs the stereotypes, in order to tell its story of children under arms. Some of the children, many of them teenagers, are part of a rebel army. Some have been kidnapped, some are volunteers, some have revolutionary ideologies, and some just want to survive. The main character, sixteen-year-old Ezra, is a troubled youth who commits terrible war crimes, but is also involved in a powerful love relationship with a female soldier. The complexity of the relationship between the characters makes this story of child soldiers ring true.

The film holds up less well when it delivers its message about how to deal with the problems of child soldiers. The scenes in which Ezra testifies before a Truth and Reconciliation Commission are completely fabricated and strange. Such testimony by children was not permitted in Sierra Leone, and the commissioners in the film are incredibly wacky. On the whole, this episode undermines the film's credibility, as does the parroting at the film's end of the view that Ezra and the rest of the children are all victims.

KONY 2012

These somewhat more complex views of child soldiers are the exceptions, and have of done little to disrupt or modify the popular narrative of the child soldier. One of the most recent embodiments of the standard narrative is the film *KONY 2012*, the very slick viral video "wanted poster" produced by the organization Invisible Children. The film targets Joseph Kony, commander-in-chief of the Lord's Resistance Army (LRA), an insurgent group that has been fighting the government of Uganda and the Ugandan army for more than twenty-five years. The Kony-led insurgency coincided with the coming to power of Yoweri Kaguta Museveni, who has been the president of Uganda since 1986. In 2005 the International Criminal Court issued a warrant for Kony, charging that he had personally issued orders to target and kill civilian populations, including those living in internally displaced persons camps in northern Uganda. Kony has been charged with numerous war crimes and crimes against humanity, including murder, rape, sexual enslavement, intentionally directing attacks against civilian populations, and, most notoriously, the forced enlistment into the LRA of children under age fifteen.

The Kony video has had more than one hundred million views on YouTube and appears to have catalyzed the African Union into launching a new regional military operation against Kony, using five thousand troops drawn from four African countries: the Central African Republic, the Democratic Republic of the Congo, South Sudan, and Uganda. Even prior to the release of the video, U.S. president Barak Obama ordered a small force of about one hundred special operations troops to support the search for Kony's rag-tag but lethal band of rebels, now estimated to number between two hundred and four hundred persons.[54] In March 2014 the president sent several CV-22 Osprey aircraft, together with an additional 150 Air Force Special Operations forces and other airmen, to join the American troops in the search.[55]

There is little doubt that Kony is a war criminal who should be captured and tried for his alleged crimes. Nonetheless, this film clearly exaggerates Kony's significance today. (He hasn't even been in Uganda for over seven years.) Criticism of the film has been pervasive. The filmmakers appear self-absorbed, overestimating their own importance; moreover, they know little about Uganda, and the film's analysis lacks complexity and nuance—it is ethnocentric and patronizing. One of the biggest problems with KONY 2012 is that it turns the whole issue of child soldiers into a discussion about criminals, when it should be a conversation about politics and social change. The film feeds into the general belief that the recruitment of child soldiers is a uniquely modern form of deviance, the result of a few "bad apples" abusing, exploiting, and terrorizing children and stampeding them into murder.

The highly public hunt for Kony also raises the issue of whether the entire problem of child soldiers can sometimes serve as a distraction from significantly more important issues. Uganda is a country whose political leadership has been charged with stealing hundreds of millions of dollars in foreign aid from the World Bank, the United States, and other countries, including money designated for the victims of Joseph Kony. Yet Uganda remains important to U.S. interests and policy in the Horn of Africa. It was the first to deploy troops under the African Union Mission in Somalia, and Ugandan troops and military command remain are key to Somalia's battle against the rebel group commonly known as al-Shabaab (the Youth). To this day the United States is Uganda's largest bilateral donor. In the meantime, as Helen Epstein reports, opposition politicians and nearly everyone else who attempts to expose the details of this systematic theft of public funds are beaten, robbed, murdered, imprisoned, tortured, and charged with treason.[56]

The Kony case is only one of several in which political interests play an important role in the child soldier issue. Rhetoric and reality are often at odds. Although President Obama recently declared child soldiers to be slaves,[57] he also waived the application of sanctions under the U.S. Child Soldier Protection Act against countries designated by the U.S. State Department as recruiters of child soldiers. On October 25, 2010, President Obama issued a waiver of sanctions against Chad, the DRC, Sudan, and Yemen, citing the importance of these countries in cooperating with key foreign policy objectives of the United States and the negative impact that sanctions would have on U.S. interests. For two countries, the presidential waivers were given in recognition of the role they played in cooperating with the United States in antiterrorism activities. President Obama stated that Chad was involved in combating trans-Saharan terrorism and in aiding in the humanitarian crisis in Darfur. Yemen was cited for its role in counterterrorism operations against al-Qaeda in the Arabian Peninsula. Broader foreign policy considerations played a role in the other two states. With respect to the DRC, the president cited a need to continue defense reform services and to influence the negative behavior patterns of the military as well as to transform the military into a nonpolitical professional force respectful of human rights. In the case of Sudan, the United States cited the need to implement the peace agreement in southern Sudan and to bring about a democratic transformation in country. All four of the countries were cited by the president as making progress in the elimination of child soldiers.[58] Waivers were issued by the White House in September 2012 for Libya, South Sudan, Yemen, and the DRC, although by October 2012 the DRC had entered into an action plan with the United Nations to bring about an end to recruitment in government forces.[59] In September 2013 the White House issued waivers for Chad, South Sudan, and Yemen, all major recruiters of child soldiers.[60] More recently, in September 2014, President Obama renewed the current policy by waiving restrictions on Rwanda, Somalia, Yemen, the Central African Republic, the Democratic Republic of the Congo, and South Sudan.[61]

Child Soldiers in Contemporary Juvenile Literature

Notwithstanding any of these political complexities, humanitarian discourse has also deeply penetrated children's literature. Books for young readers sidestep the graphic and gruesome details of adult literature, but retain the focus on the trauma of war. Like much of the adult literature, there a strong split between children's literature that focuses on child soldiers in Africa and elsewhere and those that focus on the Euro-American experience of war. In contemporary juvenile literature, there are few, if any, African child soldiers or child soldiers drawn from contemporary contexts. Where they exist, they are portrayed as hapless victims of war. In Bernard Ashley's *Little Soldier*, thirteen-year-old Kaninda Bulumba's family is murdered in an intertribal war in a fictitious African country. While he seeks revenge, he is rescued by UN forces and taken to London. At school, he is recruited by an inner-city street gang that agrees to help him take revenge on another child refugee at the school who is a member of Kaninda's enemy tribe. All is ultimately resolved when Kaninda comes to realize that his own tribe used him, and that both war and inner-city violence are meaningless.[62] In Anne de Graaf's juvenile novel *Son of a Gun* eight-year-old Liberian Lucky, his ten-year-old sister Nopi, and their schoolmates are kidnapped and forced to become child soldiers. The author's note at the end of the book tells us everything: "Can you imagine it? Children walking around with weapons? Children who are forced to hurt other children, children who are forced to defend their country?"[63] In *Chanda's Wars*, set in Ngala, a fictitious African country, Chandra, a young girl, attempts to rescue children who have been kidnapped by General Mandiki and his rebels who are hiding out across the border in a national park. The rebels are said to come out of the park only to launch attacks on their own people, burning them alive, cutting out their tongues, and kidnapping their children to use them as slaves, decoys, and human shields. The rebels kick people to death, chop them up with machetes, and nail them to trees. The rebels "feed"—a term usually used to describe animals—on raw meat. "Nobody wants peace," says one character. "If Mandiki loses he will be executed. But if Ngala wins, the foreign funds it gets to fight terrorism will disappear. Its leaders need that cash to pay for their limos and mansions." The newly kidnapped recruits are led to an initiation site tied to a single line of rope, their heads covered with burlap bags. The key moment of the initiation is the fire branding of new recruits, coupled with a ritual where the rebel leader Mandiki brandishes a human skull wrapped in monkey skin said to have been the skull of the "most powerful spirit doctor in Mozambique." During the ceremony, the rebel leader Mandiki "growls and grunts sounds . . . [that] might come from the animals in the park or from somewhere deep inside the earth."

This critique of the literary tropes is not a denial of the atrocities of war. Clearly rebel groups have engaged in terrible atrocities. The Revolutionary United Front in Sierra Leone was infamous for the maiming and slaughtering of civilians and child soldiers. Likewise, the forces of the LRA of Uganda murdered and mutilated civilians and were infamous for the abduction of children. The LRA's cult-like activities were a mixture of local religious beliefs and Christian evangelism; the backs of new recruits were sometimes carved with the sign of the cross. Abductees were sometimes brutally murdered in ways designed to induce terror into new recruits. But these terrible examples have become the staple of horror-fantasy mash-ups that combine themes from *King Kong*, *Indiana Jones*, and the *Heart of Darkness* into a horrifying typology of all child recruitment. In the end, they tell us virtually nothing about wars in Africa, child soldiers, or the motivations of rebels. The child soldier narrative is simply one element of the dystopian fantasy industry that continuously spins out tales of victimization and horror for Western readers—juvenile or adult—about hapless Africans and their troubles.

Even outside of the focus on Africa, juvenile fiction about war and child soldiers frequently harbors antiwar sentiments. Some contemporary children's literature questions whether there is anything heroic about war at all, stressing the impact of war upon children and the moral ambiguity of collective violence. Juvenile literature often conveys the sense that both children and adults, on both sides of a conflict, are caught up in events not of their making that undermine their common humanity. A prime example is Robert Westall's 1975 historical novel *The Machine Gunners*, which was awarded the Carnegie Medal in 2007 and selected by the judges of the Carnegie Medal as one of the ten most important children's novels of the past seventy years.[64] In Westall's novel, children on the coast of England capture a German gunner whose plane had been shot down by British Spitfires; they befriend him and ultimately allow him to escape (although he is recaptured later). Another example is Michael Morpurgo's *War Horse*, in which the humanity of both English and Germans, the mutual insanity of war, and the humanity of Joey the horse dominate the story.[65] In juvenile literature, as in adult literature, there are many works that stress the meaningless of armed conflict, but it is important to note that the books for juveniles set in Western contexts rarely, if ever, suggest that the children who are caught up in these wars are the pawns or dupes of nefarious adults.

Equally important, there is still a great deal of room in juvenile literature for the heroic child soldiers. These works are frequently set in World War II, the last war in which significant numbers of European children participated. In *Fire in the Hills*, the fourteen-year-old hero Roberto has escaped from a German forced labor camp and makes his way to Sicily as part of his attempt to reach his home and family in Venice. As he ventures north, he reluctantly joins with other young Italian partisans in the fight against Germany. Roberto doesn't want to die or fight or kill, but realizes that he cannot evade his responsibilities. As he puts it, he "no longer wanted to live doing the dishonorable thing."[66] *Domenic's War* by Curtis Parkinson is based upon the true story of Sandy Cellucci, a farm boy in German-occupied Italy who risked his life smuggling food to downed British airmen hidden in an old family mill.[67] In the 2010 graphic novel *Resistance*, two children, Paul and Marie, help save their Jewish friend from the Germans in Vichy France and end up becoming couriers for the French Resistance. Paul and Marie's mother is also involved in the resistance, but is unaware of her children's activities and plans. When the children's plans are revealed, she initially rejects their participation, saying, "I won't risk my children's lives," but soon relents, embracing them and crying out, "My brave, brave children. Your father would be so proud of you."[68] Shirley Hughes's 2013 novel *Hero on a Bicycle* is set near Florence, Italy, in 1944.[69] The hero in the novel is thirteen-year-old Paolo Crivelli, who, though not formally recruited into partisan ranks, helps escaped allied prisoners of war evade capture by the Germans, an act punishable by death. Both his mother and sister are equally involved in these anti-German activities, but Paolo in particular risks his life by leading the airmen into town, where they fall into a German trap and are almost killed. He risks his life again by helping the leader of a local partisan group escape execution by the Germans.

The novels hardly valorize war, which is depicted as brutal and unromantic. But they do valorize the courage of children who risk their lives in the fight against oppression. They make perfectly clear that Germans, Nazis, and other fascists are the enemy. They in no way suggest that the recruiters of children are criminals or that children have no place in armed resistance, even when detailing human and parental concerns for the terrible risks children take. Likewise, they make no attempt portray the parents of these children as criminal or immoral, even where they are complicit with or facilitate children's involvement in war. Occasionally, a war novel set in a non-Western setting has a similar resonance. Mitali Perkins's 2010 book *Bamboo People* focuses on a war in Burma undertaken by the Burmese government against the ethnic Karrenni minority.[70] The protagonists are fifteen-year-old Chiko, who is forcibly recruited into the Burmese Army and there treated with uncommon brutality, and Tu Reh, a sixteen-year-old Karenni rebel. Tu Reh finds Chiko half dead in the jungle after stepping on a land mine; the Karenni group nurses Chiko back to health and helps reunite him with his family. While the rebel forces are not uniformly kind in the way they treat their prisoner, the rebels are portrayed as fighting for a just and humane cause, and instead of killing their prisoner they allow him to be reunited with his family.

Transgressive Narratives in Fantasy and Science Fiction

There remains one additional major area in Western juvenile fiction where the child soldier is valorized. What distinguishes these works is that they are firmly set in fantasy—often dystopian fantasies. Nevertheless, they provide a highly transgressive counternarrative about child soldiers that has excited children and youth across the globe. Among the earliest of these is the 1985 science fiction novel *Ender's Game* by Orson Scott Card, which was made into a film in 2013. The plot, set in the future, is simple: the earth has fought off two attacks by insect-like aliens—the Formics or "Buggers"—in which millions of people were killed. Humanity is anticipating a third deadly attack. As the key defensive strategy, humanity creates a battle school where it recruits potential child military geniuses for battle school at about age ten. The children receive an education grounded in mathematics and computer science, but above all they participate in a succession of aggressive war games in the so-called battle room. Individual and team success in the battle room, which involves simulated battles against the Buggers, leads to individual promotion into officer ranks. The child hero of the novel, Andrew "Ender" Wiggen, is recruited to the school already marked by the military as humanity's best hope for leading a successful attack against the aliens. The battle training is frequently abusive, and various incidents lead to the deaths of trainees. Ender overcomes many personal challenges to emerge as a military leader.

The simulations become increasingly complex, and in the final practice Ender breaks the rule of engagement in the battle room, sacrifices many under his command, and destroys the Formic home planet, killing billions. Only then is it revealed that final games were not simulations but real battles, and that Ender has successfully defeated the enemy but also unintentionally committed genocide, or really xenocide, the total destruction of an alien species. It is also revealed that the Formics had mistakenly attacked earth, believing that no thinking beings inhabited the planet, but having recognized their error, the Formics had no intention of starting a third attack. Unfortunately, they were unable to communicate their intentions successfully to humanity. Ender himself becomes a celebrated military hero and is promoted to admiral, but is unable to return to earth. Instead, having belatedly discovered an egg of a Formic Queen, he resolves to colonize a new planet with Formics, in the hope of regenerating the annihilated species.

Orson Scott Card saw this book as a revolutionary text. He viewed it as story of gifted children, but one that asserts the personhood of children who are otherwise treated as an underclass subject to the decisions of adults. Adults who held different views of children, he claimed, would find the novel a difficult experience.[71] There is no doubt that the children of the school are manipulated by adults toward fulfilling the war aims of humanity, but the adult populations of earth are equally manipulated by their political leaders. The book clearly resonates with the military. It has been listed on the U.S. Marine Corps Professional Reading Program for grades from private to officer candidate and remains on the Marine Corps Commandants Professional Reading list.[72] In a very real sense, the novel blurs the psychological and technical competencies of children and adults. Children are chosen precisely because of their skills, but what appears to be appealing to military readers are the moral dilemmas of leadership and Ender's ability to cope with the problems of fear, isolation, loneliness, peer and adult pressure, and rivalry—all very real and very adult problems in the military.

Ender's Game has also been criticized as a book that absolves its hero of genocide.[73] Ender, however, doesn't quite absolve himself: "I killed ten billion buggers, whose queens, at least, were alive and wise as any man, who had not even launched a third attack against us, and no one thinks to call it a crime."[74] Ender's absolution from criminal liability comes not from being a child but from his lack of intentionality in carrying out the horrible act. But like the case with a modern-day child soldier, there appear to be many characters in the novel telling him that it is not his fault. In the end, however, he carries on not as an abused victim of war but as a tragic hero.

Another example of child soldiers clearly set in fantasy is the child fighters of Dumbledore's Army in the Harry Potter series. The central element of these tales is the resurrection of Lord Voldemort, an evil wizard with great powers and plans of world domination. The story unfolds at the Hogwarts School of Witchcraft and Wizardry, a school for young wizards led by its headmaster Albus Dumbledore. Dumbledore is also the creator and leader of the secret organization the Order of the Phoenix, which is dedicated to defeating Voldemort and his supporters, the Death Eaters. Under Dumbledore's guidance, the training of wizards at Hogwarts includes the stark recognition that the children live in a dangerous world and need practical skills and training to survive. Central to this training is an explicit recognition of children's competency and agency.

As the story progresses, Voldemort's supporters successfully infiltrate Hogwarts, undermine Dumbledore's leadership, and have him removed as headmaster. Voldemort's followers also initiate an educational revolution. Under the pretext of "protecting" young, innocent students, Dolores Umbridge, the new headmaster (and a Death Eater), creates a new curriculum that eliminates the practical use of magic and defenses against the "dark arts" and substitutes text study and "age-appropriate spells" for real training. The idea is essentially to disarm the children whose agency they fear.

Realizing the disempowering effects of the new curriculum, some students establish a school club where they secretly train for the anticipated struggle against Voldemort and his followers. Outlawed by school officials, the club becomes a clandestine organization calling itself "Dumbledore's Army." Now an underground movement, it makes plain its continued existence with a graffiti message painted on the walls of Hogwarts: "Dumbledore's Army, Still Recruiting." Over time, the club evolves into a magically armed group that engages in three major incidents of violent conflict with the Death Eaters.

The main armed conflict, the so-called Battle of Hogwarts, pits Dumbledore's Army together with the adult wizards of Hogwarts against Voldemort and his allies in a final battle for the fate of the Wizarding World. During the battle, some of the youngest students are evacuated and protected, but older students (still child soldiers) enter the battle. Later, even younger students return to join the fight. Some parents clearly object to the presence of their children in battle. One parent, fearing for her daughter's life, dismisses Dumbledore's Army as a "teenager's gang," not an army. But many children stand and fight, and some lose their lives. Critically, their deaths are cast as tragic, and no charges of abuse and exploitation subvert the nobility of their sacrifices. Instead, children who take up arms are seen as intelligent, motivated, talented, ethical, in control of their own decisions, and not coerced by adults. They fight to preserve the morality of the Wizarding World and their way of life.

The counternarrative of Dumbledore's Army offers a different perspective of child soldiers and suggests that children do, in fact, have agency and the mental capacity to take action against the wrongs they witness in their world. Of course, there are adults who do abuse children in these stories. Voldemort and his evil followers also recruit children, but the narrative makes plain that participation in armed violence is not evil per se, but that the morality of the cause is the key issue.

A third recent example, *The Hunger Games,* is a dystopian trilogy about a fantasy world in which a colonizing ruling class has institutionalized the systematic murder of children by other children at the behest of the state. In many respects, *The Hunger Games* recalls some of the most graphic horrors of children killing children found in contemporary warfare. The story is set in the futuristic nation of Panem, a grotesque fantasy version of imperial Rome, in which the pampered and privileged population of the wealthy colonial metropolis grows prosperous on the brutal enslavement of twelve outlying districts, defeated in war. Each of these districts is compelled to provide annual tribute of two children, a boy and a girl, aged twelve to eighteen. The children are chosen by lottery, and all twenty-four are forced to fight to the death in the annual Hunger Games, which are visually broadcast in real time across the nation. The games are set in specially created artificial landscapes of forest, fields, and water, in which the children, under constant televised surveillance, hunt each other down. The televised murders of children serve as a form of mass entertainment with all the glitz and celebrity of American reality TV. Under the rules of the games, the sole remaining survivor is permitted to return home enriched.

The plot focuses on sixteen-year-old Katniss Everdeen, a teenager who substitutes herself as a tribute for her even younger sister whose name has been drawn in the lottery. Katniss is forced to kill in self-defense, but defies gender stereotypes and emerges as an intelligent, moral, skillful warrior who is both self-reliant and nurturing. Katniss forges an alliance with Peeta Mellark, the male tribute from her district, and together they manage to alter the rules of the games so that they not only survive, but also emerge as symbols of resistance to the authoritarian rule of the Capitol. If the story had stopped there, Katniss might simply be a heroic child who survived a terrifying and revolting ordeal. But as the story moves forward, Katniss emerges not only as a symbol of resistance, but as a participant in an armed rebel movement that brings about the violent overthrow of the Capitol and its leaders. The *New York Times* hailed Katniss Everdeen as one of the most radical female characters to appear in American movies.[75] She is a female warrior, who fights for herself, her family, and her community.

In recent years *Ender's Game*, the Harry Potter books, and *The Hunger Games* trilogy have become international phenomena, both as literature and in film. The seven-book Harry Potter series is the best-selling book series in history, with more than 450 million copies in print, and over 36 million copies of *The Hunger Games* trilogy are currently in print. Both series illustrate the dramatic return of the child hero in wartime, although the realism of earlier child hero novels is deflected to some degree by the fantasy settings. Indeed, given the general public concern about child soldiers, fantasy may be the only setting in which the appearance of heroic child warriors is culturally acceptable. Collins has made it clear, however, that she does not want the fantasy settings of *The Hunger Games* to derail her message by opening the door to an allegorical interpretation of her work. Rejecting the suggestion that the entirety of trilogy can be interpreted as an allegory of the struggles of adolescence, she has insisted that *The Hunger Games* is, first and foremost, about war.[76]

Why do literature and film involving child combatants still thrive in an age when the recruitment of child soldiers has become an internationally recognized war crime? Part of the explanation may be that war and conflict and the extremely dystopian threats found in these works can provide a dramatic setting in which the agency and independence of children can be imaginatively rendered. In these extreme settings, the child is depicted as capable of bravery and moral decision making, and is able to demonstrate both the heroic and the sometimes brutal and bloody aspects of the warrior's role. In contrast, the vast majority of contemporary fictional and cinematic accounts of child soldiers are set in Africa. There are no brave child warriors in this literary and cinematic world, just the abused victims of war. Only in the works set in fantasy or in history does the heroic child warrior remain, and here largely in Western or Western-like settings. This allows both children and adults to imaginatively engage the action, drama, and heroic possibilities of war while keeping Africa, with its images of abused and exploited children, at a safe mental and moral distance.

Dehumanizing Child Soldiers

In contrast to stories of child soldiers in historical settings or in fantasy, most narratives of contemporary child soldiers, for adults and for children, completely remove war from the world of politics. None of these wars offer a rationale for violence; war appears virtually out of nowhere, usually as a result of adult perfidy, to engulf children and to turn them into victims and killers. It is almost as if war was a malevolent natural phenomenon akin to a tornado, which lands on a country and destroys it. It is not as if past wars and uprisings in the West, especially civil wars and revolutions, did not have dramatic displays of violence. Chateaubriand, in his memoirs of revolutionary France, for example, describes terrible scenes of murder and mayhem during the French Revolution that are hardly supportive of Hugo's view of the morality of revolutionary violence. Indeed Chateaubriand described crowds of people bearing severed heads on spikes: "A troop of ragamuffins appeared at one end of the street. . . . As they came nearer, we made out two disheveled and disfigured heads . . . each at the end of a pike. . . . The murderers stopped in front of me and stretched their pikes up towards me, singing, dancing, and jumping up in order to bring the pale effigies closer to my face. One eye in one of these heads had started out of its socket and was hanging down on the dead man's face; the pike was projecting through the open mouth, the teeth of which were biting on the iron."[77] Similarly Chateaubriand's memoirs of the July Revolution of 1830, the same one that figures so prominently in Delacroix's painting, are unequivocal in his near racialized disparagement of children and his horror at how they threw themselves into the bloody work of war: "The children, fearless because they knew no better, played a sad role during those three days. Hiding behind their weakness, they fired at point-blank range at the officers who opposed them. Modern weapons put death in the hands of the feeblest. These ugly and sickly monkeys, cruel and perverse, immoral even without the capacity to perform immorally, these three-day heroes devoted themselves to murder with all the abandon of true innocents."[78] Chateaubriand was a royalist and a foe of revolutionary violence. His scorn for children under arms did not prevail in either France or the West generally, where the democratic gains brought about through revolution trumped virtually all other considerations. Thus, despite the cruel bloodletting of the past and the prominent role played by young people in revolutionary violence, revolutionary activity was understood as meaningful and positive. Yet if Chateaubriand were alive today he could easily be writing much of the contemporary humanitarian discourse on child soldiers.

Why were we so willing to read a political and social context into the violent acts of children in the past, but strip away this context in the present? Why is it that we read only mindless barbarism into contemporary warfare? Some argue that the new wars in Africa and elsewhere are, in fact, much more horrible than the warfare of the past, and indeed the fact that war is increasingly directed toward civilians adds to our sense of fear and outrage. The set-piece portraits of African children at war in humanitarian and literary descriptions of child soldiers have been harnessed to serve modern notions of the greater good by ending children's involvement in war. But though these narratives attempt to lend the situation of child soldiers a universal "everyman" quality, these portraits of child soldiers do so by drawing upon an earlier discourse about Africa that has long served to dehumanize Africans. In the end, we are still writing Africa's script, and with it the larger story of child soldiers, in much the same way that Joseph Conrad did so many years ago.

5

Modern Child Soldiers

Millions of people around the world are involved in wars, rebellions, insurgencies, and civil conflicts. It is widely asserted that between 250,000 and 300,000 child soldiers below the age of eighteen are involved in contemporary armed conflicts, but no reliable statistics support these numbers. The figure of 300,000 was put forth by advocacy groups promoting a ban on child recruitment as a way of dramatizing the issue, and it is very likely that the actual numbers are significantly lower.[1] Whatever the exact numbers, over recent decades thousands of children have experienced and continue to experience war as soldiers.

The numbers are also very much a product of the definition of child soldier. The laws of war, also called International Humanitarian Law, criminalize recruiting or using children under age fifteen. This nearly universal standard is embodied in the Rome Treaty that established the International Criminal Court, and is widely regarded as a rule of customary international law. In tandem with this, a variety of human rights and children's rights conventions, which involve voluntary compliance, seek to raise the age bar higher, with the goal of ending the recruitment of anyone under age eighteen. The United Nations and most humanitarian and children rights groups routinely define a child soldier as anyone under age eighteen. These groups generally believe that the age provisions found in the laws of war are outmoded. However, because of this upward shift in the age at which soldiers are considered "children," many persons who today are defined as "child soldiers" would not have been classified as children in years past. Lurking beneath these definitional controversies is a far blurrier and highly contested empirical reality. To give a simple example, the United States allows youngsters who are seventeen years old to enlist in the military if they have parental permission; this practice is fully compliant with U.S. law and all of its treaty obligations. The United States does not allow soldiers under eighteen to be stationed in war zones, though compliance has not always been perfect, and during the war in Iraq some soldiers under eighteen served in a war zone. No doubt some humanitarian organizations would accuse the United States of recruiting child soldiers, but when they do so they are asserting their moral position against the recruitment of those under eighteen rather than any actual violation of international criminal law.

Child Soldiers and the Rise of Armed Groups

As we have seen in previous chapters, the trend in recruitment has been that nation-states have generally abandoned using younger soldiers. Most nations no longer systematically recruit children into their official armed forces. There have been some notable, sometimes notorious exceptions. During the Iran-Iraq War, Iran recruited some ninety-five thousand children above age twelve, and some as young as nine, to be used as human waves to clear areas of land mines. The official age of recruitment in Iran is nineteen, but government-allied paramilitary groups and even foreign Iranian allies such as Hezbollah systematically recruit volunteers with little concern about age.[2] It has also been reported that child soldiers as young as fourteen were used to violently suppress antigovernment political demonstrations in Iran in 2011.[3] Indeed, it is quite possible that some nations have shifted recruitment of children to paramilitaries in order to maintain the fiction that their armed forces have a higher age of recruitment. Nonetheless, it is clear that the age of direct child recruitment into government armed forces is coming to an end. Indeed, the goal of the 2014 UN campaign "Children, Not Soldiers" is the final eradication of child recruitment by the remaining few governments that continue to recruit.

As of 2014 only seven nations in the world were listed by the United Nations secretary-general as principal recruiters of child soldiers under eighteen years of age: Afghanistan, the Democratic Republic of the Congo

(DRC), Myanmar (Burma), Somalia, Sudan, South Sudan, and Yemen. All these countries either have signed action plans with the United Nations to end recruitment by government armed forces or are negotiating with the United Nations to develop such plans. As of 2014 there has been at least one major setback, namely in South Sudan, where civil war between the Dinka and Nuer ethic groups has resulted in increased recruitment of children.[4] Other than these seven countries, child soldier recruitment is carried out largely by non-state actors such as rebel forces, revolutionaries, guerrillas, insurgents, terrorist groups, paramilitaries, global terrorist networks, regional tribal, ethnic, and religious militants, and local defense organizations. These actors, usually termed "armed groups," still depend upon the use of youngsters as combatants. This shift is evident in a quick review of the UN list of the most persistent users and recruiter of child soldiers.[5]

The recruitment of child soldiers generally follows changes in patterns of conflict across the globe. A decade ago much attention was focused on conflicts in Africa south of the Sahara, but as even as some of these conflicts have waned, recruitment is now spreading across the Middle East, North Africa, the Horn of Africa, and the Sahel. Some of these situations reflect a continued simmering of long-term political conflicts, but another factor has been the significant erosion of the political order that held sway during the decades following the end of the colonial era. Many of the newly emergent militant groups have their origins in conflicts rooted in local grievances, but in some instances these groups have evolved into militant and near-millenarian movements with ideologies that call for radical reorganization of the system of nation-states.

In the civil war in Syria, various rebel groups such as the Free Syrian Army, the Islamic State of Iraq and Sham (ISIS), and al-Qaeda recruit child soldiers, as do a number of progovernment militias. In Iraq, both the Islamic State of Iraq (ISI) and al-Qaeda in Iraq recruit child soldiers. In Afghanistan, the most prominent recruiters are the Haqqani network and a number of Taliban armed groups. In the conflict in Sudan, armed groups that recruit child soldiers include the Sudan Revolutionary Front, a rebel alliance, as well as a few smaller militia groups that support the Sudanese government. In South Sudan various opposition groups and the Nuer White Army are known to recruit children as soldiers. In Nigeria the armed group Jama'atu Ahlis Sunna Lidda'Awati Wal-Jihad (People

Committed to the Propagation of the Prophet's Teachings and Jihad), more widely known as Boko Haram (Western Education Is Forbidden), has been identified as a major user of child soldiers, in addition to their practice of kidnapping young girls.[6] In Mali, recruiters of child soldiers include Ansar Dinea (Defenders of the Faith), a militant Islamic group with reported ties to al-Qaeda, the National Movement for the Liberation of Azawad, and the Movement for Oneness and Jihad in West Africa. In Somalia, the al-Qaeda-linked Al-Shabaab (the Youth) and its opponents the Ahlus Sunnah wal Jamaah, a Sufi paramilitary, are also recruiters of child soldiers. In the Central African Republic there are seven armed groups that recruit child soldiers. Most are part of or connected to the co-called Seleka coalition, a largely Muslim alliance. Many Seleka fighters appear to be Arabic speakers from neighboring Chad and the Sudan.[7] In addition to these insurgency groups, the Lord's Resistance Army, the notorious insurgent group that originally emerged in Uganda, has been moving through and across the borders of the Central African Republic, South Sudan, and the Democratic Republic of the Congo. In the Democratic Republic of the Congo, six non-state armed groups are involved in child recruitment.

In the Philippines, the principal recruiters are Abu Sayyaf, Bangsamoro Islamic Freedom Fighters, and Moro Islamic Liberation Front, Islamic separatist groups in the southern Philippines, and the New People's Army, the armed wing of the Communist Party of the Philippines. In Myanmar, eight armed groups recruit child soldiers. Finally, in South America, two Marxist revolutionary armed groups in Colombia are the principal recruiters of child soldiers, namely the Marxist insurgent group Ejército de Liberación Nacional (National Liberation Army) and the Fuerzas Armadas Revolucionarias de Colombia—Ejército del Pueblo or FARC (Revolutionary Armed Forces of Colombia—People's Army).

This list illustrates the diversity of armed groups recruiting child soldiers. They range from some whose stated goals are to overthrow dictatorships, resist oppression, and create democratic societies to those whose main goal is to create despotic societies backed by regimes of state terror. The variety of recruiters makes plain that child recruitment is not simply the work of evildoers who abuse children with impunity, but rather is tied to a wide variety of armed groups with an extremely mixed set of motives. It includes groups that cynically and criminally kidnap children, groups fighting against dictatorial and oppressive regimes, and others who reject or are indifferent to new and sometimes alien concepts of childhood and for whom current ideas of childhood simply do not jibe with their own understanding of the world. This does not mean that the world is a museum in which old ideas of childhood must be preserved in a diorama, but it does tell us that the entire child soldier project, with its goal of universally separating children from military service, is not simply a matter of finding and jailing a few bad apples, but is in fact an extraordinarily complex and ambitious project of directed social change.

Curbing Child Recruitment: Armed Groups and the Status of Rebels

Upon signing the Declaration of Independence of the United States in 1776, Benjamin Franklin is reputed to have said, "We must all hang together, or assuredly we shall all hang separately." Franklin was alluding to the typical fate of captured rebels in the eighteenth century. Rebellion was treason, a criminal act that led directly to the hangman's noose. Little has changed since Franklin's time. Nation-states across the globe treat rebels of every stripe as criminals and enemies of the state. The right of rebellion against oppressive governments was central to the Declaration of Independence, but no such right exists in contemporary international law. Indeed, no nation-state and no human rights group accepts a general right of rebellion against oppression, even if they are sympathetic to particular cases.[8] But as the recent armed struggles in Libya, Iraq, and Syria make plain, rebellion takes place across the globe, and nearly all rebels make use of child soldiers.[9]

Historically, rebels and most other non-state actors were unrecognized in international law. Rebellion was treated as an internal domestic matter for each nation to handle as it saw fit. The main exception to this is Article 3 of the Geneva Conventions of 1949, which required that captured rebels be treated humanely and not be subject to murder, mutilation, cruel treatment, torture, or humiliating and degrading treatment. It did not, however, preclude rebels from being executed.

Today the legal status of rebel groups remains substantially the same: they are still regarded as illegitimate. Despite the fact that rebel groups have no legitimate rights, several key international treaties now impose legal duties upon non-state military actors, usually termed "armed groups" in the language of treaties, requiring that they forgo the recruitment and use of child soldiers. Such armed groups are now bound by the laws of war as embodied by the statute creating the International Criminal Court in The Hague, even though they had no place at the table in the drafting of the statute. In essence, the international community imposes legal duties upon rebel groups without offering such groups any recognized rights or even token of legitimacy. At the same time, it is difficult to enforce international law against armed groups already regarded as illegitimate and criminal.

Despite their illegitimacy, UN officials—frequently those from the Office of the Special Representative of the Secretary-General for Children and Armed, have a strong interest in engaging non-state actors in their efforts to end the recruitment and use of child soldiers. UN officials believe that they have the best chance of reaching agreements with armed groups that have a clear political agenda of ultimately forming the government of a sovereign state. UN officials also express optimism in their ability to reach out some local self-defense groups and militias. In contrast, some armed groups, particularly self-branded "al-Qaeda" affiliates, are so linked to terrorism that negotiation is both morally and practically precluded. However, UN officials have little to offer rebel groups except moral suasion and the possibility that rebel groups that comply with international law may have an easier path to international recognition should their rebellion succeed.

UN officials face considerable political obstacles in dealing with armed groups, because they must first obtain permission from national authorities before engaging any non-state parties operating with their countries. Nation-states are typically zealous guardians of their own sovereignty and vigorously resist attempts by the international community to "meddle" in their internal affairs. For nation-states facing insurgencies, the official position is usually that violence by internal armed groups is not an "armed conflict" but a criminal matter. Even the mere discussion of the status of rebel groups by the United Nations might be deemed as treading on national sovereignty.

An instructive example comes from India, where the government responded to a UN report on the most persistent violators of international laws against the recruitment of child soldiers. The government of India objected to the inclusion of the Maoist rebels in the report, and argued that the United Nations had exceeded its authority and had no mandate to investigate and report on the situation of the Maoist rebels in central India.[10] In India's view, the Maoist rebel forces in their country were simply local criminals who should be treated as criminals and were not the legitimate concern of international institutions or international law. There is little doubt that the Maoist insurgency in India is linked to serious grievances of tribal peoples in the forested areas of eastern and central India, who are among the most economically deprived peoples of India. Some ten thousand to twenty thousand rebels are allegedly active across eastern and central India, and their avowed goal is to overthrow the Indian state. The Indian government has not deployed its regular army against the rebels, but instead uses the Central Reserve Police Force, the largest paramilitary police force in the world.[11] About fifty thousand members of the Central Reserve Police Force are involved in combating the insurgency.[12] The Indian human rights group Forum for Fact-Finding Documentation and Advocacy estimates that some eighty thousand children are affected directly and indirectly in the armed conflict in Chhattisgarh State, a center of the insurgency. The great majority of child soldiers appear to be part of the rebel groups, although there are also children in government-supported self-defense militias.[13] A 2013 report by the Asian Center for Human Rights suggests fewer children—about three thousand—have been recruited by armed groups and that government militias have been recruiting child soldiers in "the hundreds." Age ranges for combatants are from about twelve to seventeen, and younger children have been employed as spies and couriers. Nevertheless, the Indian government continues to deny that there is any situation in India that amounts to armed conflict.[14] All this makes plain that a variety of political factors affect the reporting on armed conflict by the United Nations and may result in significant underreporting.

Using Law to End the Use of Child Soldiers

The vast majority of efforts to end the use of child soldiers have focused on developing international laws banning the recruitment and use of children in armed forces and groups. The broad goal is to create a comprehensive worldwide ban on the use of children in the military. Enforcement, however, is tricky. As we have seen, two types of international treaties address the issue of child soldiers: the first is the treaties that constitute the laws of war (International Humanitarian Law), and the second is treaties that deal specifically with children's rights. The laws of war comprise international rules governing acceptable conduct during wartime both by nations and individuals. In recent years, the recruitment of children under fifteen has come to be deemed a war crime, a grave violation of the laws of war, which are clearly proscriptive, as violators face criminal penalties for child recruitment. The key treaties in this category are the 1949 Geneva Conventions, the 1977 Protocols Additional to the Geneva Convention, and 1998 Rome Statute of the International Criminal Court. The most important of the children's rights treaties are the Convention on the Rights of the Child and the Optional Protocol to the Convention on the Rights of the Child on the Involvement of Children in Armed Conflict. These treaties differ significantly from the laws of war in that they are far more aspirational than proscriptive. Violations of children's rights do not carry criminal penalties, and indeed there are very few formal mechanisms of enforcement. Instead, the treaties are designed to create new normative standards. At times the creators of these treaties are accused of trying to be "norm entrepreneurs," that is, creating new "norms" that do not in fact reflect the real practice of peoples. These accusations notwithstanding, it has generally been the goal of children's rights treaties to raise the legal age of recruitment of children from the age established in the laws of war (age fifteen) to a higher standard of age eighteen.

But treaties are tricky. As a general rule, treaties are binding only on nations that are "state parties" to the treaty, that is, the nations that have signed and ratified the treaty. The result can be a bit of a hodgepodge in which the rules of one or more treaties are binding on some nation-states but not on others. Treaty advocates, of course, hope that over time most nations will ultimately sign and ratify a treaty, thus making it fully international. So it is important to remember that not every nation is legally bound to each and every treaty. The United States, for example, is party to the Geneva Conventions of 1949, but not the 1977 Additional Protocols I and II of the Geneva Conventions, which have special provisions dealing with child soldiers. The United States is also not a party to the 1998 Rome Statue of the International Criminal Court, which provides for a universal ban on the recruitment of child soldiers under age fifteen. The U.S. government is, however, a party to the 2000 Optional Protocol to the Convention on the Rights of the Child on the Involvement of Children in Armed Conflict, but it is not yet a state party to the original 1989 Convention on the Rights of the Child. As a result, international law remains unevenly applied across the globe.

This picture is further complicated by the possibility that some provisions of a treaty may also be regarded as international customary law. This means that the provision may be regarded as universally binding even for nonparties. The Special Court for Sierra Leone, for example, has ruled that the recruitment of child soldiers under age fifteen is a war crime under international customary law. If this ruling becomes commonly accepted, then the prohibition on the recruitment of children under fifteen would be deemed a universal rule of law applicable to all.

FIRST STEPS: THE GENEVA CONVENTIONS. The story of legal attempts to ban the use of child soldiers begins with the 1949 Geneva Conventions, a set of four treaties developed over a period of many years and finalized and reaffirmed in 1949 in the wake of the catastrophe of World War II. The conventions form the cornerstone of the laws of war. The Geneva Conventions are almost entirely concerned with the problem of international aggression between the armed forces of sovereign states, the same issue that helped bring about the establishment of the United Nations. Accordingly, they do not apply to the vast majority of conflicts in the contemporary world, which are armed conflicts within sovereign states. The major exception to this is so-called Common Article 3, a section found in each of the conventions and that is applicable to non-international conflicts. The 1949 Geneva Conventions make no reference to child soldiers. They do not define childhood nor lay down a minimum age for child recruitment, despite the large numbers of child combatants in World War II.

Some provisions in Geneva Conventions indirectly provide protections for children who served as combatants. As did the Hague Convention before (discussed in chapter 3), the Geneva Conventions draw a sharp distinction between soldiers and civilians. Making these categories separate and distinct is a central tenet of modern laws of war and is intended to help ensure that civilians are protected during wartime. Accordingly, the conventions do not permit soldiers to disguise themselves as civilians or enable civilians to take up arms and then fade back into the general population. The premise of the conventions is that if regular soldiers could not distinguish among enemy soldiers, enemy soldiers disguised as civilians, or civilians who took up arms at night while appearing to be civilians during the day, then all civilians would be put at risk. As with the earlier Hague Convention, the Geneva Conventions continue the distinction between what today are referred to as "lawful" and "unlawful" combatants (although the conventions do not use these terms). The category of lawful combatants usually refers to the regular armed forces of a party to an international conflict, but may include other armed groups allied to a party to an international conflict, such as guerrilla and partisan units. To qualify as lawful combatants, fighters must openly identify themselves as soldiers and not disguise themselves as civilians. They must display fixed and distinctive insignia or signs that are recognizable at a distance. They must also carry arms openly, be under the command and control of an individual responsible for his or her subordinates, and fight according to the laws of war. Guerilla forces fighting in an international conflict may or may not be deemed lawful combatants, depending on whether they follow these rules. Lawful combatants have a privileged and protected status under the Geneva Conventions. As soldiers, they are "licensed to kill" other soldiers and may not be prosecuted for doing so.[15] If captured by the enemy, lawful combatants are entitled to the status of prisoners of war. As prisoners of war they are protected persons and not criminals.

Under the Geneva Conventions, anyone not deemed a lawful combatant is not entitled to take up arms at all. Whether they are guerrillas or members of a resistance groups, unless they are clearly identifiable as soldiers, carry out their activities openly, and follow the other rules of the Geneva Conventions, they are deemed to be civilians illegally engaged in hostilities and are labeled as unlawful combatants. Unlawful combatants have only minimal protection under the Geneva Conventions. They can be attacked, and if they are captured, they have none of the privileges of prisoners of war. Their only legal protections are found in Common Article 3 of the Geneva Conventions, which outlines minimal standards of conduct toward such individuals, who are referred to throughout the Geneva Conventions as "persons" rather than prisoners. Although the Geneva Conventions contain some protections against humiliating and degrading treatment for captured unlawful combatants, unlike prisoners of war such persons are unprotected and can be treated as criminals and executed. The only requirement is that they cannot be tried by some kind of irregular or kangaroo court. The conventions require that they be tried by a regularly constituted court, affording all the judicial guarantees that are recognized as indispensable by civilized peoples. Military forces that fail to adhere to these important provisions are themselves committing war crimes.

Like the Hague Treaty before it, the Geneva Conventions do not prohibit recruiting children into armed forces or groups. Accordingly, children who served as lawful combatants in international conflicts are, like adult combatants, entitled to prisoner of war status. However, the Fourth Geneva Convention also prohibits imposing the death penalty on persons under age eighteen for offenses against an occupying power, a provision that could protect unlawful child combatants in international conflicts. Had the Geneva Conventions been in effect during World War II, the widespread German executions of children such as Masha Bruskina and even the more limited American executions of youngsters like Heinz Petry and Josef Schorner would probably have been deemed war crimes.

Beyond these protections, the provisions of the Geneva Conventions do not generally apply to internal conflicts within a state. As discussed earlier, these conflicts are treated, at least from each sovereign state's point of view, as criminal acts of treason, as rebellion, or, more common nowadays, as terrorism. Since rebellions and insurgencies are deemed criminal under the domestic criminal laws of their states, international law has relatively little application. The Geneva Conventions offer virtually no protection to children who served as combatants in non-international conflicts. The conventions provide no prisoner of war status for belligerents, militants, rebels, or anyone else engaged in internal conflicts. All, including child combatants, are treated as the equivalent of unlawful combatants. They are entitled to the minimal protections of Common Article 3, but beyond this, they may be treated as criminals. Nothing in the conventions prevents imposing the death penalty upon such combatants, even if they are children. Children serving in virtually all the armed groups recruiting child soldiers today fall into this category.

EXTENDING PROTECTIONS TO CHILD COMBATANTS: THE 1977 ADDITIONAL PROTOCOLS. In 1977, two amendments were added to the Geneva Conventions. These amendments, known as Additional Protocol I and

Additional Protocol II, were the first systematic attempt to directly address the issue of child combatants. Additional Protocol I addresses the issue of child combatants in international armed conflict, while Additional Protocol II addresses the issue of child combatants in non-international conflicts such as civil wars, rebellions, and insurgencies. The protocols created two categories of children: younger children (below age fifteen) and older children (between ages fifteen and eighteen). The protection afforded to children by the protocols is linked to the type of conflict and the particular age category involved.

Additional Protocol I imposes only minimal requirements on sovereign states. The treaty language is not very strong and does not actually prohibit child recruitment. Instead, it discourages recruitment of younger children into national armed forced by requiring state parties to take all "feasible measures" so that children who have not attained the age of fifteen years do not take a "direct part in hostilities."[16] It also requires that they "refrain from recruiting them into their armed forces." With respect to the older children, its only requirement is that if and when states recruit older children, they should "endeavor to give priority to those who are the oldest."

The term "direct participation in hostilities" generally means active combat, such as firing at an enemy or blowing up a bridge, but does not include other important military activities, such as intelligence gathering or transportation of supplies. The term "feasible measures" subordinates the protection of children to the goal of ensuring the success of military operations. The International Committee of the Red Cross interprets Additional Protocol I as not permitting the voluntary enrollment of children under fifteen years old.[17] But the final treaty actually says nothing about the issue of voluntary enrollment.[18] The resulting treaty illustrates how hesitant states were to adopt unambiguous and binding language. The vagueness of the treaty allowed each state to decide for itself the meanings of "all feasible measures" or "direct part in hostilities."

In contrast, Additional Protocol II, which governs the use of child soldiers in internal non-international conflicts, contains much more restrictive bans on child recruitment. Not surprisingly, nation-states found it far easier to take a hard line against insurgents and rebel groups that threaten state sovereignty than unreservedly to adopt these rules for themselves.

Just as important, no representatives of armed groups were at the negotiating table to protest. Indeed, as sovereign states sign and ratify treaties, one party is always absent—the rebel groups and/or insurgents said to be bound by treaty provisions imposed them without their involvement. While it is easy for nation-states to impose rules upon insurgent groups, the enforceability of these rules is another story. Nevertheless, whatever its practical limitations, Additional Protocol II (non-international conflicts) applies to civil wars between the armed forces of a state and dissident armed forces or other organized armed groups. Its restrictions against child recruitment are clear. It states that "children who have not attained the age of fifteen years shall neither be recruited in the armed forces or groups nor allowed to take part in hostilities."[19] The treaty terms are strong and create a comprehensive ban on the recruitment by armed groups of anyone under age fifteen.[20] State parties eagerly adopted this stricter view of child recruitment by armed groups so as to criminalize an advantage that states believed such groups often had—the ability to recruit youngsters to their cause.[21]

Despite these inconsistencies in the goals of child protection, by 1977 there were legal rules in place, grounded in international criminal law, that curbed the recruitment of child soldiers. Many nations agreed to be bound by their provisions, and all agreed that these rules, with their potential for imposing criminal liability, should be applicable to insurgent forces. One key problem remained: the absence of a regular international legal system for putting offenders on trial and punishing those found guilty. In 1977, when the protocols were put in place, there had been no international war crimes trials since the Nuremberg Tribunals following World War II. Even after Nuremberg, the enforcement of international criminal law required the creation of ad hoc tribunals established in the wake of particular conflicts. These included the 1993 International Criminal Tribunal for the former Yugoslavia, the 1994 International Criminal Tribunal for Rwanda, and the 2002 Special Court for Sierra Leone. The use of ad hoc tribunals for dealing with war crimes came to an end with the establishment of the International Criminal Court in 2002.

SETTING EQUAL STANDARDS FOR STATES AND INSURGENTS: THE INTERNATIONAL CRIMINAL COURT. The creation of the International Criminal Court (ICC) in The Hague in 2002 was a key event for the issue of child soldiers. The court's jurisdiction is grounded in the 1998 Rome Statute of the International Criminal Court, which consolidates many of the traditional laws of war into a single international criminal statute. It makes the recruitment of children under fifteen years old a war crime and provides for both the trial and the imprisonment by the ICC in The Hague of persons charged and convicted of recruiting children. This treaty gives the newly created court jurisdiction over war crimes "when committed as part of a plan or policy or as part of a large-scale commission of such crimes."[22] The ICC is the only permanent international court where individuals charged with war crimes can be brought to trial. The Rome Statute defines the term "war crime" as including "grave breaches" of the Geneva Conventions as well as "other serious violations of the laws and customs" applicable to both international and non-international armed conflicts. The key provisions affecting child soldiers end the distinction between international and domestic conflicts and impose an absolute ban on the conscription, enlistment, or use of children under the age of fifteen by both the armed forces of nation-states and the armed groups of non-state actors.

Because the Rome Statue is a treaty, its ability to exercise its jurisdiction is strongest in conflict situations involving nations that have signed and ratified the treaty. It is possible, however, for the Security Council of the United Nations to refer cases to the court. In such instances the court may exercise its jurisdiction over nonparties. Many major powers, such as the United States, Russia, India, and China, are not parties to the treaty. Most of the countries of the Middle East are also not parties to the treaty. In theory, the ICC is designed to complement national criminal systems. It should exercise its jurisdiction only in circumstances where nation-states are unable or unwilling to use their domestic courts to try war crimes. The ICC has dealt with several situations involving the use of child soldiers, all of which were referred to the court by state parties of the ICC and involve rebels or insurgent leaders turned over to the ICC for prosecution.

CHILD SOLDIER RECRUITMENT CASES BEFORE THE ICC. The ICC has tried several cases involving persons charged with recruiting child soldiers and that stem from the conflicts in Uganda and in the Democratic Republic of the Congo (DRC). One of the most significant trials was that of Thomas Lubanga Dyilo, a rebel leader in the DRC and the first person ever arrested under a warrant from the ICC.[23] Lubanga was the leader of the Union of Congolese Patriots, whose military wing was the Patriotic Forces for the Liberation of Congo, an ethnic Hema militia formed during the Ituri conflict in the DRC (1999–2007). Lubanga's case was referred to the ICC by the government of the DRC. He was arrested by UN peacekeepers and transferred to The Hague for trial. He was tried solely for the war crime of "conscripting and enlisting children under the age of fifteen years and using them to participate actively in hostilities." In March 2012 he was found guilty and later sentenced to fourteen years in prison. Both his conviction and sentencing are useful for understanding the gravity of the offense under international law. For while other individuals have been charged with recruiting child soldiers, they have also been charged with numerous additional war crimes and, if convicted, may receive substantially longer prison sentences. Lubanga is only person whose sole offence was the recruitment of child soldiers.

Among those charged with recruiting child soldiers is Bosco Ntaganda, deputy chief of the General Staff and chief of staff of the Patriotic Forces for the Liberation of Congo and National Congress for the Defense of the People. On March 18, 2013, Ntaganda surrendered to U.S. embassy officials in Rwanda and is in the custody of the ICC awaiting trial beginning in June 2015. He has been charged with numerous war crimes and crimes against humanity, including murder, rape, sexual slavery, persecution based on ethnic grounds, and intentional attacks against civilians. The charges stem from attacks on Lendu and other non-Hema villages in 2002 and 2003. Ntaganda has had a complex military career. He was in the Rwandan Patriot Army and immediately prior to his arrest was leader of the March 23 Movement, an ethnic Tutsi militia. His indictment by the ICC for the war crime of recruiting child soldiers relates to the time he was with the FPLC as Lubanga's deputy and later as its leader.

Trials began on November 24, 2009, for Germain Katanga, former commander of the Front for Patriotic Resistance of Ituri, and Mathieu Ngudjolo Chui, former leader of the Nationalist and Integrationist Front. Both men were charged with war crimes and crimes against humanity including murder, sexual slavery, and the intentional killing of civilians, as well as the recruitment of child soldiers under age fifteen. Both men were leaders of the ethnic Lendu militia groups. The specific charges derive from a

2003 attack on the village of Bogoro in the DRC widely characterized as a reprisal attack against the ethnic Hema civilians. On December 18, 2012, a unanimous decision of the trial court at the ICC acquitted Chui of all charges. On March 7, 2014, Katanga was found guilty by the ICC of murder, attacking a civilian population, and destruction of property and pillaging. He was, however, acquitted of the crime of recruiting child soldiers. The court found that even though there were children within a militia group he commanded and those children were among the combatants who took part in the attack on Bogoro, there was insufficient evidence to support his conviction on these charges.[24]

In the Uganda situation, the ICC has issued arrest warrants for Joseph Kony, commander in chief of the Lord's Resistance Army (LRA); Vincent Otti, vice chairman and second in command of the LRA; Okot Odhiambo, deputy army commander of the LRA; and Dominic Ongwen, brigade commander of the Sinia Brigade of the LRA. All but Ongwen have been charged with recruiting child soldiers. Otti is now believed to be dead, and Ongwen was captured in early 2015 and transferred to The Hague for trial. Currently there is an international manhunt for Joseph Kony and Odhiambo.

The Special Court for Sierra Leone

Outside the framework of the ICC, there has been one other forum where persons have been placed on trial for recruiting of child soldiers: the Special Court for Sierra Leone, which dealt specifically with war crimes arising out of the Sierra Leone Civil War (1991–2001). At the end of the war, the UN Security Council passed Resolution 1315, which obligated the secretary-general of the United Nations to negotiate an agreement with the government of Sierra Leone to create an independent special court to prosecute individuals responsible for war crimes.

The Special Court began its work prior to the time that the Rome Treaty came into effect, and may well have been the last in the long history of ad hoc tribunals created to deal with war crimes arising from specific conflict situations. The court charged key leaders of the armed forces and groups that participated in the war with various war crimes and crimes against humanity. Separate trial chambers were established to try the principal leaders of the Revolutionary United Front (RUF), the main rebel force that initiated the civil war; the Armed Forces Revolutionary Council (AFRC), a military junta in league with the RUF; and the Civil Defense Forces (CDF), a militia that fought to restore the lawfully elected government of Sierra Leone.[25] The Special Court established an additional trial chamber to try former Liberian president Charles Taylor for his involvement in the war.[26] All of these individuals were charged under the Statute of the Special Court with "conscripting or enlisting children under the age of fifteen years into armed forces or groups or using them to participate actively in hostilities."[27] The language of the statute is identical to that used in the Rome Statute for non-international conflicts, making plain that the statute represents current international law governing personal criminal liability for recruiting child soldiers.[28]

As a result of the war crimes trials in Sierra Leone, the leaders of the RUF and the AFRC were convicted on the basis of evidence that they abducted children and forced them to become soldiers. Both the RUF and the AFRC factions were guilty of some of the most heinous war crimes in recent history. The abduction of children was just one part of a broader pattern of atrocities.[29] As the Trial Chamber in the AFRC cases stated, "the only method [of conscription] described in the evidence is abduction."[30] The Trial Chamber in the RUF cases made clear that abduction is easily encompassed by the statute since it is a form of forced conscription.[31]

The Trial Chambers in the RUF and AFRC courts never addressed the issue of voluntary enlistment. In contrast, the CDF cases involved a large number of children who voluntarily enlisted. In addition, the CDF forces, unlike the RUF and the AFRC, were not rebel forces but militias allied with the lawfully elected government of Sierra Leone. The particular CDF defendants were ultimately acquitted of all charges of recruiting child soldiers, even though they were convicted of other major war crimes. Despite these acquittals, the Special Court for Sierra Leone made clear that international criminal law contains a blanket prohibition against the recruitment of child soldiers in any context. It flatly rejected the view that a legal distinction exists between forceful conscription and voluntary enlistment. The court stated that "where a child under the age of fifteen years is allowed to voluntarily join an armed force or group, his or her consent is not a valid defense."[32] Thus, a recruiter who accepts volunteers incurs the same criminal liability as one who forcibly kidnaps his or her victims. The prohibition is absolute.

The Special Court made clear that the prohibition against the recruitment of child soldiers was absolute, regardless of the actual experience of
any child soldier. During the Civil War in Sierra Leone, the recruitment
of child soldiers was widespread. Three main armed forces and groups
were involved in the struggle. The key rebel force was the RUF; the primary government military forces were composed of the Sierra Leone Army
and the Civilian Defense Forces, a coalition of ethnic militias that fought
against the RUF. Following a military coup in Sierra Leone, the RUF joined
forces with the AFRC and its armed forces. The experiences of children in
these various situations were radically different from one another.

REVOLUTIONARY UNITED FRONT. The RUF has been the subject of considerable study and analysis. It was infamous for its abduction of children
and its widespread campaign of terror against the civilian population of
Sierra Leone. A major study of RUF recruitment practices was undertaken
by Myriam Denov, who examined seventy-six children (thirty-six boys and
forty girls), all of whom reported being abducted by the RUF.[33] The children were four to thirteen years old at the time they were taken into the
RUF, and they remained with the rebel forces for periods ranging from
a few months to eight years. Using the collected narratives of the children, Denov developed a model of forced recruitment into the RUF. She
describes an especially cruel threefold *rite de passage* by which children
(1) were separated from their former lives and incorporated and encultur-
ated into the RUF's culture of violence; (2) learned to adapt to, participate in, and sometimes resist the intensely brutal and cruel world of the
RUF fighters; and (3) finally left the RUF at war's end, transformed by their
experiences and only uneasily reintroduced to the daunting challenges of
postwar Sierra Leone.

Within this framework, children were abducted, separated, and isolated from their families and communities into RUF-controlled enclaves.
Children generally reported a period of training and ideological orientation similar to that found most armed forces and groups. This involved
weapons and physical training, including instruction in the care and use
of small arms and the careful management of ammunition. Children were
also schooled in battlefield tactics and killing techniques. There was also
a major ideological component, in which recruits were required to attend

meetings and listen to speeches and motivational lectures on the philosophy of the RUF and its social and political goals and sing war songs.

What set the RUF apart from other armed groups in Sierra Leone
was the degree to which it was infused by an extreme culture of violence,
designed to break down resistance, ensure obedience, and celebrate and
routinize cruelty and terror. The RUF, Denov states, was "indiscriminate
in its brutality."[34] It engaged in wholesale murder and terror throughout
Sierra Leone and visited daily cruelties upon its own recruits—men and
women, boys and girls. The abuse of child soldiers took place within the
larger context of abuse visited upon all members of the RUF by its chain
of command. There is little doubt that many of these child soldiers were
slaves and that, like all slaves, these children had, as David Brion Davis
observed, "no legitimate independent being except as an instrument of
their master's will."[35]

A major strength of Denov's study is that her focus is on the agency
of children, even under extreme circumstances over which they have little
control. Denov points to the strength of peer relationships among recruits
and the degree to which children and youth mentored one another, took
on key leadership positions within the RUF, actively recruited other children into the ranks of the RUF, and forged strong bonds of friendship. Her
data also point to the fluidity of roles that both boys and girls were able to
play in the RUF. Without minimizing the treatment and suffering of many
of these children and youth, it is clear that their identities and experiences
cannot be absolutely reduced to the simple categories of "victims" and
"sex slaves" that are so prominent in many accounts of child soldiers. In
some important ways both boys and girls resisted, sometimes violently, the
abusive behavior of others and were frequently able to challenge or evade
the culture of violence within the RUF in an attempt to preserve their personal identity and morality.

But demonstrating the existence of agency among the children of the
RUF does not negate a condition of slavery. Indeed, the agency of slaves
was widespread in the American chattel slave system, but strikingly, slave
agency did not necessarily challenge the system of slavery, but instead
often worked to ensure its continuity.[36] Whatever agency RUF child soldiers seemed to exercise within the culture of terror that enveloped them,
they were never able to convert this agency into explicit resistance. Many

of these children, especially girls, were slaves in any conceivable sense of the term. As Denov puts it, "among powerful patriarchal structures, girls became mere 'property' of males, with their bodies being used as resources to be exploited, and even as gifts and rewards."[37]

CIVILIAN DEFENSE FORCES. At the same time that children were being forcibly recruited into the RUF, children were also joining the Sierra Leone Civilian Defense Forces. The CDF was a loose amalgam of independent ethnic militias and self-defense groups that emerged to defend a largely unarmed and defenseless civilian population from the rapacious and violent rebels of the RUF and the predatory military forces of the Sierra Leone state. The best-known militias groups and their ethnic affiliations in Sierra Leone were the Kamajors (Mende), the Donsos (Kono), the Kapras (Temne), and the Tamboro (Koranko). These ethnic militias played a major role in defeating the RUF, but also had distinctly different local and national agendas that divided them from one another. The Mende-based Kamajors were the dominant militia group, and the CDF leadership was largely drawn from the Mende. Kamajor militias are often described as being rooted in a long-standing practice of traditional hunters who serve as guardians and protectors of villages and communities; in fact, however, they were modern forces that made use of the accoutrements of tradition. Unfortunely, the CDF, which began as a force committed to defending civilians, also came to target and victimize them. The young fighters of the CDF became marginalized bottom-feeders who resorted to depredation. The violence of all soldiers—children and adults—became a trade and an identity, and was one of the few ways that youth could actually participate in the economy.[38] But whatever their failings, the CDF forces were far less ruthless than the enemies against whom they fought.

At the end of the war, the Special Court for Sierra Leone was jointly created by the government of Sierra Leone and the United Nations. Its mandate was to try those who bore the greatest responsibility for serious violations of international humanitarian law and Sierra Leonean law during the civil war. Several of the key leaders of the RUF and the CDF stood in the dock before the Special Court for Sierra Leone, charged with (and later convicted of) orchestrating and executing numerous war crimes against civilians, including the recruitment of child soldiers.

In its examination of the conscription of child soldiers, the Special Court made it clear that the use of actual force was central to the conviction of the RUF and AFRC leaders. The evidence showed that they forcibly abducted children of a wide range of ages and that the abduction of children was only part of a broader pattern of atrocities.[39] As the Trial Chamber in the AFRC case stated, "the only method described in the evidence is abduction."[40] In the court's opinion in the RUF cases, abduction and conscription were virtually synonymous.[41] The RUF and AFRC leaders were also charged and convicted of enslavement and sexual slavery. The trial chamber made clear that the children abducted and conscripted by the RUF were also slaves, and that the crime against humanity of enslavement encompassed the forcible training for military purposes, including the forcible training of children.[42]

In contrast, before the Special Court for Sierra Leone, Kamajor violence was portrayed as a result of a self-defense force that had gone astray. The Kamajors were described as an erstwhile but authentic self-defense movement that had somehow lost its traditional moorings in village, community, and chiefdom life and, as a result, also had lost its moral compass.[43] But despite this unhappy turn of events for the CDF, it still remains clear that the recruitment of youth by the CDF was radically different from that of RUF. Both the RUF and CDF leaders were charged with war crimes and crimes against humanity, including the conscription or enlistment of child soldiers under age fifteen. But only the RUF leadership was charged and convicted of enslavement, sexual slavery, rape, and other forms of sexual violence. It was the RUF that stood out for its widespread and systematic murder, extermination, and terrorization of the civilian population and for its criminal treatment of child soldiers.

Children's Rights Treaties

Although international criminal law criminalizes the recruitment of children under fifteen years old, contemporary humanitarian and children's rights advocates actively seek to raise the age of recruitment to eighteen. Their efforts are grounded in the treaty provisions of the Convention on the Rights of the Child (CRC), which created the first international definition of the child as "any person below the age of eighteen years."[44] From this perspective, known as "Straight 18," a child soldier is defined as any person below eighteen years of age who is recruited or used by an armed force or armed group.

The CRC is one of a number of human rights treaties that seek to increase the restrictions found in the laws of war, although they do not mandate criminal penalties for violators. But the CRC illustrates the increasing power of nongovernmental organizations to shape the international legal definitions of childhood and, by extension, the definition of who is a child soldier.[45] Among the most important of these organizations are the International Committee of the Red Cross (ICRC), Amnesty International, Human Rights Watch, International Save the Children Alliance, Jesuit Refugee Service, the Quaker United Nations Office, Terres des Hommes, Defense for Children International, and World Vision International. With the exception of the ICRC, these organizations also constitute the Child Soldiers International (formerly the Coalition to Stop the Use of Child Soldiers), the principal advocacy organization on the child soldier issue. All these organizations have adopted the Straight 18 position and its call for a universal ban on military recruitment of persons below eighteen years of age.[46]

The CRC was not a complete victory for the human rights activists, because though it declared a universal definition of childhood, the treaty still allows nations to define a younger age of majority and to establish an earlier age for the attainment of the legal rights and duties of adulthood, even though this is a departure from the general rule. In fact, even when it comes to child soldiers, the CRC prohibits only recruiting soldiers who are under fifteen years old. Anti-child-soldier activists saw this as a major flaw in the treaty and successfully supplemented it with a treaty known as the 2000 Optional Protocol to the Convention on the Rights of the Child on the Involvement of Children in Armed Conflict.[47] This treaty served as a major opportunity to comprehensively apply the Straight 18 position to child soldiers. Accordingly, the Optional Protocol uses age eighteen as a target goal for banning or restricting recruitment by both armed forces and armed groups. Many nations, including the United States, have signed this treaty. However, even though both the CRC and the Optional Protocol set important international children's rights standards for curbing recruitment, there are few ways to enforce these standards. Both treaties depend on the voluntary compliance of the nations that sign them.

The Optional Protocol requires that states "shall take all feasible measures to ensure that members of their armed forces who have not attained the age of 18 years do not take a direct part in hostilities."[48] Much of the language of the Optional Protocol echoes Additional Protocol I but raises the age bar to eighteen. First and foremost, it bans the conscription by states of anyone under age eighteen.[49] In addition, it requires states to increase the minimum age of voluntary recruitment to be higher than the age fifteen that is set forth for the CRC. It also makes clear that persons who are under eighteen are entitled to special protection.[50] As is true of most children's rights treaties, enforcement is not easily achieved, although state parties are required to submit a binding declaration setting forth a minimum age for voluntary recruitment. Paralleling Additional Protocol II, the strongest restrictions in the Optional Protocol are used to squelch armed groups, banning both conscription and voluntary enlistment of those under eighteen.[51]

At around the time the Optional Protocol was created, the Straight 18 position gained strength by being included in two other treaties that applied to child soldiers. The 1999 African Charter on the Rights and Welfare of the Child unequivocally defined a child as "every human being below the age of 18 years."[52] Using age eighteen as the benchmark age for limiting recruitment, it also required that state parties "shall take all necessary measures to ensure that no child shall take a direct part in hostilities and refrain in particular, from recruiting any child."[53] Here the use of the phrase "necessary measures" requires states to take all steps needed to achieve a ban on child soldiers and not merely those that involved circumstances of armed conflict. However, the African Charter was silent on the issue of non-state actors.

In 1999, the International Labour Organization's Convention on the Worst Forms of Child Labor declared the forced or compulsory recruitment of child soldiers under age eighteen to be a "form of slavery" or a practice "similar to slavery." The convention equated the compulsory recruitment of child soldiers with a host of other evils associated with the abuse and exploitation of children, such as debt bondage, serfdom, forced labor, and child trafficking.[54] Like the African Charter, the ILO convention made no specific mention of non-state actors, although its language implies that states will have broad powers to criminalize all forms of forced recruitment by anyone, but it imposes no duty on non-state actors.

In enumerating children's rights under the CRC, it is common to speak of the convention as embodying four basic sets of children's rights: the rights of participation, protection, prevention, and provision.[55] In practice, however, the central focus of political and legal action has been protection and prevention, while participation and provisioning take a distant second place. Even more remote are such rights as freedom of conscience for children, which have been formally rejected by many state parties to the convention. This should not be surprising, because the children's rights movement differs from other such movements in a significant way. The primary forces behind the CRC are not disenfranchised groups that are seeking to gain full participatory rights in society, but rather enfranchised adults who seek to spread a protective mantle over the world's children.

Despite its complications and shortcomings, the CRC and related treaties are significant documents. The idea of children's rights has clearly come of age and is gaining momentum throughout the world. The children's rights movement seeks nothing less than the global restructuring of age categories along with the rights and duties of children and adults. Treaties signed by national leaders often tell us very little about how the peoples of the world actually experience and understand childhood. Many nations signed the CRC and other children's rights treaties because they wanted to be counted as part of the community of nations and not necessarily because the terms of the treaty actually reflect how people experience and understand childhood. From this perspective, treaties like the CRC are sometimes seen as aspirational statements of how world leaders imagine an ideal childhood. Some argue that the entire effort to redefine childhood according to the dictates of the Straight 18 position is a bureaucratic fiction with little applicability outside Western societies.[56] But for child soldiers, it has had important but mixed legal consequences.

The Criminal Liability of Child Soldiers

One of the most significant consequences of the CRC's definition of childhood is that its emphasis on child protection in international law has made it less likely that children will be held criminally liable for their actions.

Although child soldiers have committed many war crimes and other atrocities, no child soldier has ever been tried before an international tribunal. One child, however, was convicted by a so-called mixed or hybrid court. Debates over the specific age at which children incur criminal liability have a long legal history. In international law, however, the main focus has been to avoid this issue completely or, alternatively, simply to absolve children of criminal liability. The ICC in The Hague does not have jurisdiction over crimes committed by persons under age eighteen. This is because the drafters of the court's governing statute—the Rome Statute—did not want international criminal law to usurp national law with respect to offenses committed by children.[57] The drafters of the statute recognized that there is a high degree of national variation in assessing when children reach the age at which they are mature and should be criminally responsible for their actions.[58] The Rome Statute was respectful of domestic jurisdiction,[59] but more commonly international criminal law and domestic criminal law are quite at odds with one another.

The issue of the culpability of child soldiers has come up before so-called hybrid courts, established by the United Nations in the wake of specific conflicts, which are entitled to try defendants using a mixture of international and domestic law. Two of these courts have specifically addressed the culpability of child soldiers: the Special Court for Sierra Leone and the Special Panels for Serious Crimes in East Timor, established by the United Nations Transitional Administration in East Timor (UNTAET) when it served as the transitional authority between the end of the Indonesian occupation in 1999 and the independence of East Timor in 2002.

Child Soldiers before the Special Court for Sierra Leone

The civil war in Sierra Leone provided a highly visible instance of wartime atrocities. All warring parties used child soldiers extensively, and many of these children committed terrible war crimes. The UN resolution establishing the Special Court recommended that it try cases involving crimes against humanity, war crimes, and other serious violations of international humanitarian law, as well as crimes under relevant Sierra Leonean law.[60] As with virtually all international tribunals, the resolution recommended that the personal jurisdiction of the court be limited to "persons who bear the greatest responsibility for the commission of the crimes," and particularly those leaders who, in committing crimes under the court's jurisdiction, threatened the establishment and implementation of the peace process in Sierra Leone.[61] The statute also provided that children between ages fifteen and eighteen could be prosecuted for war crimes, but they would not be imprisoned even if they were convicted.[62]

The Special Court Statute was the first to deal with the criminal culpability of child soldiers, even though, in the end, no children were tried before the court. The secretary-general's response to the UN Security Council, a draft statute for the council's consideration, focused on whether child soldiers would be tried for war crimes under by the Special Court.[63] The draft statute, incorporated into the secretary-general's response, was the product of an enormous and highly emotional diplomatic and political controversy between Western diplomats and international nongovernmental organizations on the one hand, and African diplomats and civil society organizations on the other.[64] The essence of the controversy was that a broad array of child protectionist and human rights groups lobbied hard to prevent the court from exercising personal jurisdiction over any person under age eighteen, regardless of the severity and scope of the war crimes they committed.[65] These groups included Human Rights Watch, UNICEF, Save the Children, Cause Canada, and the Coalition to Stop the Use of Child Soldiers (now Child Soldiers International). All of these organizations were aware of the terrible crimes that had been committed by child soldiers during the Sierra Leone Civil War.[66] This goal of obtaining blanket immunity for war crimes committed by children under international law goes well beyond anything contained in the CRC, which did not exclude children from possible criminal sanctions.[67] In fact, both the CRC and Optional Protocol permit the recruitment of child soldiers under age eighteen,[68] but are silent as to whether child soldiers should be liable for prosecution. It can reasonably be argued that the goal of international criminal law is to bring to trial those persons most responsible for the crimes committed. As a practical matter this would ordinarily preclude children. But it hardly seems credible to argue that these treaties, which permitted the recruitment children under eighteen years of age into the military, also intended to provide a whole class of soldiers absolute prospective immunity from prosecution for war crimes they might commit.

In their zeal to protect children, the NGOs involved in influencing the crafting the Statute of the Special Court for Sierra Leone misrepresented the intention of the drafters of the Rome Statute when they eliminated criminal liability for anyone below age eighteen in the Statute for the Sierra Leone Special Court.[69] Rather than being respectful of local domestic law, the United Nations and international NGOs shared a distrust of Sierra Leone's domestic legal institutions, especially with respect to the disposition of offenses by children.[70] The NGO strategy was to prevent the prosecution of those under age eighteen. The strategy employed the new and radical notion that all persons under age eighteen must be treated solely as subjects of rehabilitation.[71] Neither the United Nations nor the NGOs had any faith in the domestic law of Sierra Leone, especially with respect to the punishment and imprisonment of offenders under age eighteen.[72] In essence, none of the international actors wanted Sierra Leone's domestic law to play a role in the issue of child soldiers.[73] A compromise solution, proposed by the United Nations, was to transfer responsibility for the prosecution of fifteen- to eighteen-year-olds to the Special Court, so that any prosecutions of children would be subject to international standards. Many Sierra Leoneans wanted some form of judicial accountability. Sierra Leone's UN ambassador Ibrahim Kamara rejected the idea that all child soldiers were traumatized victims and stated that he feared the possibility of mob violence in the absence of judicial accountability.[74] The secretary-general's report also noted the Sierra Leonean government's view that "the people of Sierra Leone would not look kindly upon a court that failed to bring to justice children who committed war crimes of that nature and spared them the process of judicial accountability."[75]

The draft statute represented a compromise. The secretary-general proposed that the question of personal jurisdiction over children be addressed by expanding the scope of personal jurisdiction from "those who bear the greatest responsibility for the commission of crimes" to "persons most responsible" for serious war crimes.[76] The latter would still include political and military leaders, but also persons further down the chain of authority, including persons ages fifteen to eighteen.[77] According to the draft statute, these children would be tried in a special juvenile chamber with guarantees of internationally recognized standards of juvenile justice and, if convicted, would not be subject to penal sanction.

The statute finally created by the Security Council retained the proposal that personal jurisdiction be extended to cover fifteen- to eighteen-year-olds, accepting in principle the concept of judicial accountability without penal sanctions. However, the statute rejected the secretary-general's recommendation that personal jurisdiction be changed to cover persons "most responsible." The statute, therefore, ensured that the Special Court would focus on the senior leadership of the warring armed forces and groups.[78] Moreover, the statute made no provision for a juvenile chamber, indicating that no one below age eighteen would be tried. In fact, that is exactly what happened. When David Crane, the first prosecutor in the Special Court, arrived in Sierra Leone, he announced that, as matter of prosecutorial discretion, he would not prosecute any person under eighteen years of age.[79] Crane's decision may well have resulted from the limited resources of the court, but in the end it guaranteed that no juvenile offenders would be subject to judicial accountability of any kind.

Special Panels for Serious Crimes in East Timor: The Trial of X

Aside from Sierra Leone, one other hybrid court, the Special Panels for Serious Crimes in East Timor, has had the authority to grapple with juvenile offenders.[80] The Special Panels arose out of the East Timorese crisis of 1999, when Indonesian-backed militias murdered large numbers of proindependence Timorese. The violence ceased when UN forces were deployed to East Timor to support the transition to independence. The United Nations established UNTAET, whose panels were authorized to try offenses committed by minors between the ages of twelve and eighteen. Under the court's rules of criminal procedure, minors between twelve and sixteen years of age were subject to prosecution for criminal offenses in accordance with UNTAET regulations on juvenile justice. However, they were subject to prosecution for only the most serious offenses, such as murder, rape, or violence resulting in serious injury.[81] Minors over sixteen years of age were subject to prosecution under adult rules of criminal procedure, but in accordance with the CRC, the court was required to safeguard the rights of minors, and to consider their status as juveniles in every decision made in a case.[82]

The only case involving a minor was that of X, a sixteen-year-old who was arrested in October 2001 and charged with having committed crimes against humanity of extermination and attempted extermination as part of a widespread and systematic attack against the civilian population of East Timor.[83] X was age fourteen at the time and a member of the local Sakunar militia; neither X's name nor gender are a matter of public record. On September 9, 1999, X participated in the killing of twenty-seven young men held prisoner by the militia. X admitted to personally killing three of the young men with a machete, but also claimed to have been forced to do so. X pled guilty to murder under Article 338 of the Indonesian penal code. Because of X's age, and the fact that X confessed and showed remorse for the killings as well, X was sentenced to only twelve months in prison. X was also given credit for the eleven months and twenty-one days he or she was held in detention and served no additional time following the trial. The United Nations reported that the United Nations Mission in Support of East Timor Human Rights Unit and Timor-Leste's Social Services were planning a reconciliation meeting between the juvenile and the families of the victims as part of the reintegration process following his release.[84] What is plain is that the norm of child protection prevailed, even though X's victims were defenseless young men, and that the crimes themselves, as the sentencing judges put it, were committed "with strange cold blood."

The Treatment of Child Soldiers in Domestic Courts

Child soldiers accused of war crimes have not fared as well in domestic (non-international courts) and have at times been aggressively prosecuted. In 2002, the government of Uganda brought treason charges against two boys, age fourteen and sixteen, who were members of the LRA.[85] In a letter to the Ugandan minister of justice on February 19, 2003, Human Rights Watch urged the government to immediately drop the treason charges and release the boys to a rehabilitation center.[86] Human Rights Watch also requested that the government issue a public statement that children would not be subject to treason charges.[87] The Ugandan government decided not to proceed in these cases.[88] However, the government did not establish a national policy. In 2009 the Ugandan government charged another child soldier with treason,[89] a child who, according to Human Rights Watch, was abducted at age nine by the rebel forces of the Allied Democratic Front, and who was arrested at age fifteen.[90] The DRC is reported to have executed a fourteen-year-old child soldier in 2000.[91] In another instance in the DRC, four children, ages fourteen to sixteen at the time of their arrest, were sentenced to death by the DRC's Court of Military Order.[92] Following a meeting with Human Rights Watch representatives on May 2, 2001, the lives of these children were spared.[93]

Compliance with the child protectionism of international law is a problem not just in developing countries. For the first time in many years, the wars in Iraq and Afghanistan brought American soldiers face to face with child soldiers. No doubt many child soldiers were killed in combat, but a large number were captured, which raised the issue of how captive children should be treated under U.S. law. In the United States, where prosecuting child offenders as adults is widespread in domestic criminal law, the treatment of captured child soldiers was frequently abusive and harsh. In 2008, the United States reported that since 2002 it had held approximately twenty-five hundred juvenile combatants who were below eighteen years of age at the time of their capture. About twenty-four hundred were held in Iraq, ninety in Afghanistan, and between fifteen and twenty-two at Guantanamo Bay in Cuba.[94] As of April 2008, about five hundred juveniles were still being held by the United States in Iraq, although an unknown number had been transferred to Iraqi custody with little or no follow-up on case dispositions. In this same period at least ten juveniles were being held at the Bagram Theater Internment Facility in Afghanistan. Of the Guantanamo detainees, three juveniles under age sixteen were transferred back to Afghanistan in January 2004, and three others were sent to their home countries between 2004 and 2006. Two of them, Mohamed Jawad and Omar Khadr, were held for trial under the Military Commissions Act of 2006.[95] As of December 31, 2009, the United States reported that it had fewer than five individuals under the age of eighteen in detention in Iraq and Afghanistan. As of January 2010, the government claimed that it had greatly reduced the number of juveniles held in detention and that it had released or turned over virtually all the juveniles it held in Iraq to the government of Iraq for prosecution.[96] On September 29, 2012, nearly ten years after his capture and detention, Khadr, the last remaining former child soldier held at Guantanamo, was repatriated to Canada to serve out the prison sentence meted out by a U.S. military commission.

Virtually all detainees held by the United States, including the juveniles, were labeled "enemy combatants" by the George W. Bush administration.[97] What the Bush administration meant by this term was an unlawful combatant who would not be entitled to the protections legally afforded to prisoners of war under the Geneva Conventions. Indeed, the administration announced that such unlawful combatants would not have even the minimal protections of Common Article 3, the only provision of the Geneva Conventions that was specifically created to provide humane standards for captured unlawful combatants. This was a complete subversion of the application of the laws of war that require captive prisoners to be treated as lawful combatants unless otherwise shown not to be entitled to prisoner of war status. Following Bush's decision, virtually all armed opposition to the U.S. invasion of Afghanistan was criminalized. Moreover, President Bush ordered that when these detainees were put on trial it would not be practical to "apply the principles of law and the rules of evidence generally recognized in the trial of criminal cases in the United States district courts."[98] Hundreds, if not thousands, of detainees were held with little or no distinction made as to whether they were lawful combatants, unlawful combatants, or even combatants at all. On February 2, 2002, the president issued another order declaring that Common Article 3 of the Geneva Conventions applied to neither al-Qaeda nor Taliban detainees. These detainees, the president asserted, were not legally entitled to humane treatment.[99] This presidential order led directly to the abuse of numerous detainees, including children. One of them, Yasser Talal al-Zahrani, hanged himself shortly after arriving at the prison camp.[100] But the most well known instances are those of two child soldiers who came before U.S. military commissions: Mohamed Jawed and Omar Khadr.

MOHAMED JAWAD: TORTURED FOR SPORT. Mohamed Jawad was detained as a child soldier and charged with attempted murder. He was charged with throwing a hand grenade at a passing American convoy on December 17, 2002. But it is only because he was categorized as an unlawful combatant that he could be criminally charged. Had Jawad been treated as an ordinary soldier—a lawful combatant—he would have been perfectly entitled to throw a hand grenade at a military convoy without criminal penalty. Of course, U.S. soldiers in the convoy would have been lawfully permitted to kill him as well.

There was a great deal of uncertainty about Jawad's age. No written records existed of his birth. His family claimed that he was twelve years old when he was detained. A bone scan taken about a year after his detention indicated that he was age eighteen at the time of the scan, and this would have made him approximately seventeen at the time of detention. But bone scan evidence is often inaccurate, so the best that can be said is that he was somewhere between twelve and seventeen when he was detained. Jawad was initially arrested by the Afghan police. He was taken for interrogation to an Afghan police station, where both armed Afghan police officers and government officials threatened him and his family with death if he did not confess to throwing the hand grenade. He allegedly confessed, and was then turned over to U.S. authorities. Shortly thereafter, he was interrogated at a U.S. military base, where he was said to have confirmed his confession. Jawad was then transferred to the Bagram Theater Internment Facility in Afghanistan and after that to Guantanamo Bay, where he was systematically abused.

The abusive treatment of Jawad took place during a well-documented period of widespread maltreatment of detainees by the U.S. military in Iraq and Afghanistan and at Guantanamo Bay. The abuse of detainees began early in the war against terror and stemmed from the presidential orders denying the right of detainees to humane treatment. Among the more extreme examples of abuse were the killings of two Afghan detainees, Mullah Habibullah and Dilawar of Yakubi, who were chained and suspended from the ceiling and beaten to death over a five-day period in December 2002.[101] Both the U.S. Army and the U.S. Senate Armed Services Committee confirmed that these two detainee deaths were homicides.[102]

In response to widespread public reports of detainee abuse, the Department of Defense opened an investigation of the allegations. In 2005, Vice Admiral Albert Church, the navy inspector general, issued a report that proved the existence of a pervasive system of detainee abuse by U.S. military personnel.[103] According to the Church Report, the abuses were carried out members of all armed services, including active-duty, reserve, and National Guard personnel. The great majority of abuses happened in Afghanistan and Iraq, with a smaller number at Guantanamo Bay. The Church Report focused on serious abuse, meaning forms of abuse that could potentially lead to death or grievous bodily harm. These included actions that resulted in fractured or dislocated bones, deep cuts, or serious damage to internal organs, as well as sexual assaults and threats of death or grievous bodily harm. The report disregarded lesser injuries such as such as black eyes and bloody noses.[104]

In 2008, the U.S. Department of Justice issued a report of its own investigation of FBI involvement in the interrogations of detainees in Afghanistan and Iraq and at Guantanamo Bay. At Guantanamo Bay, FBI agents either saw or became aware of a variety of abusive techniques used against detainees, including depriving detainees of food, water, and clothing; exposure to cold and heat; death threats; short shackling to the floor to induce pain and stress; choking; and strangling. One FBI agent personally witnessed a female interrogator bending back the thumb of a detainee and grabbing his genitals while the detainee grimaced in pain.[105] The FBI also reported on a so-called pep rally where FBI agents observed Guantanamo Bay interrogators being told to get as close to the legal limits of torture as possible.[106]

This pattern of abuse was applied to juveniles like Jawad, who were routinely subjected to inhumane and degrading treatment. Upon transfer to American custody, he was forced to remove his clothing, was strip-searched, and was later ordered to pose naked for photographs in front of witnesses. He was blindfolded and hooded and subjected to interrogation techniques designed to "shock" him into the extremely fearful state associated with his initial arrest. For example, while he was blindfolded, interrogators told him to grasp a water bottle that he believed was actually a bomb that could explode at any moment. Again he was told that if he ever wanted to see his family, he should cooperate and confess.

This pattern of abuse continued when he was transferred to Bagram.[107] Jawad actually arrived there only a few days after Mullah Habibullah and Dilawar of Yakubi had been beaten to death by U.S. interrogators. At Bagram, he was forced into so-called stress positions, and his interrogators forcibly hooded him, placed him in physical and linguistic isolation, pushed him down stairs, chained him to a wall for prolonged periods, and subjected him to death threats. Jawad was also subjected to sleep deprivation, becoming so disoriented that he could not tell night from day, and was psychologically pressured by the sounds of screams from other prisoners and rumors of them being beaten to death.

After Jawad was transferred to Guantanamo Bay, he was treated as an adult prisoner and housed with them, in violation of the U.S. treaty obligation under the Optional Protocols. He never received rehabilitation treatment, special education, or other rights due to him as a juvenile. Instead, military records show a pattern of forced interrogation during which Jawad repeatedly cried, asked for his mother, fainted, complained of dizziness and stomach pain, and was given an IV. In addition, he was subjected to psychological assessment by the Behavioral Science Consultation Team at Guantanamo Bay for the sole purpose of exploiting his vulnerabilities for further interrogation.

According to both the Church Report and the FBI, a key method of abuse at Guantanamo was a system of sleep deprivation program called the Frequent Flyer Program by interrogators and guards. This program, the FBI reported, was designed to disorient detainees and make them cooperative. The Detainee Incident Management System records at Guantanamo Bay revealed that Jawad was subject to this program and was shackled and moved 112 times from cell to cell over a period of two weeks—an average of eight moves a day. This abuse had no purpose. Lieutenant Colonel Darrel Vandeveld, former lead prosecutor in the military commission case against Jawad, described it as "gratuitous mistreatment." The abuse of Jawad was unrelated to any effort to collect intelligence from him. No interrogations were actually undertaken around the times he was being tortured. Indeed, there was no belief that he actually had any special intelligence. According to Major David Frakt, Jawad's defense counsel, the only reason for torturing Jawad was for sport. As a result Jawad tried to kill himself by repeatedly banging his head against his cell wall.[108] The entire episode was, as the journalist Anthony Lewis put it, official American sadism.[109]

On October 28, 2008, the government's case against Jawad received a major setback when Colonel Stephen Henley, the judge of the military commission set to try Jawad, ruled that the alleged confession that Jawad had made to the Afghan police at the time of his detention was obtained by torture. The Military Commission Rules of Evidence preclude the admission into evidence of statements obtained by torture. Accordingly, the oral or written statements made by Jawad were suppressed by the court.[110] A few weeks later, on November 19, 2008, Henley ruled that statements made later by Jawad to U.S. authorities were inadmissible as evidence as well, as they were also the result of the preceding death threats.[111]

Without Jawad's confession, the case against him began to collapse. The government would now have to produce actual witnesses to the events in question. But the prosecutor failed to locate any eyewitnesses who supposedly told U.S. investigators that they saw Jawad throw the grenade. Even Jawad's military prosecutor came to doubt whether Jawad had ever even confessed in the first place. There were also both media accounts and intelligence reports that other Afghans had been arrested for the crime and had confessed. The prosecutor became convinced that the statements attributed to Jawad in his original interrogation had simply been made up by one of the Afghan policemen.

Major Frakt petitioned the U.S. courts for a writ of habeas corpus, asking for an order that Jawad be released from custody. As stated in the petition to the court, Jawad was an Afghan citizen who had been taken into U.S. custody as a teenager in December 2002 on the basis of a false "confession" that officials had obtained from him through torture, and had been illegally removed from his homeland to the U.S. Naval Base at Guantanamo Bay to face an illegal military tribunal for a nonexistent "war crime." At the initial hearing, an exasperated Judge Ellen Segal Huvelle described the government case as "unbelievable." Referring to Jawad's continued detention without any evidence, she stated, "This guy has been there seven years, seven years. He might have been taken there at the age of maybe 12, 13, 14, 15 years old. I don't know what he is doing there . . . I don't understand your case." She demanded that the government produce any witness to testify that Jawad had thrown a grenade at anyone.[112] No witnesses were ever produced. No one was able to show that Jawad was ever a combatant for any military or terrorist group. On July 30, 2009, Judge Huvell ordered that Jawad be released from detention, that he be treated humanely, and that he be returned to Afghanistan.[113] Jawad's return and resettlement to Afghanistan was at best a difficult experience, and he may well have fled into the tribal areas of Pakistan.[114]

OMAR KHADR: A CHILD SOLDIER TRIED AT GUANTANAMO. The first child soldier put on trial by the United States since the end of World War II was Omar Khadr. Khadr was captured in Afghanistan at age fifteen and was criminally charged with the "intentional murder" of U.S. Army Sergeant Christopher Speer during the course of a firefight with U.S. troops. According to the charges, Khadr was trained by an al-Qaeda operative in the use of small arms and explosives, and he and other al-Qaeda members planted improvised explosive devices where U.S. troops were expected to travel. The charges stated that on July 27, 2002, U.S. troops surrounded Khadr and other al-Qaeda members in their compound and in the ensuing firefight, Khadr threw a grenade, killing Speer. In addition to Sergeant Speer, two Afghan Militia Force members accompanying U.S. forces were shot and killed in the firefight, and several other U.S. service members were wounded. Khadr was very badly wounded during the firefight, but was treated, hospitalized, and detained as an enemy combatant. Like Mohamed Jawad, Khadr was charged with a number of criminal offenses, including murder, because he was regarded as an unlawful combatant.

According to reports, Khadr's family and father, Ahmed Said Khadr, were deeply connected with al-Qaeda. An al-Qaeda news service also featured him in its "Book of 120 Martyrs in Afghanistan" and he was praised as a fighter for the poor. Ahmed Said Khadr emigrated from Egypt to Canada where he married a Palestinian woman. Omar Khadr was born in Canada and was a Canadian citizen. The elder Khadr returned with Omar to Pakistan, where he became an al-Qaeda commander and was killed by Pakistani troops in a 2003. The al-Qaeda website praises him for "tossing his little child [Omar] in the furnace of the battle."[115]

Because no eyewitness could identify Omar Khadr as the person that killed Sergeant Speer, the case against him depended heavily on his alleged confession. As in the Jawad case, a key element in Khadr's defense was that his confession was involuntary. It is clear that he was often handled harshly as a detainee, so the key question was whether his confession could be used as evidence against him despite this harsh treatment. Khadr made numerous allegations that he was tortured and subjected to cruel, inhumane, and degrading treatment throughout the course of his capture and ultimate detention at Guantanamo Bay. Among the most serious of his charges were that he was threatened with rape and sexual violence and that he was told that uncooperative detainees are sent to Afghanistan to be raped and that "they like small boys in Afghanistan." In a different interrogation, Khadr also alleged that he was told that someone identified as "Soldier Number 9" would be sent to interrogate and rape him or that he would be sent to Egypt, Syria, Jordan, or Israel to be raped.[116]

During his detention at Bagram, Khadr was alleged to have confessed to throwing the hand grenade that killed Sergeant Speer as well as to helping build and plant improvised explosive devices. The principal issue prior to trial was whether Khadr's admissions were obtained through torture or other forms of abuse. Some of Khadr's claims of having been tortured or abused were corroborated at his pretrial hearing in May 2010. Particularly important was the testimony of Interrogator No. 1, who was later identified as John Claus, the same interrogator who was involved in the beating death of Dilawar. Claus's interrogation of Khadr took place in the summer of 2002 after Khadr had been released from a military hospital. Claus admitted that he had interrogated the badly wounded Khadr, who was fifteen years old at the time, and that he had told Khadr a fictitious tale of an Afghan kid who was sent to an American prison where he was gang-raped and died. Claus testified, "We'd tell him about this Afghan who gets sent to an American prison and there's a bunch of big black guys and big Nazis." He said that he described the Afghan kid as "a poor little kid . . . away from home, kind of isolated." Claus went on to tell Khadr that he had sent the kid to an American prison because he was disappointed in his truthfulness and that when the American prisoners discovered that the Afghan kid was a Muslim, they raped him in their rage over the September 11, 2001, attacks.[117]

A former army combat medic testified that he found Khadr chained by the arms to the door of a five-square-foot cage at a U.S. lockup in Afghanistan, hooded and weeping. Khadr's wrists were chained just above eye level with just enough slack to allow his feet to touch the floor.[118] But despite substantial evidence of abuse, the military judge ruled that the incriminating statements made by Khadr during his detention were voluntary.[119] The judge did not reject the truthfulness of testimony of abuse and torture but only that Khadr's admissions of his involvement in the killing of Sergeant Speer's was not connected with that abuse. With this key ruling in place, which would have allowed his admission to be used in evidence, the government and the defense began to negotiate a plea bargain.

Both the U.S. government and Khadr had strong reasons for reaching a plea bargain. The United States was reluctant to be the first Western country in modern history to put a former child soldier on trial. Moreover, in its abuse and mistreatment treatment of both Khadr and Jawad, the United

States had already violated its treaty obligations under the Optional Protocol, which required that persons under the age of eighteen be given special protection. The United Nations had reminded the United States of its failure to live up to its treaty obligations. Radhika Coomaraswamy, the special representative of the secretary-general for children in armed conflict, told the Military Commission that the Khadr case was a "classic child soldier narrative" in which a child is recruited by the adults of unscrupulous groups to fight in battles that the child barely understands. She argued that although the actions of Khadr's father were central to the abuse and harm done to him, the United States, as a signatory to the Optional Protocol, was required to assist the reintegration of child soldiers with their families and communities. Coomaraswamy also pointed out that no child could be tried before the ICC and that the Special Court for Sierra Leone had also declined to try children under eighteen years old.[120]

The United States was also under some pressure from Canada. Khadr's family had lived in Canada, and Khadr was a Canadian citizen. Canada initially refused to intervene in the matter. As a consequence, he was interrogated while being denied access to Canadian consular officials, legal counsel, and his family. The Canadian Department of Foreign Affairs and International Trade officials reported that, like Jawad, Khadr had been subjected to the Frequent Flyer Program. Khadr also faced a possible sentence of death, but because of pressure from Canada his case was not designated a capital case. Finally, on April 23, 2009, the Canadian Supreme Court ruled that Khadr had being illegally detained at Guantanamo Bay, that he had been tortured and deprived of legal counsel, and that the government of Canada should seek his repatriation to Canada.[121]

On October 13, 2010, Khadr reached a plea bargain agreement with military prosecutors.[122] Khadr admitted to all the crimes he was charged with as an unlawful combatant and agreed that he had no legal basis to commit any warlike acts.[123] In his admission, he stipulated that he was fifteen years old when he was sent by his father to serve as a translator for known members of al-Qaeda, and that he had been trained in the use of rocket-propelled grenades and other weapons and explosives by a member of al-Qaeda. Khadr also stipulated that he shared al-Qaeda's goal of killing all Americans and Jews anywhere they can be found. Khadr further admitted numerous other acts, including planting improvised explosive devices, collecting information on U.S. forces, spying on U.S. troop movements, and finally engaging in the firefight and throwing the Russian hand grenade at American troops that killed Sergeant Speer.

In the end, Khadr agreed to a prison sentence of eight years with no credit given for his detention since 2002. According to his plea agreement, he was to spend the first of these years in U.S. custody, but that if requested by the Canadian government, the remaining seven years could be spent in Canada. Ironically, the procedural rules of the Military Commission required that the military jury determine his sentence without knowledge of the prior plea bargain. The jury had no knowledge that Khadr was entitled to the lesser of two sentences: the eight years agreed to in the plea bargain or the one to be handed down by the jury. On October 31, 2010, the military jury sentenced him to forty years in prison. The humanitarian and human rights community derided this harsh sentence of a child soldier as "stunningly punitive."[124] Khadr began serving the first year of his eight-year sentence at Guantanamo Bay in January 2010. Khadr was transferred to Canada in 2012 and since his transfer has repudiated all the admissions he made in the plea bargain, claiming that he pled guilty to killing Sergeant Speer only because he was left with the "hopeless choice" of remaining in indefinite detainment at Guantanamo.[125] As of 2015 he remains in prison in Canada, but may soon be released on bail.

These cases show the striking gap between international and domestic forums. The United States has a reputation as a supporter of human rights and a proponent of abolishing the use of child soldiers, but this broad idealism has been sorely tested in practice and is not reflected in the record of the hard facts of its foreign policy or in its treatment of child soldiers during the war on terror. When the United States has had to actually come to grips with the reality of child soldiers, it has readily set aside its ideals and treaty commitments.

The last century has seen the gradual elimination of child soldiers in the armed forces of the world. But it is important to remember that the entire modern humanitarian campaign against child soldiers turns on the idea that the recruitment of youngsters in war is not normative. Much of this is based upon the somewhat erroneous ideas that in the nineteenth century American and European armies fought by a set of rules that made hard and fast distinction between children and adults, soldiers and civilians, and war and crime. However, these rules, if they ever fully existed, tell us something only about interstate warfare at a particular period in human history and much less about how the vast majority of conflicts—mostly not between states—were carried out. In much of history, warfare was dominated by what is now termed irregular warfare— and this pattern has not changed. Most conflicts in the past never involved set-piece battles between the armed forces of nation-states, and that is still very much the situation today. In fact, "irregular" warfare may be growing as states "outsource" their aggression to a wide variety of military proxies, including terrorists and irregular armed groups. In many urban settings, armed gang enclaves operate as autonomous mini-states backed by sophisticated weapons, and the boundaries between militias, criminal gangs, child gang members, and child soldiers is increasingly blurry. If David Kilcullen is correct that the coming age of warfare will be the age of the urban guerrilla, the child soldier problem, so identified with rural insurgencies, may well become one of the urban landscapes.[126]

6

The Politics and Culture of Childhood Vulnerability

Despite the keenly felt and plaintively voiced concerns of humanitarian, human rights, and children's rights organizations, it is clear that there are substantially fewer child soldiers in the world today than in the past. The contemporary numbers are a mere fraction of the vast numbers of young-sters who served in the armies of yesteryear. Whatever is at the heart of the modern child soldier crisis, it is not a matter of numbers—it is, rather, a problem of both imagination and place. Child soldiers have moved out of the ranks of Western and European armed forces and groups and into the armed groups and forces of the poorest nations on earth. This shift, this change in place, is the setting for the modern cultural production of the image of child soldiers. Child soldiers now inhabit only one side of the great North-South socioeconomic and political divide; they are found almost exclusively in the part of the world that has three-quarters of the world's population and only one-fifth of the world's income—the Global South.[1] When a young Sierra Leo-nean soldier wrote in nail polish on the butt of his rifle "War is my food," he was broadcasting to the world the harsh context of economic inequality and exploitation that characterizes the modern world of the child soldier.

The Cultural Construction of Contemporary Child Soldiers

The cultural construction of the child soldier is grounded in the discourse of humanitarian, human rights, children's rights advocacy, and law. This discourse imagines and posits the existence of a universal child whose development, needs, and well-being are all indifferent to context. The most striking features of this image of the child are its mobility, transferability, and disconnectedness from history. Using this cultural model, children's rights advocates have little difficulty in codifying simple, universally applicable, bright-line distinctions between childhood and adulthood. In contrast, many fields involved in the study of children, such as anthropology and history, take as their central orientation the idea that there are a multiplicity of concepts of childhood and adulthood, each codified and defined by age, ethnicity, gender, history, location, and numerous other factors. Whereas the idea of the "rights of the child," a concept based upon a putative universal child, seems self-evident and obvious to modern-day children's rights advocates, it often seems facile, overly simplistic, and ethnocentric to anthropologists and historians. Concerns about childhood, cast in the language of a human rights and humanitarian imperative, pay little attention to the enormousness of the issues of social and cultural changes contained in the transnational restructuring of age categories. Like many other avowed human rights imperatives, the discourse surrounding the idea of chidren's right tends to ignore, demonize, or marginalize the historical experiences and moral and legal imperatives of other cultures.[2]

For rights advocates, aversion to the idea of the child soldier is a simple and logical extension of the concept of a universal child. Indeed, the very concept of the "child soldier" is intentionally constructed to conflate what in the West are two antithetical and irreconcilable terms. The first, "child," generally refers to a young person between infancy and youth and is almost inseparable from ideas about immaturity, simplicity, and the absence of full physical, mental, or emotional development. The second, "soldier," refers to adult men and women who are trained combatants. As a result, the concept of the child soldier fuses two very contradictory and powerful ideas, namely the "innocence" of childhood and the "evil" of warfare. Thus, from the outset, in the modern Western imagination the very idea of the child soldier seems both aberrant and abhorrent.[3] This language is now so deeply embedded in a Western discourse of deviancy that it is virtually impossible to treat it as an artificial codification, often divorced from the experiences of real children and clashing with local understandings about the involvement of young people in war.

The Abused and Vulnerable Child

Both humanitarian discourse and international law categorize child sol-diers primarily as victims of criminal adult abuse. From this perspective the essential character of this child soldier is composed of victimhood and vulnerability, and differences in the real experience of child sol-diers collapse under the essentialist rubric. Such an approach contrasts sharply with the modern understanding of children found throughout the humanities and social sciences, which positions children as active players and participants in society. Central to these contemporary stud-ies is the concept of agency, which builds upon children's interpretative capacity and their ability to act upon such interpretations.[4] "Agency" is more a general orientation toward the child than an operational concept, and broadly refers to children's capacity to make choices, express their own ideas, take direction in their lives, and play a part in bringing about changes in the wider society.[5] The idea of agency serves as a corrective to earlier paradigms of children and childhood wherein children were largely understood to be passive actors with little ability to direct their own lives. Humanitarian discourse and international law have little or no ability (or desire) to incorporate ideas of agency into their understand-ing of child soldiers. As a result, the child soldier who volunteers is con-flated with the child soldier who is kidnapped; the teenager is conflated with the vulnerable toddler.

The gap between empirical description and humanitarian advocacy is vast. Humanitarian advocates insist that the issue be primarily framed as a matter of childhood innocence distorted and subverted by adult culpabil-ity. Even legal scholars who have a clear understanding of these difficulties are often unable to abandon the model.[6] This approach has clearly led to convictions in international tribunals, and for the worst abusers of chil-dren such convictions are appropriate and just. But few ethnographers and other close observers of war zones would agree that the issue of child soldiers can be reduced to that of adults abusing and terrifying innocent children into committing violent acts.[7] Yet, the theme of the innocent child and the blameworthy adult serves as the operational shibboleth of the child soldier problem. Indeed, given the horrendous reality of war, mythologiz-ing the innocence of child combatants demands equal mythologizing of the blameworthiness of adults. As with all binary modes of thought, the vaunted innocence of the child rests upon the exaggerated culpability of the adult.[8]

Despite differences in outlook and policy among advocacy groups, nearly all humanitarian and human rights efforts on the child soldier issue are shaped by a common belief that all persons under age eighteen are particularly vulnerable and innocent and that modern warfare is especially horrible. Though barely rooted in fact, these core beliefs profoundly shape the international conversation about child soldiers. Advocates for banning child recruitment equate childhood with vulnerability, and recognizing this equation is central to understanding humanitarian views of the child soldier. Although it is self-evident that young children are both vulnerable and in need of nurturing, it is only by international definition that these attributes of infancy, toddlerhood, and early childhood have been extended to apply all persons under age eighteen. From the perspective of the essential vulnerability of the child, recruiting child soldiers at any age is seen as the action of abusive and corrupt adults who thereby bring harm to innocent children. It is a perspective primarily calculated to assign legal and moral culpability and blame, and it frames virtually all discussions of child soldiers.

Throughout the humanitarian literature, examples abound that routinely conflate the issue of child soldiers with the most horrific forms of child sexual abuse.[9] These include sexual trafficking and child prostitution, and other forms of criminal misconduct in which ruthless and unprincipled adults exploit immature, innocent, and susceptible children. Child soldiers are frequently depicted as being "used" or "manipulated," or as "cheap and disposable."[10] The latter term conceptually conflates them with the throwaway items of modern society such as disposable diapers, electronics, razors, plastic cups, or wristbands. The term "disposable" is commonly employed to describe other forms of exploited children such as child laborers, prostitutes, street children, human shields, and even children trapped in the criminal justice or child welfare systems.

Building on the premise that children are especially vulnerable, humanitarian child advocates focus on the forced and abusive exploitation of children who are recruited to become child soldiers. What has emerged is a generic composite that, though drawn from real instances, has been transformed into an archetype of the child soldier experience that has rapidly spread throughout the media and popular culture. Child soldier recruitment is typically described as forcing recruits to engage in specific acts of terror such as compelling them to kill family, friends, loved ones, and fellow villagers in gruesome ritual acts designed to permanently alienate the recruit from family, home, and community life. Following this the children are portrayed as suffering from the vilest forms of child abuse, including slave labor, sexual slavery, forced use of drugs, and forced murder including ritual killings.[11] The result of this abuse, it is frequently claimed, is the emergence of societies inundated with psychologically scarred children who contribute to long-term social instability.[12]

Child Slaves and Child Robots

Child soldiers are frequently depicted as slaves or as commodities or even robots. The International Labour Organization's 1999 Convention on the Worst Forms of Child Labor declared the forced or compulsory recruitment of child soldiers under age eighteen to be a "form of slavery" or a practice "similar to slavery." The convention equated the compulsory recruitment of child soldiers with a host of other evils associated with the abuse and exploitation of children such as debt bondage, serfdom, forced labor, and child trafficking.[13] At times, child soldiers are said to be "harvested" like crops or animals. Child soldiers are commonly described as the most expendable form of "cannon fodder."[14] Parents are sometimes treated as abetting child exploitation and recruitment. When a child soldier who had volunteered for the Mai-Mai Patriotic Resistance in the Congo reported that he was encouraged to fight by his parents, Joseph N. Giza, of the Congolese NGO Heal Africa, treated this as simply incredible. "Can you imagine," exclaimed Giza, "sending your children to a war you are busy running away from? The children were used as cannon fodder."[15] Child soldiers are sometimes said to be "programmed" and trained to function like robots. They are described as being "programmed to kill," "programmed to lie about their age," and "programmed to feel little revulsion for their actions and to think of war and only war."[16] They are said to be "programmed to develop a mindset that resists any acknowledgment of injury and sickness, be it physical or psychological."[17] Some child soldiers are described as living in a trance-like state while reciting programmed messages.[18] The idea of the child soldier as a programmed cyborg is so deeply embedded in public consciousness that the Australian ethicist Robert Sparrow defines child soldiers as "autonomous robots," which he imagines as the next generation of smart weapons.[19]

There has been some pushback against this kind of unrelieved packaging of child soldiers as helpless victims who can be easily morphed into mechanized monsters. Clearly this mode of describing child soldiers completely dehumanizes child soldiers and turns them into mere instruments of criminality. No doubt, there are situations in which children are brutally exploited, such as the Palestinian child suicide bombers of Hamas and Palestinian Islamic Jihad, the kidnapped recruits of the Revolutionary United Front in Sierra Leone, or the cult-like Lord's Resistance Army, which at one time was an important factor in the violence in Uganda. But even in this latter situation, which stands out as one of the worst-case situations of forced child recruitment, data from the Survey of War Affected Youth provide a far more complicated portrait than is typically found in hyperbolic reporting in the media.[20]

In situations where adults and children are struggling to meet basic needs, reintegration efforts that focus on psychological needs and healing the enduring traumas of child soldiers may not be very productive. Counseling youngsters in general should be less about healing psychological wounds or mental illness than helping young people socially practically integrate into civil life.[21] All forms of counseling and help need to be focused on support of the key goal, namely to enable former child soldiers to make decent lives for themselves in a context characterized by chronic and often extreme poverty. It is increasingly clear that there is little to be gained from seeing child soldiers as "damaged goods," a notion that blinds us to children's ability to take charge of their own lives. Unfortunately, though humanitarian groups often make pro forma declarations in support of children's agency and empowerment, they fall short in respecting children's ability to participate in decision making.

Modern Warfare and the New Barbarism

As I have shown, the claim that the presence of child soldiers on the battle-field is a modern novelty is simply not borne out by any reasonable and nonideological assessment of the existing historical data. But for those who, a priori, convinced themselves that they were seeing something especially new and cruel, an equally new explanation for the phenomenon was required. One of the principal tenets of contemporary views of child soldiers is that child soldiers exist because modern or "new" wars differ significantly from "old wars," namely traditional nineteenth-century European warfare. This dualism has been theorized in a variety of ways. One version draws its inspiration from Robert Kaplan's notion that many modern wars, especially in Africa, are rooted in atavistic local hatreds that are essentially inchoate, irrational, and unknowable. This approach reaches deep into nineteenth tropes about war in Africa. While superficially moribund, these tropes continue to deeply resonate within so-called civil society, which is implacably hostile to so-called harmful cultural practices, which, upon inspection, frequently turn out to be cultural perspectives inconsistent with Western norms.

Kaplan's approach, criticized as the "New Barbarism" by Paul Richards, is a concept that caricatures "Bad Africans" and harkens back to nineteenth-century notions of the savage horde that remain widespread in the Western imagination.[22] In its specific construction of warfare, the underlying premise of the Kaplan model is that the eighteenth- and nineteenth-century European wars, so-called traditional wars or "old wars," were rule-bound and limited, while "new wars" are anomic and chaotic.[23] Kaplan's understanding of old wars is built upon the views of the nineteenth-century German soldier and military theorist Carl von Clausewitz, who regarded war as an extension of politics by other means.[24] But new wars, in the light of the New Barbarism thesis, are not treated as such. Indeed they are widely understood as apolitical. At worst, they are mindless, and at best they are an extension of criminality by other means. Mary Kaldor, perhaps the leading theorist on new wars, asserts that old wars were state-building endeavors, while new wars serve to destroy or undermine state creation.[25] Paul Colliers and Anke Hoeffler argue that new wars are essentially built around rebel greed and that there is really nothing to distinguish rebels from bandits and pirates.[26] The use of child soldiers is essentially deemed a novel characteristic of the anomie and normlessness of these wars.

But this theoretical dualism simply ignores the presence of child soldiers in old wars. Clausewitz himself was a child soldier, having been born in 1780 and serving in battle at age twelve or thirteen during the early years of the Rhine Campaign (1792–1793), a war between a coalition of European monarchies and France. There is very little empirical evidence to substantiate the notion of a once-upon-a-time golden age of progressive warfare. Such claims seem no more credible than the fairy tale idea that war was once governed by a code of knightly chivalry.[27] The reality is that the manner in which wars were fought often depended on the nature of the adversary. Though America and Europe may have adopted more restrained forms of warfare for their European or American enemies, they behaved with unrestrained brutality toward the colonized and the conquered.[28] The American war of acquisition on the Great Plains ended with the massacre of the Lakota at Wounded Knee. Similar patterns of wide-scale atrocities of near genocidal proportion were carried out by the U.S. military against men, women, and children in the Philippines during the nineteenth century and justified by the assertion that they were uncivilized and could be treated without regard to their humanity.[29] The murderous British reaction to the Mau Mau Rebellion in Kenya stands as ample testimony to the barbarity of so-called civilized societies.[30] These and numerous other examples give lie to the notion that modern-day irregular warfare is qualitatively more heinous than in the past or that modern-day rebels hold a particularly monstrous place in the morality of warfare.

The Diversity of the Child Soldier Experience

None of this bloody history should serve to whitewash the horrors of modern warfare. All wars are dirty, and civilian deaths and terrorist episodes exist in every conflict. Some wars involve terrorism on a vast scale, and some involve the worst abuses of child soldiers. But even here it is crucial not to ignore the very different experiences of child soldiers. In the previous chapter I discussed the striking differences in the experiences of child soldiers in Sierra Leone. Moreover, the situation in Sierra Leone stands in stark contrast to the experience of children in revolutionary movements in Mozambique or in Eritrea, in which the wars were fought through revolutionary groups that systematically mobilized the rural population in support of the war. Child soldiers were present in all of these struggles, but their experiences were quite different.

Women who as children served in FRELIMO's Destacemento Feminino or "Female Detachment" saw their participation in combat as empowering and liberating, and they continued to see it this way as adult women. Many interpreted their war experiences as liberating them from both colonial rule and the male structures of dominance in "traditional" Mozambique society. These women viewed their involvement as children in combat and other revolutionary acts as the key experiences that led to full citizen participation in the political life of Mozambique.[31] Their narratives are reminiscent of the celebratory portraits of boy soldiers in nineteenth-century America. Schoolgirls and peasant women who joined the Eritrean People's Liberation Front were specifically recruited for combat roles and temporarily enjoyed a kind of rough equality with male combatants. Unhappily, after independence they failed to achieve full citizenship and were pushed back into extremely conservative gender roles. Nevertheless, their experience under arms endowed them with both "critical perspectives" toward Eritrean society and the skills to engage in collective action.[32] The data on female ex-combatants from the Tigray People's Liberation in Ethiopia show that the girls and young women who served as soldiers became more self-confident, independent, and politically aware than those who did not serve. All the subjects studied had been recruited at ages ranging from five to seventeen, with an average age of recruitment of 12.68 years.[33] None of the individuals from any of these conflicts regarded themselves as having been powerless or having been victimized.[34] Ironically, every single activity these girls participated in, from cooking to transporting war materials and supplies to learning to use weapons and attacking civilian settlements, would nowadays be reframed as criminal abuse.

Conrad Redux: The Africanization of the Child Soldier

Child soldiers are recruited across the globe, but much of the contemporary gaze remains firmly fixed on conflicts in Africa. The focus on Africa is so ubiquitous that virtually the entire child soldier issue has been Africanized. It is unclear exactly why this is the case. Certainly, some contemporary armed groups in Africa such as the Revolutionary United Front in Sierra Leone and the LRA in Uganda provide chilling examples of the abuse of children. But these extraordinary cases have come to serve as the universal archetype of children's experiences as soldiers. There are strong links between the central concepts of the New Barbarism—that Africa and other places where child soldiers fight are inherently chaotic and apolitical—and nineteenth-century descriptions of Africa. Many of the reports of violence and the recruitment of child soldiers found in the advocacy literature echo Joseph Conrad's *Heart of Darkness*.[35] Conrad took Africans out of real history and politics and suspended them between the human and the animal. Like contemporary humanitarians, Conrad had an idealistic purpose in writing *Heart of Darkness*—to offer a critique of the colonial exploitation of Africa. Yet the African novelist Chinua Achebe decried Conrad's stripping of Africans of their humanity as well as his description of Africa as a "metaphysical battlefield devoid of all recognizable humanity." As Achebe tells us, "You cannot diminish a people's humanity and defend them" at one and the same time.[36] Contemporary treatments of child soldiers— almost all geared to Western audiences—have a lingering tendency to look at Africa and the other conflict zones where child soldiers are found with Conradian eyes, and see only a heart of darkness. Conrad was hardly alone. It is striking that Western discourse about war in Africa, whether precolonial, colonial, or postcolonial, has remained remarkably consistent since the middle of the nineteenth century. Central to this discourse is that warfare in Africa—in contrast to the West—is invariably cast as irrational and meaningless.[37]

The neo-Conradian vision of the New Barbarism completely removes war from the world of politics. It offers less of a theory than an orientation that relies upon ideas about ancient rivalries and other atavistic attitudes. The idea that war is merely a criminal conspiracy is the central pillar of contemporary war crimes trials. The origins of this theory rest in the Nuremberg trials of the horrific crimes of the German war machine in World War II, but it has slowly morphed into a general theory of warfare in Africa. In other accounts, war appears virtually out of nowhere, usually as a result of adult perfidy, to engulf children and to turn them into victims and killers. It is as if war was a malevolent natural phenomenon akin to a tornado that lands on a country and destroys it. The descriptions of wars that involve child soldiers impart a kind of random and feral meaninglessness to war that unmistakably echoes Conrad's representations of the near-riotous inhumanity of Africans. Why do we invoke the tropes of mindless barbarism only in contemporary warfare, in the poorest places on earth? No doubt, the portraits of children at war central to humanitarian and human rights narratives of child soldiers are designed to serve modern notions of the greater good—ending child participation in armed conflict. But despite attempts to lend the situation of child soldiers a universal "everyman" quality, humanitarian portraits of child soldiers draw on an earlier discourse about Africa that served to dehumanize Africans.

The Role of Humanitarian Groups and "Civil Society"

From the perspective of humanitarian and human rights groups who have helped shape international law, the ban on child soldiers is consistent with what they believe are (or should be) universal ideas about childhood. Others, however, argue that these are relatively recent ideas about childhood, developed in the West over the past century, which are being exported and imposed on other peoples of the world. If we understand that the attempt to ban the use of child soldiers is a form of directed social change, we are better able to analyze the difficulties of achieving compliance with the ban under international law. We can also begin to better understand the role of humanitarian and human rights groups in shaping both the perception of the problem and the proposed solutions.

Humanitarian and human rights groups are part of the many thousands of nongovernmental organizations (NGOs) that collectively define themselves as "civil society." In international matters, there exists a unique and important connection between the United Nations, its agencies and offices, and civil society. The United Nations is, in effect, the political hub of civil society, providing legitimacy and an international forum to NGOs and allowing them to influence the development of UN policy and participate in shaping UN-sponsored treaties and international legal instruments. The principal organizations of civil society have routine access to the preparatory and working groups that develop and follow international conferences. In many respects they function as the international equivalent of lobbyists in the U.S. Congress. It is in this capacity that civil society plays a significant role in shaping the awareness and attitudes toward the issue of child soldiers. Public awareness of child soldiers comes primarily from newspapers accounts, novels, films, and the reports of humanitarian and human rights organizations that report and advocate on the issue. Child Soldiers International is the predominant organization in the humanitarian and human rights efforts to end the recruitment of child soldiers. Its member organizations have invested considerable energy, passion, and resources to shape public awareness of the issue and to bring about changes in international law and policy to help curb the recruitment of children into armed forces and armed groups.

The principal organizations of civil society are deeply integrated in the work of the General Assembly and the administrative agencies of the United Nations. They consider themselves to be partners in the UN system and are regarded as such in the United Nations, despite the fact that they have no mandate from any political community. There has also been a shift, in the past couple of decades, in both the power these groups wield and the kinds of political activities in which they engage. Most of these groups do not take any contributions from governments, but because of their growing power in the international arena, humanitarian groups and other members of civil society often function as political actors, pursuing specific political agendas. The organizations of civil society position themselves as caretakers and upholders of the moral values of transnationalism, but are frequently accused of being partisan in particular conflicts. This is a significant departure from the more traditional model of humanitarian groups, in which they were perceived to be neutral and politically impartial.[38] In addition, these humanitarian organizations use political "spin" to interpret events and sway public opinion and sympathy, including techniques such as extensively cherry-picking facts, assuming the truth of things that have yet to be proven, and shaping the interpretations of international law to meet advocacy goals. Without doubt, these organizations play valuable roles in combating the use of child soldiers, but it is crucial for researchers to recognize that these groups are first and foremost advocacy groups, not necessarily objective reporters of facts, law, or policy.

It is also important to remember that many advocacy groups are not underfunded organizations that are seeking to get their voices heard. Many of them wield considerable economic power and influence. In 2013, Human Rights Watch had annual budget of over 65 million dollars and net assets of more than 228 million.[39] Amnesty International US alone spent 47 million dollars on its programs, administrative expenses, and fund-raising.[40] Amnesty International in the United Kingdom had expenditures of 55 million pounds in 2012.[41] Many poor countries are extraordinarily dependent on foreign aid, and advocacy groups often influence the direction and flow of aid. As a purely practical matter, some countries may need to agree with the views of advocacy groups into order to receive continued aid. All these factors shape the way such countries and the public at large view and respond to the child soldier problem.

Our Western understanding of child soldiers, and even of war itself, has been affected by more than a half century of peace (mostly) in the West. We have, understandably and luckily, lost our visceral understanding of war. Our modern-day experience of war is mediated by cultural and geographical distance, professional volunteer armies, civil society, and human rights organizations—all of which, in a variety of ways, serve to ascribe war to a distant and alien "other." Across the political spectrum leaders often work to compartmentalize our experiences of war, as for example the nearly two-decade ban in the United States—beginning in 1991—on media coverage of the return of coffins of U.S. soldiers killed in war. While particular conflicts, such as the recent battles between Israel and Hamas, garner microscopic attention, there is little sustained public attention or reflection on the long-distance war carried out by U.S., British, and other NATO forces during the "humanitarian" intervention in Kosovo, which resulted in the bombings of hospitals, schools, busses, libraries, neighborhoods, the Chinese Embassy, and even a passenger train. In Kosovo, NATO and U.S. forces used both cluster munitions and depleted uranium bombs to kill more than two thousand civilians, including eighty-eight children. Even more horrific were the thousands of civilians—men, women, and children—killed by Great Britain, the United States, and their allies in Iraq. Obviously, there is nothing new about warfare or hypocrisy, but in recent years all these processes of distancing, demonizing, sanitizing, and "othering" have transformed us into distant observers, ultimate noncombatants, with little firsthand knowledge of the kind of warfare that often thrusts children into combat in their homelands. From the safety of the West, we may have reached a point where we can barely comprehend the agility and resourcefulness of the children Anna Freud encountered during the years of the Nazi air blitz in London.[42] So instead of real children at war, we now have an invented discourse about imagined children who have become the focus of Western and international sympathy, charity, intervention, and pity. If anthropologists, historians, and others have anything to contribute to the study of children at war, it may well be to bring a sense of humility to our analysis and to use our abilities make sense of the complexity of the lives of both children and adults caught up in the drama and tragedy of armed conflict.[43]

NOTES

CHAPTER 1   A TALE OF TWO ORPHANS

1. Jill Lepore, "Bound for Glory: Writing Campaign Lives," *New Yorker*, October 20, 2008, accessed September 2, 2014, http://www.newyorker.com/magazine/2008/10/20/bound-for-glory.

2. Jon Meacham, *American Lion: Andrew Jackson in the White House* (New York: Random House, 2009), 11.

3. James Parton, *The Life of Andrew Jackson*, vol. 1 (New York: Mason Brothers, 1860), 70. James Parton, one of Jackson's nineteenth-century biographers, describes the setting of the conflict, drawing his descriptions from written records and oral histories of friends of Jackson and from oral histories of the incidents in which he was involved.

4. Ibid., 75.

5. Letter from Robert Brownfield to William Dobein James, quoted in William Dobein James, *A Sketch of Brigadier General Francis Marion and a History of His Brigade* (Charleston: Gould and Milet, 1821), 78–80.

6. Parton, *Life of Andrew Jackson*, 70.

7. Ben Rubin, "The Rhetoric of Revenge: Atrocity and Identity in the Revolutionary Carolinas," *Journal of Backcountry Studies* 5, no. 2 (2010): 1–46.

8. Ibid., 2.

9. "Memoir of Major Thomas Young: A Revolutionary Patriot of South Carolina," *The Orion: A Monthly Magazine of Literature and Art* 3, nos. 2–3 (1843): 84–88 and 100–105, also available at http://sc_tories.tripod.com/thomas_young.htm.

10. Parton, *Life of Andrew Jackson*, 70.

11. Amos Kendall, *The Life of Andrew Jackson* (New York: Harper & Brothers, 1843), 44.

12. Ibid., 85.

13. Augustus C. Buell, *A History of Andrew Jackson*, vol. 1 (New York: Charles Scribner's Son, 1904), 49.

14. Kendall, *Life of Andrew Jackson*, 44.

15. Parton, *Life of Andrew Jackson*, 78.

16. Ibid., 75–76.

17. Buell, *History of Andrew Jackson*, 52

18. Parton., *Life of Andrew Jackson*, 87.

19. Ibid., 89.

20. James Parton attributes Robert Jackson's death to smallpox, while Amos Kendall asserts that Robert never recovered from the wounds he received from the British officer. See Parton, *Life of Andrew Jackson*, 94 and Kendall, *Life of Andrew Jackson*, 50.

21. Parton, *Life of Andrew Jackson*, 94–95.

22. Ibid.,

23. Edwin G. Burrows, *Forgotten Patriots: The Untold Story of American Prisoners during the Revolutionary War* (New York: Basic Books, 2008), 7.

24. Wallabout Bay lies between the Williamsburg and Manhattan Bridges adjacent to the Brooklyn Navy Yard.

25. Burrows, *Forgotten Patriots*, 202–203.

26. Ibid., 200–201.

27. Albert G. Green, ed., *Recollections of the Jersey Prison Ship* (New York: P. M. Davis, 1831), 84–85.

28. Danske Dandridge, *American Prisoners of the Revolution* (Charlottesville, VA: Michie Company, 1910), 82–88.

29. Jackson was the first president to be elected with near universal white male suffrage in the United States. Full democracy did not emerge until the passage of the Nineteenth Amendment in 1920 providing for women's right to vote.

30. Lepore, "Bound for Glory."

31. Ishmael Beah, *A Long Way Gone: Memoirs of a Boy Soldier* (New York: Farrar, Straus and Giroux, 2007), 123.

32. Ibid., 119.

33. Ibid., 164–169.

34. Michael Clancy, "Fact Check: UNICEF Cannot Confirm Beah's Camp Brawl Claim," *Village Voice*, March 19, 2008, http://blogs.villagevoice.com/runninscared/2008/03/unicef_cannot_c.php.

35. Chris Blattman, "Credibility: A Long Way Gone?," *Chris Blattman* (blog), March 5, 2008, http://chrisblattman.com/2008/03/05/credibility-a-long-way-gone.

36. Graham Rayman, "Boy Soldier of Fortune: A Celebrated Memoir Threatens to Blow into a Million Little Pieces," *Village Voice*, March 18, 2008, http://www.villagevoice.com/2008–03–18/news/boy-soldier/full.

37. Talk given by Ishmael Beah at the session titled "War and Child Soldiers: A Dialogue with Ishmael Beah, Author of *A Long Way Gone*" at the annual meetings of the American Anthropological Association, Montreal, Canada, November 17, 2011.

38. Steven Mintz, *Huck's Raft: A History of American Childhood* (Cambridge, MA: Harvard University Press, 2004), 29–29.

39. Ibid., 51. See also Harold E. Selesky, *War and Society in Colonial America* (New Haven: Yale University Press, 1990).

40. Mintz, *Huck's Raft*, 69.

41. Ibid., 62–63.

42. Joseph Plumb Martin, *Private Yankee Doodle* (Fort Washington, PA: Eastern National, 2002).

43. M. M. Quaifem, "A Boy Soldier under Washington: The Memoir of Daniel Granger," *Mississippi Valley Historical Review* 16, no. 4 (1930): 538–560.

44. Ibid., 539.

45. Ibid.

46. William Evans, "Peter Francisco: The American Soldier," *William and Mary Quarterly* 13, no. 4 (1905): 213–216.

47. Ethnic and social class factors may have figured importantly in Francisco's disappearance from the pantheon of American Revolutionary War heroes. See Wesley Joyner, "The Legend and Life of Peter Francisco: Fame, Fortune, and the Deprivation of American's Original Citizen Soldier" (master's thesis, Virginia Commonwealth University, 2007).

48. Travis Bowman, *Hercules of the Revolution* (Davidson, NC: Bequest, 2009).

49. Caroline Cox, "Boy Soldiers of the American Revolution: The Effects of War on Society," in *Children and Youth in a New Nation*, ed. James Marten (New York: New York University Press, 2009), 18.

50. Harold Selesky, *A Demographic Survey of the Continental Army That Wintered at Valley Forge, Pennsylvania, 1777–1778* (Washington, DC: Nation Park Service, 1987), http://www.nps.gov/vafo/historyculture/demographic-survey.htm.

51. Ibid., 19.

52. Ibid., 27.

53. D. M. Keesee, *Too Young to Die: Boy Soldiers of the Union Army 1861–1865* (Huntington, VA: Blue Acorn Press, 2001).

54. David B. Parker and Alan Freeman, "David Bailey Freeman," *Cartersville Magazine*, Spring 2001, http://www.ifreeman.com/freeman/whois.htm.

55. Margaret Downie Banks, "Avery Brown (1852–1904), Musician: America's Youngest Civil War Soldier," *America's Shrine to Music Newsletter*, February 2001, http://www.usd.edu:80/smm/AveryBrown.html.

56. "Last Veteran of '61 to Leave the Army," *New York Times*, August 8, 1915, 18.

57. "Willie Johnston," accessed April 23, 2014, U.S. Army Center for Military History, http://www.history.army.mil/html/moh/civwaral.html.

58. "Benjamin Levy," accessed April 23, 2014, U.S. Army Center for Military History, http://www.history.army.mil/html/moh/civwaral.html.

59. "James Machon," accessed April 23, 2014, U.S. Army Center for Military History, http://www.history.army.mil/html/moh/civwaral.html.

60. "John Angling." accessed April 23, 2014, U.S. Army Center for Military History, http://www.history.army.mil/html/moh/civwaral.html.

61. Ezra Warner, *Generals in Blue: Lives of the Union Commanders* (Baton Rouge: Louisiana State University Press, 1964).

62. "Albert Woolson, Honorary Commander-in-Chief 1953/1954," Sons of Union Veterans of the Civil War, last modified 1999, http://suvcw.org/pcinc/woolson.htm.

63. James McPherson, *Battle Cry of Freedom: The Civil War Era* (Oxford: Oxford University Press, 2003), 306n.4.

64. Benjamin Gould, *Investigations in the Military and Anthropological Statistics of American Soldiers* (New York: Hurd and Houghton, 1869).

65. George L. Kilmer, "Boys in the Union Army," *Century* 70 (1905): 269–275.

66. Charles King, "Boys of the War Days," in *A Photographic History of the Civil War*, vol. 8, ed. Francis Trevelyan Miller (Springfield, MA: Patriot Press, 1911), 189–201.

67. Judith Pizzaro, Roxanne Cohen Silver, and JoAnn Prause, "Physical and Mental Health Costs of Traumatic War Experiences among Civil War Veterans," *Archives of General Psychiatry* 63, no. 2 (2006): 193–200. Age at first enlistment was obtained from military records, and ranged from 9 to 71 years. This variable was categorized into five age groups of approximately equal size to highlight the effect of younger ages: 9 to 17 years (n = 3,013), 18 to 20 years (n = 3,694), 21 to 25 years (n =3,435), 26 to 30 years (n = 2,225), and 31 years and older (n = 2,660).

68. Bell Irvin Wiley, *The Common Soldier in the Civil War. Book II: The Life of Johnny Reb* (New York: Grosset and Dunlop, 1943), 331.

69. Susan Hull, *Boy Soldiers of the Confederacy* (New York: Neale, 1905).

70. John Lincoln Clem, "From Nursery to Battlefield," *Outlook*, July 4, 1914, 546–547.

71. Benedict Anderson, *Imagined Communities: Reflections on the Origins and Spread of Nationalism* (London: Verso, 1991); George L. Mosse, *Fallen Soldiers: Reshaping the Memory of World Wars* (Oxford: Oxford University Press, 1990).

72. Robert Hertz, *Death and the Right Hand*, trans. Rodney Needham and Claudia Needham (Glencoe, IL: Free Press, 1960), 27–86 and 117–154.

73. Danny Kaplan, "Commemorating a Suspended Death: Missing Soldiers and National Solidarity in Israel," *American Ethnologist* 35, no. 3 (2008): 413–427.

74. Ibid., 423, citing Irit Dekel, "Collectivism and Anonymity: The Israel Unknown Soldier" (paper, American Sociological Association, Atlanta, August 16–19, 2003).

75. Drew Gilpin Faust, *This Republic of Suffering: Death and the American Civil War* (New York: Vintage Books, 2008), 6.

76. Ibid. 7, 9, 17.

77. Ibid.

78. Ibid., 10–11.

79. "Luther C. Ladd, a Massachusetts Volunteer, Killed at Baltimore (First Victim of the War)," *Harpers Weekly* 5, no. 231 (June 1, 1861): 241.

80. Gene Thorp, "First Civil War Deaths Took Place in Baltimore," *Washington Post*, April 19, 2011, http://www.washingtonpost.com/blogs/house-divided/post/first -civil-war-deaths-took-place-in-baltimore/2011/04/18/AFeOpQ4D_blog.html.

81. Richard Watson Musgrove, *History of the Town of Bristol, Grafton County, New Hampshire*, vol. 1 (Bristol, NH: R. W. Musgove, 1904), 223–223.

82. *Life of Luther C. Ladd, Who Fell in Baltimore, April 19, 1861 Exclaiming All Hail to the Stars and Stripes* (Concord, NH: P. B. Cogswell, 1862), 18.

83. "The Battle of Baltimore," *New York Times*, April 21, 1861, accessed April 8, 2014, http://www.nytimes.com/1861/04/21/news/the-battle-of-baltimore-detailed -account-of-the-affair.html?pagewanted=all.

84. *Boston Travellor*, May 8, 1861, quoted in Frank Moore, ed., *The Rebellion Record*, vol. 1 (New York: G. B. Putnam, 1862), 111.

85. Faust, *This Republic of Suffering*, 11.

86. "Luther Ladd," in *Massachusetts Register No. 94* (Boston: Adams, Sampson, 1862), 155.

87. Ibid., 196.

88. Moore, *Rebellion Record*, 35.

89. Henry Allen Ford, *Poems of History* (New York: William Shepard, 1883), 413–414. The poem is also sometimes attributed to Clarence Butler. See Frank Moore, *Anecdotes, Poetry, and Incidents of the War: North and South* (New York: Arundel, 1882), 164–165.

90. B. B. Wade, "All Hail the Stars and Stripes," *Knickerbocker* 60, no. 2 (July 1862): 149–150.

91. G. Gumpert, "*The Dying Volunteer*" (Philadelphia: G. Andre, 1861), Library of Congress Performing Arts Encyclopedia, http://lcweb2.10c.gov/diglib/ihas/loc.natlib .ihas.200001165/default.html.

92. J. P. Webster, "*The Dying Volunteer*" (Chicago: H. M. Higgens, 1863), accessed September 27, 2014, Library of Congress Performing Arts Encyclopedia, http://lcweb2 .10c.gov/diglib/ihas/loc.natlib.ihas.200002223/default.html; A.E.A. Muse, "The Dying Volunteer" (New Orleans: Louis Grunwald, 1865), accessed September 27, 2014, Library of Congress Performing Arts Encyclopedia, http://lcweb2.10c.gov/ diglib/ihas/loc.natlib.ihas.200002470/default.html; Andrew Boyd, "The Dying Volunteer" (Boston: Oliver Ditson, n.d.), accessed April 8, 2014, Library of Congress Performing Arts Encyclopedia, http://lcweb2.10c.gov/diglib/ihas/loc.natlib .ihas.200001216/default.html.

93. John Benson Lossing, *Pictorial History of the Civil War in the United States of America* (Philadelphia: George W. Childs, 1866), 426.

94. "The Lowell Celebration: Dedication of the Monument to the First Martyrs of the Rebellion Address by Gov. Andrew," *New York Times*, June 18, 1865, accessed April 8, 2014, http://www.nytimes.com/1865/06/18/news/lowell-celebration-dedication -monument-first-martyrs-rebellion-address-gov.html.

95. A child of the regiment was any child raised by a regiment, especially its noncommissioned officers and soldiers, and raised and trained to be a soldier. The expression sometimes refers to street children who have been recruited into the military. as in Victor Hugo's *Les Misérables*. "That is pure gamin, and there are many varieties in the gamin genus. The notary-gamin is called 'leap-the-gutter'; the cook-gamin is called 'scullion'; the baker-gamin is called 'doughey'; the footman gamin is called 'tiger'; the sailor-gamin is called 'powder monkey'; the soldier-gamim is called 'a child of the regiment'; the tradesman gamin is called 'errand-boy'; the courtier-gamin is called 'page'; the royal-gamin is called 'dauphin'; and the divine-gamin is called 'St Bambino.'" Victor Hugo, *Les Misérables* (London: Hurst and Blackett, 1862), 99. In this context it appears to refer to the deep emotional connection felt between the adults of the regiment and its drummer boy.

96. "Military Funeral," *Brooklyn Daily Eagle*, June 15, 1861, 2.

97. Ibid.

98. *The Little Drummer Boy, Clarence McKenzie: The Child of the 13th Regiment New York State Militia and the Child of the Mission Sunday School* (New York: Reformed Protestant Dutch Church, 1861), 124.

99. Ibid., 125.

100. "The Reverend Dr. McClelland Dead," *New York Times*, September 7, 1916, 9.

101. *Little Drummer Boy*, 126–129.

102. Ibid.

103. "A Child of the Regiment," *New York Times*, November 3, 1884, accessed April 8, 2014, http://select.nytimes.com/gst/abstract.html?res=FA0C13FA3F5B1 0738DDDAA0894D9415B8484F0D3&scp=3&sq=clarence%20mckenzie&st=cse.

104. "Private Joseph Darrow," Find a Grave, accessed April 8, 2014, http://www .findagrave.com/cgi-bin/fg.cgi?page=gr&GSln=Darrow&GSfn=Joseph&GSbyrel= in&GSdy=1861&GSdyrel=in&GSob=n&GRid=10162975&.

105. Edwin Warriner, *Old Sands Street Methodist Episcopal Church of Brooklyn, New York: An Illustrated Centennial Record* (New York: Phillips & Hunt, 1885), 353.

106. Bernhard J. Nadal, *The Christian Boy-Soldier: The Funeral Sermon of Joseph E. Darrow Preached in Sands Street Methodist Episcopal Church, Brooklyn, on the 27th of October, 1861* (New York: Steam, 1862), 9.

107. Ibid., 10.

108. Ibid., 11–14.

109. Ibid., 14.

110. J. David Hacker, "Recounting the Dead," *New York Times, Opinionator* (blog), September 20, 2011, http://opinionator.blogs.nytimes.com/2011/09/20/recounting -the-dead/#more-105317.

111. Lionel Rose, *The Erosion of Childhood: Child Oppression in Great Britain 1860–1918* (London: Routledge, 1991), 27–28.

112. *The Scouts Book of Heroes* (London: C. Arthur Pearson, 1919), 46.

113. "Jack Cornwall: The Boy Hero of Jutland Battle," *Mercury* (Hobart, Tasmania), October 24, 1916, 5.

114. John Tussaud, *The Romance of Madame Tussaud's* (New York: George H. Duran, 1920), 336.

115. "Painting Tells the Story of Boy Hero in Battle," *Miami Daily News*, January 31, 1926, 16. The episode of Giancomo Casabianca was enshrined in the 1826 poem "Casabianca" by British poet Felicia Dorothea Hemans (1793–1835), widely known as "The Boy Stood on the Burning Deck." For full text of the poem, see Felicia Dorothea Hemans, *The Poetical Works of Felicia Dorothea Hemans* (London: Oxford University Press, 1914), 396. The opening lines are, "The boy stood on the burning deck / Whence all but he had fled; / The flame / that lit the battle's wreck / Shone round him o'er the dead." This poem became deeply embedded in the culture of schooling from the mid-nineteenth to mid-twentieth centuries, a culture that continued to sentimentalize and venerate boy heroes. So many generations of schoolchildren both in Great Britain and America were required to recite Hemans's poem that it became the object of children's revenge, its heroic lines subverted by widespread parody: "The boy stood on the burning deck / His legs were covered with blisters / His father was in the public house / With beer all down his whiskers." See Iona Opie and Peter Opie, *The Lore and Language of School Children* (Oxford: Clarendon, 1961), 93.

116. Martin van Creveld, *The Culture of War* (New York: Ballantine Books, 2008), 202.

117. Katharine Tynan, *Late Songs* (London: Sidgwick & Jackson, 1917), 11.

118. C. A. Renshaw, *England's Boys: A Woman's War Poems* (London: Erskine MacDonald, 1916), 18.

119. Ibid., 29.

120. Mary A. Conley, *From Jack Tar to Union Jack: Representing Naval Manhood in the British Empire, 1870–1918* (Manchester: Manchester University Press, 2009), 166.

121. Ibid.

CHAPTER 2   THE STRUGGLE OVER CHILD RECRUITMENT

1. William Gouge, *Of Domestical Duties* (1622; repr., Pensacola, FL: Chapel Library, 2006), 11.

2. John Demos, *A Little Commonwealth: Family Life in Plymouth Colony* (Oxford: Oxford University Press, 1999).

3. Stephanie Coontz, *The Way We Never Were: American Families and the Nostalgia Trap* (New York: Basic Books, 1992), 10; Lawrence Stone, *The Family, Sex and Marriage in England 1500–1800* (London: Harper and Row, 1977), 653–654.

4. John Grinspan, "The Wild Children of Yesteryear," *New York Times*, May 31, 2014, http://www.nytimes.com/2014/06/01/opinion/sunday/the-wild-children-of-yesteryear.html.

5. Janet Dolgin, "Transforming Childhood: Apprenticeship in American Law," *New England Law Review* 31 (1997): 1114.

6. David William Archard, "Children's Rights," in *The Stanford Encyclopedia of Philosophy (Winter 2010 Edition)*, http://plato.stanford.edu/archives/sum2011/entries/rights-children.

7. Lawrence Friedman, *The History of American Law*, 3rd ed. (New York: Touchstone, 2005).

8. An Act Concerning the Care and Education of Neglected Children (May 29, 1866), *Massachusetts Acts* c. 283 (Boston: Secretary of the Commonwealth, 1866), http://archives.lib.state.ma.us/handle/2452/100205.

9. An Act for the Prevention of Cruelty to, and Better Protection of, Children, 1889, 44 Vict.52 and 53, United Kingdom General Public Acts, http://www.legislation.gov.uk/ukpga/1889/44/pdfs/ukpga_18890044_en.pdf.

10. These developments are described in detail in John E. B. Myer, "A Short History of Child Protection in America," *Family Law Quarterly* 42, no. 3 (2008): 449–463. See also John E. B. Myer, *Child Protection in America: Past, Present, and Future* (New York: Oxford University Press, 2006).

11. Mary Ann Glendon, *The Transformation of Family Law* (Chicago: University of Chicago Press, 1989), 28–34.

12. Ibid., 36.

13. John Witte, "Honor Thy Father and Thy Mother? Child Marriage and Parental Consent in Calvin's Geneva," *Journal of Religion* 86, no. 4 (2006): 580–605.

14. Glendon, *Transformation of Family Law*, 36.

15. An Act for the Better Preventing of Clandestine Marriage, 1753, 26 Geo. II. c. 33.

16. David Lemmings, "Marriage and the Law in the Eighteenth Century: Hard-wicke's Marriage Act of 1753," *Historical Journal* 36, no. 2 (1996): 344.

17. Ibid.

18. William Blackstone, *Commentaries of the Laws of England*, vol. 1 (Philadelphia: Robert Bell, 1771), 463.

19. George Elliot Howard, *A History of Matrimonial Institutions Chiefly in England and the United States, with an Introductory Analysis of the Literature and the Theories of Primitive Marriage and the Family* (Chicago: University of Chicago Press, 1904), 395–396.

20. *The Revised Statues of the State of South Carolina*, c. 85 § 11 (Charleston: Republican Publishing Company, 1873), 441.

21. Ibid., c. 133 § 2, 735.

22. Stephanie Coontz, *Marriage, a History: How Love Conquered Marriage* (New York: Penguin, 2006), 172.

23. *Maynard v. Hill*, 125 U.S. 190, 210–211 (1888), http://supreme.justia.com/cases/federal/us/125/190/case.html.

24. S. T. Ansell, "Legal and Historical Aspects of the Militia," *Yale Law Journal* 26 (1917): 471–479.

25. Blackstone, *Commentaries*, 1:410, 413.

26. J. W. Fortescue, *A History of the British Army*, vol. 1 (London: Macmillan, 1899), 5.

27. Ibid., 577.

28. Marvin R. Kreidberg and Merton G. Henry, *History of Military Mobilization in the United States Army, 1775–1945* (Washington, DC: Government Printing Office, 1955), 3

29. An Act for the Better Regulating and Disciplining of the Militia (April 30, 1757), in *Statutes at Large of All the laws of Virginia* (Richmond: Franklin Press, 1820), 93.

30. An Act for Forming and Regulating the Militia in the Colony of Massachusetts Bay (January 22, 1776), in *Acts and Resolutions, Public and Private, of the Province of Massachusetts Bay* c. 10, 445 (Boston: Secretary of the Commonwealth, 1776), http://archives.lib.state.ma.us/handle/2452/117005.

31. *Journals of the Continental Congress, 1774–1789* (Washington, DC: Library of Congress, 1904–1937), 90, http://memory.loc.gov/ammem/amlaw/lwjclink.html.

32. Ibid., 187–188.

33. William Stryker, ed., *Official Register of the Officers and Men of New Jersey in the Revolutionary War* (Trenton, NJ: William Nicolson, 1872), 18.

34. Ibid., 19.

35. Martin, *Private Yankee Doodle*, 1–17.

36. An Act for regulating the Military Establishment of the United States, April 30, 1790, in *U.S. Statutes at Large* 1 (1790): 119.

37. Ibid., § 3.

38. An Act Fixing the Military Peace Establishment of the United States, March 16, 1802, in *U.S. Statutes at Large* 2 (1802): 134–135.

39. Frederick Morse Cutler, *The History of Military Conscription with Special Reference to the United States* (Worcester, MA: Clark University, 1922); Frederick Morse

Cutler, "Military Conscription, Especially in the United States," *Historical Outlook* 14, no. 5 (May 1923): 170–175.

40. An Act to Provide for Calling Forth the Militia, to Execute the Laws of the Union, Suppress Insurrections and Repel Invasions, May 2, 1792, *U.S. Statutes at Large* 1:264–265.

41. An Act More Effectually to Provide for the National defense by Establishing a Uniform Militia throughout the United States, May 8, 1792, *U.S. Statutes at Large* 1:272–274.

42. "An Act to Raise and Additional Military Force," January 11, 1812, *U.S. Statutes at Large* 2:671–672.

43. "An Act Supplementary to an Act Entitled 'An Act for the More Perfect Organization of the Army of the United States,'" January 20, 1813, *U.S. Statutes at Large* 2:791–792.

44. "An Act Making Further Provisions for Filling the Ranks of the Army of the United States," December 10, 1814, *U.S. Statutes at Large* 3:146–147.

45. Roane County Tennessee Archives Military Records—War of 1812—Enlistment, accessed June 3, 2014, http://files.usgwarchives.net/tn/roane/military/warof1812/enlistment/warof181296nmt.txt.

46. Ed Gilbert, *Frontier Militiaman in the War of 1812: Southwestern Frontier* (Oxford: Osprey, 2008), 11; Richard W. Stewart, ed., *The United States Army and the Forging of a Nation, 1775–1917*, vol. 1 (Washington, DC: U.S. Army Center for Military History, 2005), 132–134.

47. *United States v. Bainbridge*, 1 Mason 71, 24 F.Cas. 946 (1816).

48. "An Act Supplementary to the Act Entitled 'An Act to Provide Additional Armament for the Further Protection of the Trade of the United States and for Other Purposes,'" June 30, 1798, *U.S. Statutes at Large* 1:575. Section 5 of the act provided that "the President of the United States may, at his discretion, increase or vary the quotas of seamen, landsmen and marines, to be employed on board the frigates, and may permit a proportion of boys for them, and the other vessels of the navy of the United States, according to the exigencies of the public service."

49. See, for example, "An Act Authorizing the Employment of and Additional Naval Force," January 31, 1809, *U.S. Statutes at Large* 2:514. Section 2 provides that the president is "authorized and empowered, in addition to the number of petty officers, able seamen, ordinary seamen and boys, at present authorized by law, to appoint, and cause to be engaged and employee! as soon as may be, three hundred midshipmen, three thousand six hundred able seamen, ordinary seamen and boys." See also "Act to Amend the Act, Entitled 'An Act to Amend the Act Authorizing the Employment of an Additional Naval Force,'" May 15, 1820, *U.S. Statues at Large* 2:606. The specific wording of the statute was, "*Be it enacted by the Senate and House of Representatives of the United States of America, in Congress assembled,* that the second section of the act, entitled 'An act authorizing the employment of an additional naval force,' passed on the thirty-first day of January, eighteen hundred and nine, be, and the same is hereby, amended, so far as to authorize the enlistment of able seamen, ordinary seamen, and boys, during

the continuance of the service or cruise for which they shall be enlisted; not, however, to exceed the period of three years."

50. *United States v. Bainbridge*, 948.

51. Ibid., 950–951.

52. Ibid., 950.

53. Ibid., 948–951.

54. *In re John McLave*, 8 Blatch 67, 3 Alb. L.J. 75, 16 F.Cas. 235, (1870).

55. *Army and Navy Chronicle*, vol. 1 (Washington, DC: B. Homans, 1835), 21.

56. "An Act to Provide for the Enlistment of Boys for the Naval Service and to Extend the Term of the Enlistment of Seamen," March 2, 1837, *U.S. Statutes at Large* 5:153.

57. "An Act Making Appropriations for the Naval Service for the Year Ending the Thirtieth of June Eighteen Hundred and Fifty Nine," June 12, 1858, *U.S. Statutes at Large* 11:314, 318.

58. *Morrissey v. Perry* 137 U.S. 157 (1890), http://caselaw.lp.findlaw.com/cgi-bin/getcase.pl?court=us&vol=137&invol=157.

59. George S. Boutwell, *Revised Statutes of the United States, Passed at the First Session of the Forty-Third Congress, 1873–'74* (Washington, DC: Government Printing Office, 1878), 205.

60. *The King v. the Inhabitants of Rutherfield Greys*, 1 Barnewall & Cresswell 345 (1823), in *Reports of Cases Argued and Determined in English Court of Common Law* (Philadelphia: T & J. W. Johnson, 1872), 148–150.

61. *New York State Annual Report of the Attorney General* (Albany: J. B. Lyon, 1919), 207–211.

62. "An Act Making Appropriations for the Support of the Army," September 28, 1850, *U.S. Statutes at Large* 9:504.

63. "An Act Making an Appropriation for Completing the Defense of Washington," February 13, 1862, *U.S. Statutes at Large* 12:339.

64. "An Act Authorizing Additional Enlistments in the Navy of the United States," August 6, 1861, *U.S. Statutes at Large* 12:315.

65. "An Act to Establish and Equalize the Grade Line Officers of the United States Navy," July 16, 1862, *U.S. Statutes at Large* 12:583.

66. James M. McPherson, *Ordeal by Fire: The Civil War and Reconstruction* (New York: Knopf, 1982), 356.

67. "An Act for Enrolling and Calling Out the National Forces, and for Other Purposes," March 3, 1863, *U.S. Statutes at Large* 12:731–737.

68. *Second Report of the Provost Marshal General to the Secretary of War on the Operations of the Selective Service System to December 20, 1918* (Washington, DC: Government Printing Office, 1919), 376–377. See also U.S. Congress. *House Committee on Military Affairs Hearings* (Washington, DC: Government Printing Office, 1946), 55n12.

69. *Second Report of the Provost Marshal General*, 378.

70. Present value was calculated by measuring multiplying one dollar by the percentage increase in the CPI from 1865 to 2011. This represents the most

conservative method of estimating the cost. See http://www.measuringworth
.com/uscompare.

71. Eugene C. Murdock, "New York's Civil War Bounty Brokers," *Journal of American History* 53, no. 2 (1966): 266.

72. Ibid., 261.

73. Ibid., 263–265.

74. "A Shocking Case of Kidnapping by Bounty Brokers," *New York Times*, August 7, 1864, http://www.nytimes.com/1864/08/07/news/a-shocking-case-of -kidnapping-by-bounty-brokers.html?scp=9&sq=boys%20bounty&st=cse.

75. Murdock, "New York's Civil War Bounty Brokers,"269.

76. "Astounding Frauds on Government," *New York Times*, February 8, 1865, http:// www.nytimes.com/1865/02/08/news/astounding-frauds-government-arrest -twenty-seven-bounty-brokers-their.html?scp=3&sq=bounty+brokers+boy&st =cse&pagewanted=all.

77. Martin W. Ofele, *True Sons of the Republic: European Immigrants in the Union Army* (Santa Barbara, CA: Praeger, 2008).

78. Eugene H. Berwanger, *The British Foreign Office and the American Civil War* (Lexington: University Press of Kentucky, 1994), 139.

79. Murdock, "New York's Civil War Bounty Brokers," 267.

80. "War Department Special Agency, Henry Isaacs Off for the Old Capital Spurious Mother Sponsor for a Recruit," *New York Times*, March 1, 1865, http://www .nytimes.com/1865/03/01/news/war-department-special-agency-henry-isaacs -off-for-old-capital-spurious-mother.html?scp=2&sq=bounty+brokers+&st=p& pagewanted=all.

81. "Pensioners for Revenue," *New York Times*, April 29, 1894, http://query.nytimes.com/ mem/archive-free/pdf?res=9406E7DF1531E033A2575AC2A9629C94659ED7CF.

82. "More Pensions Than Soldiers," *New York Times*, April 19, 1894, http://query .nytimes.com/mem/archive-free/pdf?res=F70D15F73D5C17738DDDA0099 4DC405B8485F0D3.

83. "An Act for Enrolling and Calling Out the National Forces," March 3,1863, *U.S. Statutes at Large* 12:731.

84. "An Act to Amend an Act Entitled 'An Act for Enrolling and Calling Out the National Forces, Approved March 3, 1863,'" February 24, 1864, *U.S. Statutes at Large* 12:6.

85. "An Act Further to Regulate the Enrolling and Calling Forth of the National Forces," July 4, 1864, *U.S. Statutes at Large* 13:379.

86. Dennis Thavenet, "The Michigan Reform School and the Civil War: Officers and Inmates Mobilized for the Union Cause," *Michigan Historical Review*13, no. 1 (1987): 21–46.

87. The actual ages of enlistees are not available, but the facts that the average age of boys in the school was 14.8 years and the average length of stay at the school was 10.9 months indicate that many of these were underage. See M. L. Elbridge, "History of the Massachusetts Nautical Reform School," in *Transactions of the National Congress on Penitentiary and Reformatory Discipline, Cincinnati, 1870*, ed. Enoch C. Wines (Albany: Weed Parson, 1871), 350–358.

88. Thavenet, "Michigan Reform School," 26–27.

89. "An Act to Provide a Military Force," in *Acts of the Legislature of the State of Michigan, 1861* (Lansing, MI: John A. Kerr, 1861), 545–547.

90. Thavenet, "Michigan Reform School," 31–32.

91. "An Act to Secure Homesteads to Actual Settlers on the Public Domain," May 20, 1862, *U.S. Statutes at Large* 12:392.

92. Rhode Island Historical Society, "Providence Reform School Records: 1850–1885," http://www.rihs.org/mssinv/Mss214sg3.htm.

93. *Report Made to the Senate Relative to the Enlistment of Boys from the Reform School into the Army of the United States* (Providence, RI: Hiram H. Thomas, 1865), 1–4.

94. Ibid., 8–10.

95. Ibid.

96. Ibid., 5, 19–20.

97. *Report of the Committee Appointed to Enquire into the Subject of Boy Enlistment* (London: Harrison and Sons, 1876).

98. Ibid., 3.

99. Ibid., 25, appendix D.

100. Ibid., 7, 18.

101. R. H. Nichols and F. A. Wray, *The History of the Foundling Hospital* (London: Oxford University Press, 1935), 320–321.

102. Gillian Pugh, *London's Forgotten Children: Thomas Coram and the Foundling Hospital* (Stroud, UK: Tempus, 2007).

103. *Register of Enlistment into Military Bands and Lists of Boys Sent to the Training Ships Goliath and Exmouth: 1858–1902*, SMSD/178 (London: London Metropolitan Archives, n.d.).

104. The cartoon is available at http://punch.photoshelter.com/image/I0000nTHJ70gjei0.

105. George Coppard, *With a Machine Gun to Cambrai* (London: HMSO, 1969), 1.

106. Victor Silvester, *Dancing Is My Life* (London: Heinemann, 1958), 16.

107. Richard Van Emden, *Boy Soldiers of the Great War* (London: Headline, 2005), 321.

108. Ibid., 319.

109. Ibid., 321.

110. Nicoletta F. Gullace, "White Feathers and Wounded Men: Female Patriotism and the Memory of the Great War," *Journal of British Studies* 36, no. 2 (1997): 180.

111. "Boy Soldiers," Spartacus Education, http://spartacus-educational.com/FWWboy.htm.

112. Francis Beckett, "The Men Who Would Not Fight," *Guardian*, November 11, 2008, http://www.guardian.co.uk/world/2008/nov/11/first-world-war-white-feather-cowardice.

113. Max Arthur, *Forgotten Voices of the Great War* (London: Lyons Press, 2004), 19.

114. Ibid., 63.

115. Tom Bevan, *Doing His "Bit": A Story of the Great War* (London: Thomas Nelson, 1917), 52.

116. Virginia Woolf, *Three Guineas*, in *The Selected Works of Virginia Woolf* (Hertford-shire, UK: Hare, 2007), 918nIII.

117. David Sibley, *The British Working Class and Enthusiasm for War, 1914–1916* (London: Routledge, 2005), 118.

118. Nicoletta Gullace, *The Blood of Our Sons* (London: Palgrave Macmillan, 2002).

119. Cate Haste, *Keep the Home Fires Burning: Propaganda in the First World War* (London: Allen Lane, 1977), 57.

120. Susan Evans, *Mothers of Heroes, Mothers of Martyrs: World War I and the Politics of Grief* (Montreal: McGill-Queens University Press, 2007), 77–84.

121. Ibid.

122. *House of Commons Hansard (debate) October 12, 1915, Volume 74: 1173–1177*, http://hansard.millbanksystems.com/commons/1915/oct/12/recruiting#S5CV0074P0 _19151012_HOC_92.

123. *House of Commons Hansard (debate) October 19, 1915, Volume 74: 1626–27*, http://hansard.millbanksystems.com/written_answers/1915/oct/19/recruiting #S5CV0074P0_19151019_CWA_11.

124. *House of Commons Hansard (debate) October 12, 1915, Volume 74: 1173–1177*, http://hansard.millbanksystems.com/commons/1915/oct/12/recruiting#S5CV0074P0 _19151012_HOC_92.

125. Ibid.

126. *House of Commons Hansard (debate) June 28 1916, Volume 83: 823–24*, http://hansard .millbanksystems.com/commons/1916/jun/28/under-age-soldiers#S5CV0083P0 _19160628_HOC_123.

127. *House of Commons Hansard (debate) October 12, 1915, Volume 74:1173–1177*, http://hansard.millbanksystems.com/commons/1915/oct/12/recruiting#S5CV0074P0 _19151012_HOC_92.

128. *House of Commons Hansard (debate), March 14, 1916, Volume 80:1865–66*, http://hansard.millbanksystems.com/commons/1916/mar/14/boy-recruits #S5CV0080P0_19160314_HOC_89.

129. *House of Commons Hansard (debate) October 19, 1915, Volume 74:1626–27*, http://hansard.millbanksystems.com/written_answers/1915/oct/19/recruiting #S5CV0074P0_19151019_CWA_11.

130. Coppard, *With a Machine Gun to Cambrai*, 19.

131. ANZAC, "Boy Soldiers." http://www.anzacs.net/BoySoldiers.htm.

132. A full account of the history of the Bevistein case is found in David Lister, *Die Hard, Aby* (Barnsley, South Yorkshire: Pen & Sword Books, 2005).

133. *House of Commons Hansard* (debate) *May 4, 1916, Volume 82:128–129*, http://hansard .millbanksystems.com/commons/1916/may/04/court-martial-sentences-of-death.

134. Frank Crozier, *The Men I Killed* (London: Michael Joseph, 1937), 42.

135. Ibid., 123.

136. Chris Comber, "Worthing War Memorial Roll of Honor" (2006), http://www.roll -of-honour.com/Sussex/WorthingST.html.

137. Press clippings, Papers, Correspondence, and Press Cuttings Relating to the Life and Careers of Arthur Basil Markham, MP Markham 22/Code PA3143, Archival

Material of British Library of Political and Economic Science, London School of Economics.

138. *An Act to Make Provision with Respect to Military Service in Connexion with the Recent War, 1916* (5 & 6 Geo. C. 104), UK Parliamentary Archives, HL/PO/PU/1/1916/5&6G5c1044.

139. The specific number is 4,970,902. *Statistics of the Military Effort of the British Empire during the Great War* (London: HMSO, 1922), 364.

140. "Letter from George C. Curnock to Sir Arthur Markham," November 2, 1915, Markham 22/Code PA3143.

141. Richard Rinaldi, *The United States Army in World War I—Order of Battle* (Takoma Park, MD: Tiger Lily, 2005), 5.

142. *Second Report of the Provost Marshal General,* 6.

CHAPTER 3   CHILD SOLDIERS IN WORLD WAR II

1. "Nationalist Veteran," *Spanish Civil War,* University of Texas, Austin, accessed September 21, 2012, http://journalism.utexas.edu/coursework/spanish-civil-war/nationalist-veteran.

2. George Orwell, *Homage to Catalonia* (New York: Harcourt, 1969), 26.

3. A. K. Starinov, *Behind Fascist Lines: A Firsthand Account of Guerilla Warfare during the Spanish Revolution* (New York: Ballantine Books, 1995), 33.

4. Gerhard Rampel, *Hitler's Children: The Hitler Youth and the SS* (Chapel Hill: University of North Carolina Press, 1989), 256.

5. The best known film, *Kadetten* (Cadets), was directed by Karl Ritter, a Nazi Party member with a long history of making fascist and propaganda films, focused on young Prussian cadets captured by the Russians during the Seven Years' War (1756–1763) who escape their captors and heroically engage them in battle. See William Gillespie, *Karl Ritter: His Life and "Zeitfilms" under National Socialism* (Potts Point, Australia: German Films Dot Net, 2012) and Guido Knopp, *Hitler's Children* (Stroud, UK: Sutton, 2004), 97.

6. Hubert Meyer, *The 12th SS: The History of the Hitler Youth Panzer Division,* vol. 1 (Mechanicsburg, PA: Stackpole Books, 2005), 12.

7. Knopp, *Hitler's Children,* 4.

8. Guido Knopp, *Hitler's Kinder* (Munich: Bertelesmann, 2000), 58–59.

9. Ibid.

10. Knopp, *Hitler's Kinder,* 193.

11. Rampel, *Hitler's Children,* 232.

12. Christer Bergström, Andrey Dikov, and Vladimir Antipov, *Black Cross Red Star: Air War over the Eastern Front: Everything for Stalingrad,* vol. 3. (Hamilton, MT: Eagle Editions, 2006).

13. Meyer, *12th SS*

14. Karl H. Schlesier, *Flakhelfer to Grenadier: Memoir of a Boy Soldier, 1943–1945* (Lexington, KY: K. H. Schlesier, 2011).

15. Ibid., 12.

16. Alexander Perry Biddescomb, *Werewolf: The History of the National Socialist Guerilla Movement, 1944–1946* (Toronto: University of Toronto Press, 1998), 59.

17. Anthony Beever, *The Fall of Berlin 1945* (New York: Penguin, 2002), 316.

18. Ian Kershaw, *The End: The Defiance and Destruction of Hitler's Germany, 1944–1945* (New York: Penguin, 2011), xvii.

19. Ibid.

20. Beever, *Fall of Berlin*, 181.

21. Rampel, *Hitler's Children*, 241.

22. Ibid., 242.

23. Beever, *Fall of Berlin*, 346.

24. Ibid., 189.

25. Kershaw, *The End*, 311.

26. Daniel Jonah Goldhagen, *Hitler's Willing Executioners: Ordinary Germans and the Holocaust* (New York: Vintage, 1997), 364–368.

27. Biddescomb, *Werewolf*, 6–14.

28. Ibid., 162–164.

29. "2 Hitler Youth Shot by Allies as Spies," *New York Times*, June 5, 1945, 12.

30. Rampel, *Hitler's Children*, 248; "Execution of Two Hitler Youths for Espionage," *Canberra Times*, June 6, 1945, 1.

31. David Kahn, *Hitler's Spies: German Military Intelligence in World War II* (New York: Da Capo Press, 2000), 363–64.

32. Howard Katzlander, "PW Baby Cage: Captured Wehrmacht GIs between the Ages of 12 and 17 Get Special Indoctrination in Democracy at This PW School Sparked by a Yank Pfc," *Yank: The Army Weekly* 4, no. 18 (October 19, 1945): 16–17.

33. Edward N. Peterson, *The Many Faces of Defeat* (New York: Peter Lang, 1990), 32.

34. Josh Waletsky, *The Partisans of Vilna: The Untold Story of Jewish Resistance during World War II* (Washington, DC: Ciesla, 1986), DVD.

35. UN War Crimes Commission, *Law Reports of the Trials of War Criminals*, vol. 8 (London: HMSO, 1949), 36, 38.

36. *Hague Convention (IV) Respecting the Laws and Customs of War on Land and Its Annex: Regulations Concerning the Laws and Customs of War on Land*, October 18, 1907, http://www.unhcr.org/refworld/docid/4374cae64.html.

37. UN War Crimes Commission, *Law Reports*, 58.

38. Ibid., 75.

39. Ibid., 2, 25.

40. Bill Keller, "Echo of '41 in Minsk: Was the Heroine a Jew?," *New York Times*, September 15, 1987, https://www.nytimes.com/1987/09/15/world/echo-of-41-in-minsk-was-the-heroine-a-jew.html?pagewanted=3&src=pm.

41. For many years Masha Bruskina's identity was officially suppressed in the Soviet Union owing to her Jewish background. See Nechama Tec and Daniel Weiss, "A Historical Injustice: The Case of Masha Bruskina," *Holocaust and Genocide Studies* 11, no. 3 (1997): 366–377.

42. Barbara Jancar-Webster, *Women & Revolution in Yugoslavia, 1941–1945* (Denver, CO: Arden Press, 1990).

43. Elizabeth Sevier, *Resistance Fighter: A Teenage Girl in World War II France* (Manhattan, KS: Sunflower University Press, 1998).

44. Howard Fast, *The Incredible Tito: Man of the Hour* (New York: Lev Gleason, 1944).

45. Robert Capa, *Funeral of 20 Teenage Partisans of the Liceo Sannazaro, in the Vomero District, Naples 1943*, photograph, Art Institute of Chicago, http://www.artic.edu/aic/collections/artwork/71864?search_no=2&index=0.

46. Olga Kucherenko, *Little Soldiers: How Soviet Children Went to War, 1941–1945* (New York: Oxford University Press, 2011), 2.

47. Rivka Perlis, *The Pioneering Zionist Youth Movements in Nazi-Occupied Poland* [in Hebrew] (Tel Aviv: Kibutz Hameuchad, 1987), 457.

48. Israel Gutman, "Youth Movements," in *Encyclopedia of the Holocaust*, ed. Israel Gutman (New York: Macmillan, 1990), 1697–1703.

49. Perlis, *Pioneering Zionist Youth Movements*, 181.

50. Ibid.

51. Chaika Grossman, *The Underground Army*, 1965, trans. Shmuel Berri (New York: Holocaust Library, 1987), 1.

52. Havka Folman Raban, *They Are Still with Me*, trans. Judy Grossman (Western Galilee, Israel: Ghetto Fighters Museum, 2001) 48–62.

53. R. Domski, "The Aims of Jewish Youth, 1940" (Archive Ref JM/215/1) Jerusalem: Yad Vashem, the Holocaust Martyr's and Heroes Authority, http://www.yadvashem.org/odot_pdf/Microsoft%20Word%20-%20599.pdf.

54. Avihu Ronen, "'Youth Culture' and the Roots of the Idea of Resistance in the Ghetto (Youth Movements in Zaglembie during the Holocaust)" [in Hebrew], *Zionism: Studies in the History of the Zionist Movement and of the Jewish Community in Palestine* 16 (1991): 141–165.

55. Lucy S. Dawidowicz, *The War Against the Jews 1933–1945* (New York: Holt, Rinehart and Winston, 1975), 264.

56. Israel Gutman, *Resistance: The Warsaw Ghetto Uprising* (New York: Houghton Mifflin, 1994), 123.

57. Ibid.

58. Elaine Sciolino, "Young Resistance Fighter Becomes Icon of France's Center-Right," *New York Times*, October 23, 2007, http://www.nytimes.com/2007/10/23/world/europe/23france.html.

59. Paolo Brogi, "Il ponte sull'Aniene intitolato a Ugo Forno, eroe dodicenne del 1944," *Corriere della Sera*. June 10, 2010, http://roma.corriere.it/roma/notizie/cronaca/10_giugno_5/ponte-intitolato-go-forni-brogi-1703146566178.shtml.

60. Cesare De Simone, *Roma, città prigioniera: i 271 giorni dell'occupazione nazista: 8 settembre '43—4 giugno '44* (Milan: Mursia, 1994). See also Marco Marzilli, "Hugo Forno," Historiamilitaria.it, http://digilander.libero.it/historia_militaria/forno.htm.

61. *Per Non Dimenticare, Ugo Forno*, accessed October 7, 2014, http://www.ugoforno.it/.

62. Nina Tumarkin, *The Living and the Dead: The Rise and Fall of the Cult of World War II in Russia* (New York: Basic Books, 1994), 77.

63. "Kosmodemyanskaya," *Time*, March 2, 1942, 25.

64. Matthew Cooper, *The Phantom War: The German Struggle Against Soviet Partisans 1941–1944* (London: McDonald and James, 1979). See appendix 9, "Extracts from the 11th Army's Memorandum on the use of Troops Against Partisans 15 December 1941."

65. "Secret Order on the Conduct of Troops in Eastern Territories by Field Marshal von Reichenau, October 10, 1941," in *Nazi Conspiracy and Aggression*, vol. 8 (Washington, DC: Government Printing Office, 1946), 585–587, www.loc.gov/rr/frd/Military_Law/pdf/NT_Nazi_Vol-VIII.pdf.

66. There are numerous accounts of Zoya's death available in English with some variation in detail. These include the account written by her mother, Lyubov Kosmodemyanskaya, *The Story of Zoya and Shura* (Moscow: Foreign Languages Publishing House, 1953), http://gammacloud.org/features/zoya/story-zoya-shura/index.htm; "Teenage Soviet Hero Executed 61 Years Ago," *Pravda* (English), November 26, 2002, http://english.pravda.ru/news/russia/26-11-2002/18360-0. See also Mike Bessler, ed., *Red Youth: Young Heroes of the Great Patriotic War, Zoya Kosmodemyanskaya* (Kettering, OH: Erythros Press, 2012).

67. Martin Amis, *Koba the Dread: Laughter and the Twenty Million* (New York: Vintage, 2003), 200.

68. Maxim D. Shraver, *An Anthology of Jewish-Russian Literature*, vol. 1 (Armonk, NY: M.E. Sharpe, 2007), 561.

69. Roger D. Markwick and Euridice Charon Cardona, *Soviet Women on the Frontline in the Second World War* (New York: Palgrave Macmillan, 2012), 124.

70. Joseph Foster, "Zoya," *New Masses*, May 1, 1945, 29–30.

71. Tec and Weiss, "Historical Injustice." What follows is drawn from this study.

72. James V. Wertsch, *Voices of Collective Remembering* (Cambridge: Cambridge University Press, 2002), 72.

73. Timothy Snyder, *Bloodlands: Europe Between Hitler and Stalin* (New York: Basic Books, 2010), 339, 345.

74. María Tumarkin, "Productive Death: The Necropedagogy of a Young Soviet Hero," *South Atlantic Quarterly* 110, no. 4 (2011): 885–899.

75. Elizabeth S. Senlavskala, "Heroic Symbols: The Reality and Mythology of War," *Russian Studies in History* 37, no. 1 (1998): 61–87; Maksim Kondratyev, "USSR's Iconic Partisan Zoya Kosmodemyanskaya Made Her Death Her Biggest Accomplishment," *Pravda* (English), September 14, 2009, http://english.pravda.ru/history/14-09-2009/109252-zoya_kosmodemyanskaya-1/; Tumarkin, *Living and the Dead*, 78.

76. For analyses of the material iconography of the Zoya story, see Adrienne M. Harris, "The Lives and Deaths of a Soviet Saint in the Post-Soviet Period: The Case of Zoia Kosmodem'ianskaia," *Canadian Slavonic Papers* 53, nos. 2–4 (2011): 273–304; and Adrienna M. Harris, "Memorializations of a Martyr and Her Mutilated Bodies: Public Monuments to Soviet War Hero Zoya Kosmodemyanskaya, 1942 to the Present," *Journal of War and Culture Studies* 5, no. 1 (2012): 73–90.

77. Marek Haltof, *Polish Film and the Holocaust: Politics and Memory* (New York: Berghahn, 2012), 66.

78. Zbigniew Wroblewski, *Under the Command of "Gozdawy"* [in Polish] (Warsaw: University Press of Trade Unions, 1989).

79. An interview with Jerzy Bartnik is available on the website of the Warsaw Rising Museum at http://ahm.1944.pl/Jerzy_Bartnik/. A rough translation can be obtained through Google Translate.

80. Elżbieta Wiącek, "In the Labyrinth of Memory Cultural Representations about the Warsaw Rising of 1945 in Polish Film and Media Narration," *History Research* 2, no. 6 (2012): 398–414, 403.

81. Peter Martyn, "Warsaw 1989 to September 2001: Successive Statuary and Monument Memorialization for the National Capitol," in *Power and Persuasion: Sculpture in Its Rhetorical Context*, ed. Ursula Szulakowska (Warsaw: Institute of Art of the Polish Academy of Sciences, 2004), 225–248, 236n16.

82. Jasper Goldman, "Warsaw: Reconstruction as Propaganda," in *The Resilient City: How Modern Cities Recover from Disaster*, ed. Lawrence J. Vale and Thomas J. Camanella (New York: Oxford University Press, 2005), 135–158, 154.

83. See Jorge Hackmann and Marko Leht, "The Myth of Victimhood and the Cult of Authenticity: Sacralizing the Nation in Estonia and Poland," in *Rethinking the Space for Religion: New Actors in Central and Southeast Europe on Religion, Authenticity and Belonging*, ed. Catherina Raudvere, Kryzstof Stala, and Trine Stauning Willert (Lund, Sweden: Nordic Academic Press, 2013), 126–162.

CHAPTER 4   THE CHILD SOLDIER IN POPULAR CULTURE

1. Herman Melville, "The March into Virginia Ending in the First Manassas," in *American War Poetry: An Anthology*, ed. Lorrie Goldensohn (New York: Columbia University Press, 2006), 65–66.

2. van Creveld, *Culture of War*, 246–247.

3. Wilfred Owen, *Poems* (New York: Viking, 1921), 11. See also Jon Stallworthy, *Twelve Soldier Poets of the First World War* (New York: Constable, 2002).

4. Erich Maria Remarque, *All Quiet on the Western Front* (New York: Ballantine Books, 1987).

5. Lewis Milestone, *All Quiet on the Western Front* (Culver City, CA: RKO-Pathé, 1930), DVD.

6. Herbert Cobb, *Paths of Glory* (New York: Penguin, 2010).

7. Vsevolod Pudovkin, *The End of St. Petersburg* (Moscow: Mezhrabpom-Rus, 1927), DVD.

8. Richard Reid, *War in Pre-colonial Eastern Africa* (Athens: Ohio University Press, 2007), 2–21.

9. Delacroix's painting can be accessed at Wikipedia, accessed October 28, 2007, http://fr.wikipedia.org/wiki/Eug%C3%A8ne_Delacroix.

10. Jean-Jacques Yvorel, "De Delacroix à Poulbot, l'image du gamin de Paris," *RHEI: Revue d'histoire de l'enfance irrégulière* 4 (2002): 39–71.

11. Margaret Mead and Martha Wolfenstein, *Childhood in Contemporary Cultures* (Chicago: University of Chicago Press, 1955), 7.

12. Hugo, *Les Misérables*, 1028.

13. Ibid.

14. Ibid., 883.

15. Ibid., 887.

16. Ibid., 939.

17. Libby Murphy, "Gavroche and the Great War: Soldier *Gouaille* and the Legend of the *Poilu*," *Journal of War and Culture* 2, no. 2 (2009): 121–133.

18. Harry Castlemon, *Frank on a Gun-Boat* (Philadelphia: Porter & Coates, 1864).

19. Dale Freeman, *Oliver Optic 1822–1897, Children's Author* (Boston: University of Massachusetts Joseph P. Healey Library Publications, 2004), 13. http://scholarworks .umb.edu/cgi/viewcontent.cgi?article=1010&context=hlpubs.

20. Oliver Optic, *The Soldier Boy; or, Tom Somers in the Army* (New York: Hurst, 1864), 133–134, http://www.gutenberg.org/ebooks//14595.

21. Ibid., 135.

22. Ibid., 333.

23. Edna Forbes, *Johnny Tremain* (1943; repr., New York: Dell, 1980), 256.

24. Andrei Tarkovsky, *Ivan's Childhood* (Moscow: Mosfilm, 1962), DVD.

25. Elem Klimov, *Come and See* (Moscow: Mosfilm, 1985), DVD.

26. Chris Abani, *Song for Night: A Novella* (New York: Akashic Book, 2007); Uzodinma Iweala, *Beasts of No Nation* (New York: Harper Perennial, 2005); Delia Jarrett-Macauley, *Moses, Citizen and Me* (London: Granta, 2005); Emmanuel Dongala, *Johnny Mad Dog* (New York: Farrar, Straus and Giroux, 2005).

27. Other works of fiction contain episodes in which child soldiers appear. These include Chimamanda Ngozi Adichi, *Half of a Yellow Sun* (New York: Knopf, 2006); Helon Habila, *Measuring Time* (New York: Norton, 2007); and Ahmadou Kourouma, *Allah Is Not Obliged* (New York: Anchor, 2007).

28. Iweala, *Beasts*, 2, 8, 21, 47, 51.

29. Joseph Conrad, *Heart of Darkness* (1899; repr., Mineola, NY: Dover, 1990), 32.

30. Iweala, *Beasts*, 45.

31. Jarrett-Macauley, *Moses, Citizen and Me*, 36–37.

32. Ibid., 58–61.

33. Ibid., 208.

34. See David Rosen, *Armies of the Young: Child Soldiers in War and Terrorism* (New Brunswick, NJ: Rutgers University Press, 2005); Paul Richards, *Fighting for the Rain Forest* (Portsmouth, NH: Heinemann, 1996).

35. Dongala, *Johnny*, 64.

36. Patrick S. Gilmore, "When Johnny Comes Marching Home Again" (sheet music, 1863), U.S. Library of Congress, Patriotic Melodies, http://lcweb2.loc.gov/diglib/ ihas/loc.natlib.ihas.200000024/default.html.

37. George M. Cohan, "Over There" (sheet music, 1917), U.S. Library of Congress, Patriotic Music, http://lcweb2.loc.gov/diglib/ihas/loc.natlib.ihas.200000015/ default.html; Edward F. Cline, dir., *Private Buckaroo* (Universal City, CA: Universal Studios, 1942), DVD.

38. Dalton Trumbo, *Johnny Got His Gun* (New York, 2007).

39. Ibid., 145.

40. Ibid., 2.

41. Edward Zwick, *Blood Diamond* (Burbank, CA: Warner Brothers, 2006), DVD; Jean-Stéphane Sauvaire, *Johnny Mad Dog* (Paris: MNP Enterprise, 2008), DVD.

42. Ken Nguyen, *War Witch* (Montreal: Telefilm, 2012), DVD.

43. Emmanuel Jal, *War Child: A Child Soldier's Story* (New York: St. Martin's, 2009); Wole Soyinka, *Of Africa* (New Haven: Yale University Press, 2009), 87.

44. Jal, *War Child*, 183–184.

45. Ibid., 157–159.

46. John Keegan, *The Face of Battle* (New York: Barnes & Noble, 1976), 46–54.

47. Jal, *War Child*, 255.

48. Biyi Bandele, *Burma Boy* (London: Jonathan Cape, 2007).

49. Ken Saro-Wiwa, *Sozaboy* (New York: Longman, 1994).

50. Kourouma, *Allah Is Not Obliged*.

51. Catrina Martins, "The Dangers of the Single Story: Child-Soldiers in Literary Fiction and Film," *Childhood* 18, no. 4 (2011): 434–446.

52. Aminatta Forna, *The Memory of Love* (New York: Atlantic Monthly Press, 2010), 367.

53. Newton I. Aduaka, *Ezra* (Vienna: Amour Fou Filmproduktion, 2007), DVD.

54. Jeffrey Gettleman, "In Vast Jungle, U.S. Troops Aid in Search for Kony," *New York Times*, April 9, 2012, http://www.nytimes.com/2012/04/30/world/africa/kony -tracked-by-us-forces-in-central-africa.html?pagewanted=all.

55. Helene Cooper, "More U.S. Troops to Aid Uganda Search for Kony," *New York Times*, March 24, 2014, A7.

56. Helen Epstein, "Murder in Uganda," *New York Review of Books*, April 3, 2014.

57. Barak Obama, "Remarks at the 8th Annual Clinton Global Initiative Meeting," September 25, 2012, accessed March 5, 2014, http://www.c-span.org/video/ ?308392-2/president-obama-remarks-clinton-global-initiative.

58. U.S. President, Memorandum, "Presidential Determination with Respect to Section 4040(c) of the Child Soldier Prevention Act of 2008, No. 2011-4," *Federal Register* 74, no. 234 (October 25, 2010): 75855–63, http://www.gpo.gov/fdsys/ pkg/FR-2010-12-07/pdf/2010-30828.pdf; U.S. President, Proclamation, "National Alzheimer's Disease Awareness Month, 2013, Proclamation 9050," *Federal Register* 78, no. 214 (November 5, 2013): 66611, http://www.gpo.gov/fdsys/pkg/FR-2013 -11-05/pdf/2013-26670.pdf.

59. U.S. President, Memorandum, "Presidential Determination with Respect to the Child Soldiers Prevention Act of 2008" (White House, September 29, 2012), http:// www.whitehouse.gov/the-press-office/2012/09/28/presidential-memorandum -presidential-determination-respect-child-soldier.

60. U.S. President, Memorandum, "Presidential Determination–Child Soldiers" (White House, September 30, 2013), http://www.whitehouse.gov/the-press-office/ 2013/09/30/presidential-memorandum-determination-respect-child-soldiers -preventio-0.

61. U.S. President, Memorandum, "Determination with Respect to the Child Soldiers Prevention Act of 2008" (White House, September 30, 2014), http://www.humanrights.gov/2014/09/30/presidential-memorandum-determination-with-respect-to-the-child-soldiers-prevention-act-of-2008/.

62. Bernard Ashley, *Little Soldier* (New York: Scholastic Press, 2007).

63. Anne de Graaf, *Son of a Gun* (Grand Rapids, MI: Eerdmans, 2012), 91.

64. Robert Westall, *The Machine Gunners* (1975; repr., London: Pan Macmillan, 2001).

65. Michael Morpurgo, *War Horse* (New York: Scholastic Press, 2011).

66. Donna Jo Napoli, *Fire in the Hills* (New York: Penguin, 2006).

67. Curtis Parkinson, *Domenic's War* (Toronto: Tundra Books, 2006).

68. Carla Jablonski and Leland Purvis, *Resistance* (New York: First Second, 2010), 72–73.

69. Shirley Hughes, *Hero on a Bicycle* (Somerville, MA: Candlewick, 2013).

70. Mitali Perkins, *Bamboo People* (Watertown, MA: Charlesbridge, 2010).

71. Orson Scott Card, *Ender's Game* (New York: Tom Doherty Associates, 1991), xx.

72. *United States Marine Corps Commandant's Professional Reading List—All Hands* (Quantico, VA: Library of the Marine Corps, 2013), http://lgdata.s3-website-us-east-1.amazonaws.com/docs/2215/631428/Commandants-Professional-Reading-List-All-Hands.pdf.

73. John Kessel, "Creating the Innocent Killer: *Ender's Game*, Intentions, and Morality," *Foundation, the International Review of Science Fiction* 33, no. 90 (Spring 2004), http://tentoinfinity.com/2013/10/18/creating-the-innocent-killer-by-john-kessel/.

74. Card, *Ender's Game*, 309.

75. A. O. Scott and Manohla Dargis, "A Radical Female Hero from Dystopia," *New York Times*, April 4, 2012, http://www.nytimes.com/2012/04/08/movies/katniss-everdeen-a-new-type-of-woman-warrior.html?pagewanted=all&_r=0.

76. Susan Dominus, "Suzanne Collins's War Stories for Kids," *New York Times*, April 8, 2011, http://www.nytimes.com/2011/04/10/magazine/mag-10collins-t.html?pagewanted=all&_r=0.

77. Robert Baldick, *The Memoires of Chateaubriand* (New York: Knopf, 1961), 105.

78. François René de Chateaubriand, *Mémoires d'outre-tomb* (Paris, 1841, 1951), 430, cited in Yvorel, "De Delacroix."

CHAPTER 5   MODERN CHILD SOLDIERS

1. G. Scott and S. Reich, "Think Again: Child Soldiers: What Human Rights Activists Never Tell You about Young Killers," *Foreign Policy*, May 22, 2009, http://www.foreignpolicy.com/articles/2009/05/21/think_again_child_soldiers.

2. Child Soldiers International, *Child Soldiers Global Report 2001—Iran* (2001), http://www.refworld.org/docid/498805f02d.html.

3. Robert Tait, "Iran 'Using Child Soldiers' to Suppress Tehran Protests," *Guardian*, March 13, 2011, http://www.guardian.co.uk/world/2011/mar/13/iran-child-soldiers-tehran-protests.

4. Isma'il Kushkush, "In South Sudan, a Ghost of Wars Past: Child Soldiers," *New York Times*, June 7, 2014, http://www.nytimes.com/2014/06/08/world/africa/in -south-sudan-a-ghost-of-wars-past-child-soldiers.html.

5. "Children and Armed Conflict: Report of the Secretary General" (UN General Assembly, Security Council, A/68/878-S/2014/339, May 15, 2014), http://unispal .un.org/UNISPAL.NSF/0/AD785413FF8594C685257D090069FD10.

6. *"Who Will Care for Us": Grave Violations Against Children in Northeastern Nigeria* (New York: Watchlist on Children and Armed Conflict, 2014), http://watchlist .org/wordpress/wp-content/uploads/2111-Watchlist-Nigeria_LR.pdf.

7. Human Rights Watch, "'I Can Still Smell the Dead': The Forgotten Human Rights Crisis in the Central African Republic" (New York: Human Rights Watch, 2013), http://www.hrw.org/sites/default/files/reports/car0913_ForUpload.pdf.

8. Bertil Dunér, "Rebellion: The Ultimate Human Right?," *International Journal of Human Rights* 9 (2005): 264.

9. Doug Saunders, "Ill-Equipped Teenagers Members of the Libyan Anti-Gadhafi Rebels," *Globe and Mail*, June 10, 2012, http://www.theglobeandmail.com/news/world/ill -equipped-teenagers-members-of-the-libyan-anti-gadhafi-rebels/article2092964/.

10. "Naxal Problem Not an Armed Conflict, India Tells UN," *Times of India*, June 18, 2010, http://articles.timesofindia.indiatimes.com/2010-06-18/india/28276362 _1_conflict-with-humanitarian-consequences-children-and-armed-conflict -radhika-coomaraswamy.

11. "India's CRPF Urges New Intelligence Wing," *UPI*, May 19, 2008, http://www.upi .com/Top_News/Special/2008/05/19/Indias-CRPF-urges-new-intelligence-wing/ UPI-67201211222492/tab-listen.

12. "5,000 Hardcore Maoists with Armed Militia in Chhattisgarh," *Rediff News*, April 8, 2010, http://news.rediff.com/report/2010/apr/08/chhattisgarh-igp-on -the-naxalites.htm.

13. Ueli Zemp and Subash Mohapatra, "Child Soldiers in Chhattisgarh: Issues, Challenges and FFDAs Response," http://www.otherindia.org/dev/images/stories/ feda_child.pdf. This article is no longer available online, but a copy can be obtained from the author.

14. "India's Child Soldiers" (New Delhi: Asian Center for Human Rights, 2013), http://www.achrweb.org/reports/india/JJ-IndiasChildSoldiers2013.pdf.

15. Knut Dormann, "The Legal Situation of 'Unlawful/Unprivileged Combatants,'" *International Review of the Red Cross* 85 (2003): 45.

16. *Protocol Additional I to the Geneva Conventions of 12 August 1949, and Relating to the Protection of Victims of International Armed Conflicts*, June 8, 1977, 1125 U.N.T.S. 3, Article 77.

17. Astrid J. M. Delissen, "Legal Protection of Child-Combatants after the Protocols: Reaffirmation, Development, or a Step Backwards?," in *Humanitarian Law of Armed Conflict: Challenges Ahead*, ed. Astrid J. M. Delissen and Garard J. Tangje (Boston: Martinus Nihoff, 1991), 153.

18. *Commentary on the Additional Protocols of 8 June 1977 to the Geneva Conventions of August 12, 1949* (Geneva: Martinus Nijhoff, 1987), 901 §§ 3185–3186.

19. *Protocol Additional II to the Geneva Conventions of 12 August 1949, and Relating to the Victims of Non-international Armed Conflicts*, June 8, 1977, 1125 U.N.T.S. 609, Article 4.

20. *Additional Protocols Commentary*, 1380, § 4557.

21. Howard Mann, "International Law and the Child Soldier," *International and Comparative Law Quarterly* 36 (1987): 32–50.

22. *Rome Statute of the International Criminal Court*, 2187 U.N.T.S. 90 (July 17, 1998): Article 8.

23. *Prosecutor v. Thomas Lubanga Dyilo*, International Criminal Court, Case No. ICC-01/04-01/06-2, Warrant of Arrest (February 10, 2006).

24. *Prosecutor v. Germain Katanga*, International Criminal Court, Case No. ICC-01/04-01/07, Judgment (March 7, 2014).

25. Stephen J. Rapp, "The Compact Model in International Criminal Justice: The Special Court for Sierra Leone," *Drake Law Review* 57 (2008): 24.

26. *Prosecutor v. Taylor*, Special Court for Sierra Leone, Case No. SCSL-2003-01-I, Indictment (March 7, 2003).

27. *Statute of the Special Court for Sierra Leone*, 2178 U.N.T.S. 145 (January 16, 2002): Article 4(c) prohibits "conscripting or enlisting children under the age of 15 years into armed forces or groups or using them to participate actively in hostilities."

28. *Rome Statute*, Article 8(2)(e)(vii).

29. Rapp, "Compact Model," 14–15.

30. *Prosecutor v. Brima*, Special Court for Sierra Leone, Case No. SCSL-04-16-T (June 20, 2007), Judgment, 1276.

31. *Prosecutor v. Sesay*, Special Court for Sierra Leone, Case No. SCSL-04-15-T, Judgment, 186 (March 2, 2009).

32. *Prosecutor v. Fofana*, Special Court for Sierra Leone, Case No. SCSL-04-14-A, Judgment (May 28, 2008), 140

33. Myriam Denov, *Child Soldiers: Sierra Leone's Revolutionary United Front* (Cambridge: Cambridge University Press, 2012).

34. Ibid., 123.

35. David Brion Davis, *Inhuman Bondage: The Rise and Fall of Slavery in the New World* (New York: Oxford University Press, 2006), 31.

36. For an extended critical discussion of agency in the context of chattel slavery, see Walter Johnson, "On Agency," *Journal of Social History* 37, no. 1 (2003): 113–124.

37. Denov, *Child Soldiers*, 132.

38. Danny Hoffman, *The War Machines: Young Men and Violence in Sierra Leone and Liberia* (Durham, NC: Duke University Press, 2011).

39. Rapp, "Compact Model," 11–49.

40. *Prosecutor v. Brima, Special Court for Sierra Leone*, Case No. SCSL 04-16-T, Trial Court Judgment, June 20, 2007, ¶ 275.

41. *Prosecutor v. Sesay, Special Court for Sierra Leone*, Case No. SCSL 04-15-T, Trial Court Judgment, March 2, 2009, ¶¶ 1699–1701

42. Ibid., 1488, 1694, 1695, and 2156.

43. Hoffman, *War Machines*, 86.

44. *Convention on the Rights of the Child*, 1577 U.N.T.S. 3 (November 20, 1989), Article 1.

45. Angela Banks, "The Growing Impact of Non-state Actors on the International and European Legal System," *International Law FORUM du droit international* 5 (2003): 293–299.

46. Matthew Happold, "Child Soldiers: Victims or Perpetrators?," *University of La Verne Law Review* 29 (2008): 56–87.qw

47. *Optional Protocol to the Convention on the Rights of the Child on the Involvement of Children in Armed Conflict*, G.A. Res. 263, U.N. GAOR, 54th Sess., Annex 1, U.N. Doc. A/27531 (May 25, 2000).

48. Ibid., Article 1.

49. Ibid., Article 2.

50. Ibid., Article 3.

51. Ibid., Article 4. It provides that "armed groups, distinct from the armed forces of a State, should not, under any circumstances, recruit or use in hostilities persons under the age of 18 years."

52. African Charter on the Rights and Welfare of the Child, Organization of African Unity Doc. CAB/LEG/24.9/49 (November 29, 1999), Article 2.

53. Ibid., Article 22.

54. *Convention Concerning the Prohibition and Immediate Action for the Elimination of the Worst Forms of Child Labour*, ILO Convention No. 182 (June 17, 1999), Articles 1 and 3(a).

55. Geraldine Van Bueren, *International Law on the Rights of the Child* (Boston: Martinus Nijhoff, 1995), 15.

56. Heather Montgomery, *An Introduction to Childhood: Anthropological Perspectives on Children's Lives* (West Sussex, UK: Wiley-Blackwell, 2009), 14.

57. Ilene Cohn, "The Protection of Children and the Quest for Truth and Justice in Sierra Leone," *Journal of International Affairs* 55, no. 6 (2001): 1–34.

58. Ibid.

59. Ibid., 7.

60. UN Security Council Resolution 1315, U.N. Doc S/RES/1315 (August 14, 2000).

61. Ibid.

62. *Statute of the Special Court for Sierra Leone*, Article 7.

63. *Report of the Secretary General on the Establishment of a Special Court for Sierra Leone*, UN Doc S/2000/915 (October 4, 2000).

64. "UN Says Sierra Leone War Crimes Court Should Be Able to Try Children," Agence France-Presse, October 5, 2000, http://www.globalpolicy.org/security/issues/sierra/court/001005af.htm.

65. A notable exception to this was Amnesty International. Cohn, "Protection of Children," 16

66. An example of the types of atrocities committed by children during the war is found in the recent and uncontested testimony of Alex Teh at the trial of former Liberian president Charles Taylor before the Special Court for Sierra

Leone. Teh describes the gruesome murder of a young boy by other children, members of the so-called Small Boys Unit (SBU) of the rebel forces of the Revolutionary United Front: "I saw some other SBU boys coming closer to me with another small boy and the boy was crying, screaming, he was screaming. He asked them, 'What have I done In the Labyrinth of Memory Cultural Representations abo?' They didn't say anything to him, but the boy was screaming. At first they had to put his right arm on a log. They took a machete and amputated it at the wrist. The boy was screaming and they took the left arm again and put it on the same log and sliced it off. He was still screaming and shouting. They took the left leg and put it on the same log and cut it off at the ankle. At last they took the right leg again and put it on the same log and cut it off with a machete. Some held him by his hand at that time now and I am speaking about the same SBU boys. They are the same people doing this. Some held his other hand, legs. They were swinging the boy. They threw him over into a toilet pit. I was there, I saw it myself." *Prosecutor v. Taylor*, Special Court for Sierra Leone, Case No. SCSL 2003-01, Transcript of Record at 699–700, January 8, 2008.

67. Cohn, "Protection of Children," 7.
68. *Convention on the Rights of the Child*, Article 38.
69. Cohn, "Protection of Children," 6.
70. For an example of the reflexive dismissal of local norms of justice, see Chen Reis, "Trying the Future, Avenging the Past: The Implications of Prosecuting Children for Participation in Internal Armed Conflict," *Columbia Human Rights Law Review* 28 (1996–1997): 625–656.
71. Many of the claims made by NGOs seem in retrospect to have been quite fanciful. For example, it was asserted that "the prosecution of children would run counter to Sierra Leone's cultural values of healing and forgiveness" and "local communities would doubt the legitimacy and effectiveness of a Special Court that disregarded the traditional shared vision of the child as a vital channel of peace and reconciliation." Cohn, "Protection of Children," 11.
72. See Richard Wilson, "Children and War in Sierra Leone: A West African Diary," *Anthropology Today* 17, no. 5 (2001): 21–22.
73. Ibid.
74. "UN Says Sierra Leone War Crimes Court Should Be Able to Try Children."
75. *Report of the Secretary General on the Establishment of a Special Court for Sierra Leone*, 7.
76. Ibid., 5–6.
77. Ibid., 6
78. *Special Court Statute*, Article 1.
79. Special Court for Sierra Leone, "Special Court Prosecutor Says He Will Not Prosecute Children," *IRIN*, November 2, 2002, http://www.essex.ac.uk/armedcon/story_id/000024.html.
80. UN Transitional Administration in East Timor, *On Establishment of Panels with Exclusive Jurisdiction over Serious Criminal Offenses*, Regulation 2000/1,

June 6, 2000, http://www.jornal.gov.tl/lawsTL/UNTAET-Law/Regulations%20English/Reg2000-15.pdf.

81. UN Transitional Administration in East Timor, *Transitional Rules of Criminal Procedure*, Regulation 2000/30, September 25, 2000, http://www.un.org/en/peacekeeping/missions/past/etimor/untaetR/Reg10e.pdf.

82. Ibid., Article 45 (4).

83. For the details of this case, see *Prosecutor v. X.*, Amended Indictment, Case No. 04/2002, October 23, 2002, and *Prosecutor v. X.*, Judgment, Case No. 04/2002, February 12, 2002, War Crimes Study Center, University of California, Berkeley, Special Panels for Serious Crimes Documents, accessed October 13, 2014, http://wcsc.berkeley.edu/east-timor/east-timor-2/. See also *The Case of X: A Child Prosecuted for Crimes Against Humanity* (Dili, East Timor: Judicial System Monitoring Program, 2005), accessed October 13, 2014, http://www.essex.ac.uk/armedcon/story_id/000386.pdf.

84. United Nations, "Timor-Leste Court Sentences Juvenile for Killings after UN-Run Ballot in 1999," December 3, 2002, http://www.un.org/apps/news/story.asp?NewsID=5524&Cr=timor&Cr1.

85. "Uganda: Human Rights Watch Urges Government to Drop Treason Charges Against Child Abductees," Human Rights Watch, March 4, 2003, http://www.hrea.org/lists/child-rights/markup/msg00173.html.

86. Ibid.

87. Ibid.

88. Matthew Happold, "The Age of Criminal Responsibility for International Crimes Under International Criminal Law," in *International Criminal Accountability and the Rights of Children*, ed. Karin Arts and Vesselin Popovski (The Hague: Hague Academic Press, 2006).

89. "Letter to Ugandan Minister of Justice Regarding Abducted Child," Human Rights Watch, January 6, 2009, http://www.hrw.org/en/news/2009/01/06/letter-ugandan-minister-justice-regarding-abducted-child.

90. Ibid.

91. "Democratic Republic of Congo: Massive Violations Kill Human Decency," Amnesty International, May 31, 2000, http://www.amnesty.org/en/library/asset/AFR62/011/2000/en/f9c8bebf-748a-4c0c-9a37-3ca3a3dad950/afr620112000en.pdf.

92. "Congo: Don't Execute Child Soldiers: Four Children to Be Put to Death," Human Rights Watch, May 2, 2001, http://www.hrw.org/en/news/2001/05/02/congo-dont-execute-child-soldiers.

93. Ibid.

94. "More Youth at Guantánamo Than U.S. Claimed," University of California-Davis, News and Information Center, June 7, 2011, http://www.news.ucdavis.edu/search/news_detail.lasso?id=9918; "The Pentagon Can't Count: 22 Juveniles Held at Guantánamo," Andy Worthington, November 22, 2008, http://www.andyworthington.co.uk/2008/11/22/the-pentagon-cant-count-22-juveniles-held-at-guantanamo.

95. United Nations, Committee on the Rights of the Child, *Written Replies by the Government of the United States of America concerning the List of Issues re the Optional Protocol*, June 2, 2008, http://www2.0hchr.org/english/bodies/crc/docs/AdvanceVersions/CRC.C.OPAC.USA.Q.1.Add.1.Rev.1.pdf.

96. United Nations, Committee on the Rights of the Child, *Periodic Report of the United States*, January 22, 2010, http://www.state.gov/documents/organization/135988.pdf.

97. U.S. President, Presidential Order, "Detention, Treatment, and Trial of Certain Non-citizens in the War Against Terrorism," Military Order, *Federal Register* 66 (November 16, 2001): 57833–36, http://federalregister.gov/a/01-28904.

98. Ibid.

99. U.S. President, Memorandum, "Human Treatment of al Qaeda and Taliban Detainees," Memorandum, February 7, 2002, http://www.pegc.us/archive/White_House/bush_memo_20020207_ed.pdf.

100. Ibid.

101. Douglas Jehl, "Army Details Scale of Abuse of Prisoners in an Afghan Jail," *New York Times*, March 12, 2005, http://www.nytimes.com/2005/03/12/politics/12detain.html.

102. *Inquiry into the Treatment of Detainees in US Custody* (Washington, DC: U.S. Senate Committee on Armed Services, 2008), http://www.armed-services.senate.gov/imo/media/doc/Detainee-Report-Final_April-22-2009.pdf.

103. *Review of Department of Defense Detention Operations and Detainee Interrogation Techniques (Church Report)* (Washington, DC: U.S. Department of Defense, 2005), http://www.cfr.org/publication/11092/church_report.html.

104. Ibid., 88–89.

105. *A Review of the FBI's Involvement in and Observations of Detainee Interrogations in Guantanamo Bay, Afghanistan, and Iraq* (Washington, DC: U.S. Department of Justice, 2008), 175, http://www.justice.gov/oig/special/s0805/final.pdf.

106. Ibid., 174.

107. Details of the detention and abuse of Mohamed Jawad are drawn from the "Amended Petition for Writ of Habeas Corpus on Behalf of Mohammed Jawad," *In Re Guantanamo Detainee Litigation*, Misc. No. 08-442 (TFH), U.S. Court for the District of Columbia, January 13, 2009, https://www.aclu.org/files/pdfs/natsec/amended_jawad_20090113.pdf.

108. David R. Frakt, "Closing Argument at Guantanamo: The Torture of Mohammed Jawad," *Harvard Human Rights Journal* 22 (2009): 417.

109. Anthony Lewis, "Official American Sadism," *New York Review of Books* 55, no. 14 (2008), http://www.nybooks.com/articles/archives/2008/sep/25/official-american-sadism.

110. *United States v. Mohammad Jawad*, Ruling on Defense Motion to Suppress Out of Court Statements of the Accused to Afghan Authorities, October 28, 2008, http://www.defense.gov/news/d20081104jawadd022suppress.pdf.

111. *United States v. Mohammad Jawad*, Ruling on Defense Motion to Suppress Out of Court Statements Made by the Accused while in U.S. Custody, November 19, 2008, http://www.defense.gov/news/d20081223Jawadexhibitsa-h.pdf.

112. *Baca v. Obama*, Transcript of Hearing before the Honorable Ellen Segal Huvelle, U.S. District Court Judge, Civil Case No. 05-2385, July 16, 2009, http://www.aclu .org/pdfs/safefree/jawad_transcriptofhearing.pdf.

113. *Baca v. Obama*, Order Granting Petition of Habeas Corpus, Civil Case No. 05-2385, July 30, 2009, https://www.aclu.org/files/pdfs/safefree/sakibachavobama _order.pdf.

114. Michael Paterniti, "The Boy from Gitmo," *GQ*, February 2011, http://www.gq .com/news-politics/newsmakers/201102/boy-from-guantanamo.

115. "Khadr Patriarch Disliked Canada, Says al-Qaeda Biography," *CBC News*, February 7, 2008, http://www.cbc.ca/world/story/2008/02/07/khadr-bio.html.

116. *United States v. Omar Ahmed Khadr*, Supplemental Defense Motion, March 8, 2010, http://www.defense.gov/news/Khadr_D-094.pdf.

117. Carol Rosenberg, "Interrogator Says Khadr Was Told He'd Likely Be Raped in U.S.," *Miami Herald*, May 6, 2010, http://www.miamiherald.com/2010/05/06/ 1616825/interrogator-says-he-told-detainee.html and http://www.mcclatchydc .com/2010/05/06/93670/interrogator-says-khadr-was-told.html. See also Amy Davidson, "How to Scare a Child Soldier," *New Yorker*, Close Read (Blog), May 6, 2010, http://www.newyorker.com/online/blogs/closeread/2010/05/how-to-scare -a-child-soldier.html.

118. Carol Rosenberg, "Medic: I Saw Omar Khadr Shackled as Punishment," *Miami Herald*, May 3, 2010, http://www.mcclatchydc.com/2010/05/03/93346/medic -found-canadian-detainee.html.

119. *United States v. Omar Ahmed Khadr*, Ruling on Defense Suppression Motion, August 17, 2010, http://www.defense.gov/news/D94-D111.pdf.

120. "Letter from Radhika Coomaraswamy, the Special Representative of the Secretary General for Children in Armed Conflict to the Members of the Military Commissions," October 27, 2010, http://www.cbc.ca/news/pdf/omar-khadr -letter.pdf.

121. *Khadr v. the Prime Minister of Canada*, Case No. 2009 FC 405, Reasons for Judgment and Judgment, April 23, 2009, http://library.law.utoronto.ca/documents/ Mackin/Repat_Khadr_v_Canada_PM_FedTD.htm.

122. *United States v. Omar Ahmed Khadr*, "Offer for Pretrial Agreement," October 13, 2010, http://www.defense.gov/news/Khadr%20Convening%20Authority %20Pretrial%20Agreement%20AE%20341%2013%200ct%202010%20%28redacted %29.pdf.

123. *United States v. Omar Ahmed Khadr*, "Stipulation of Fact," October 13, 2010, http:// media.miamiherald.com/smedia/2010/10/26/19/stip2.source.prod_affiliate.56 .pdf.

124. Carol Rosenberg, "Despite 40-Year Sentence, Khadr Likely to Go Home in a Year," *Miami Herald*, October 31, 2010, http://www.mcclatchydc.com/2010/10/31/ 102932/jury-sentences-child-soldier-to.html.

125. Michelle Shepard, "Omar Khadr: No Memory of Firefight in Afghanistan," *Toronto Star*, December 13, 2013, http://www.thestar.com/news/canada/2013/12/13/omar_khadr_no_memory_of_firefight_in_afghanistan.html.

126. David Kilcullen, *Out of the Mountains: The Coming Age of the Urban Guerilla* (New York: Oxford University Press, 2013), 97.

CHAPTER 6 THE POLITICS AND CULTURE OF CHILDHOOD VULNERABILITY

1. For a broader discussion of the issues related to the North-South divide, see Lorraine Macmillan, "The Child Soldier in North-South Relations," *International Political Sociology* 3 (2009): 36–52.

2. Sally Merry, "Human Rights Law and the Demonization of Culture (and Anthropology along the Way)," *PoLAR: Political and Legal Anthropology Review* 26, no. 1 (1999): 55–77.

3. Most "child soldiers" are adolescents who are legally defined as children.

4. Myra Bluebond-Langner, *The Private Worlds of Dying Children* (Princeton, NJ: Princeton University Press, 1978).

5. Allison James and Adrian James, *Key Concepts in Childhood Studies* (London: Sage, 2012), 9.

6. Mark Drumble, *Reimagining Child Soldiers in International Law and Policy* (New York: Oxford University Press, 2012).

7. See, for example, Chris Coulter, *Bush Wives and Girl Soldiers* (Ithaca, NY: Cornell University Press, 2008); Denov, *Child Soldiers*; Alcinda Honwana, *Child Soldiers in Africa* (Philadelphia: University of Pennsylvania Press, 2006); Hoffman, *War Machines*; Luca Jourdan, "Mayi-Mayi: Young Rebels in Kivu, DRC," *Africa Development* 36, nos. 3–4 (2011): 89–111; Mats Utas, "Victimcy, Girlfriending, Soldiering: Tactic Agency in a Young Woman's Social Navigation of the Liberian War Zone," *Anthropological Quarterly* 78 (2005): 403–430; Henrik Vigh, *Navigating Terrains of War: Youth and Soldiering in Guinea-Bissau* (New York: Berghahn, 2000).

8. My discussion of the discourse of innocence and blameworthiness regarding child soldiers has benefitted from several conversations with Susan Rosenbloom, associate professor of sociology at Drew University, who has worked extensively with minority youth.

9. *Adult Wars, Child Soldiers* (New York: UNICEF, 2000).

10. Youth Advocate Program International, "Children Affected by Armed Conflict," accessed October 14, 2014, http://yapi.org/youth-wellbeing/children-affected-by-armed-conflict-child-soldiers/.

11. *Trafficking in Persons Report* (Washington, DC: U.S. Department of State, 2004). http://www.state.gov/g/tip/rls/tiprpt/2004/34021.htm; and "Campaign Against Torture," Amnesty International, October 18, 2000, http://www.amnesty.org/en/library/asset/ACT40/016/2000/en/51e8fe04-d0d2-4dc8-96a5-06d8253746ff/act400162000en.pdf.

12. Robert Kaplan, "The Coming Anarchy: How Scarcity, Crime, Overpopulation, and Disease Are Rapidly Destroying the Social Fabric of Our Planet," *Atlantic*

Monthly, February 1, 1994, http://www.theatlantic.com/magazine/archive/1994/02/the-coming-anarchy/304670/.

13. *Convention concerning the Prohibition and Immediate Action for the Elimination of the Worst Forms of Child Labour*, ILO Convention No. 182, adopted by the ILO General Conference, Geneva, June 17, 1999, Articles 1 and 3(a).

14. "Somalia: Warring Parties Put Children at Grave Risk," Human Rights Watch Press Release, February 21, 2012, http://www.hrw.org/fr/node/105208.

15. Michelle Faul, "Traumatized Child Soldiers Return Home in Congo," *AP News*, March 7, 2009, http://www.newsvine.com/_news/2009/03/07/2517439-traumatized-child-soldiers-return-home-in-congo.

16. Alcinda Honwana, *Okusiakala ondalo yokalye: Let Us Light a New Fire: Local Knowledge in the Post-war Healing and Reintegration of War-Affected Children in Angola* (Luanda, Angola: Christian Children's Fund, 1998), 21.

17. Dahr Jamail, "A Morally Bankrupt Military: When Soldiers and Their Families Become Expendable," *Truthout*, November 11, 2009, http://www.truth-out.org/1111097.

18. Kalsoon Lakhani, "Pakistan's Child Soldiers," *Foreign Policy*, March 29, 2010, http://afpak.foreignpolicy.com/posts/2010/03/29/pakistans_child_soldiers.

19. Robert Sparrow, "Killer Robots," *Journal of Applied Philosophy* 24 (2007): 62–77.

20. Christopher Blattman, "Making Reintegration Work for Youth in Northern Uganda," Survey of War Affected Youth, November 2007, http://chrisblattman.com/documents/policy/sway/SWAY.ResearchBrief.Reintegration.pdf.

21. Michael Wessels, *Child Soldiers: From Violence to Protection* (Cambridge, MA: Harvard University Press, 2006).

22. See Sarah Steinbock-Pratt, "The Lions in the Jungle: Representations of Africa and Africans in American Cinema," in *Africans and the Politics of Popular Culture*, ed. Toyin Falola and Augustine Agwuele (Rochester, NY: University of Rochester Press, 2009), 214–236, 223.

23. Kaplan, "Coming Anarchy," 14–76; Richards, *Fighting for the Rain Forest*.

24. Carl von Clausewitz, *On War* (Princeton, NJ: Princeton University Press, 1989).

25. Mary Kaldor, *New and Old Wars: Organized Violence in a Global Era* (Cambridge: Polity Press, 1989).

26. Paul Colliers and Anke Hoeffler, "Greed and Grievance in Civil War," *Oxford Economic Papers* 56, no. 4 (2004): 563–595; Paul Collier and Nicholas Sambanis, eds., *Understanding Civil War: Evidence and Analysis*, vol. 1—*Africa* (Washington, DC: World Bank, 2005).

27. See Peter Singer, *Children at War* (Berkeley: University of California Press, 2006) for the view that war was once governed by a code of knightly chivalry that precluded the harming of women and children. For a far more empirical assessment of the behavior of knights, in which their pillaging, looting, and murder, especially of the poor, made them widely feared warlords and sources of uncontrolled violence, see Richard W. Kaeuper, *Chivalry and Violence in Medieval Europe* (Oxford: Oxford University Press, 2001).

28. Peter Maguire, *Law and War: An American Story* (New York: Columbia University Press, 2000), 7.

29. Paul Kramer, *The Blood of Government: Race, Empire, the United States, and the Philippines* (Chapel Hill: University of North Carolina Press, 2006). Testimony before Congress with respect to widespread cruelty including the killing of civilians, the use of dum-dum bullets, water boarding (then called the water cure), and the killing of prisoners was widely covered in the media. See, for example, "Cruelty in the Philippines," *New York Times*, May 20, 1902, 3.

30. Robert Edgerton, *Mau Mau: An African Crucible* (New York: Free Press, 1989); Caroline Elkins, *Imperial Reckoning: The Untold Story of Britain's Gulag in Kenya* (New York: Henry Holt, 2005).

31. Harry G. West, "Girls with Guns: Narrating the Experience of War of FRELIMO's 'Female Detachment,'" *Anthropological Quarterly* 73, no. 4 (2000): 180–194.

32. Victoria Bernal, "Equality to Die For? Women Guerilla Fighters and Eritrea's Cultural Revolution," *PoLAR: Political and Legal Anthropology Review* 28, no. 2 (2000): 61–76.

33. Angela Veale, *From Child Soldier to Ex-Fighter* (Pretoria, South Africa: Institute for Security Studies, 2003), 25–26.

34. Ibid., 64–65.

35. Conrad, *Heart of Darkness*.

36. Caryl Phillips, "Out of Africa," *Guardian*, February 22, 2003, http://www.theguardian.com/books/2003/feb/22/classics.chinuaachebe.

37. Reid, *War in Pre-colonial Eastern Africa*, 2–21.

38. Thomas G. Weiss, "Principles, Politics, and Humanitarian Action," *Ethics and International Affairs* 13, no. 1 (1999): 1–22.

39. Human Rights Watch, "Financial Statements Year Ended June 30, 2013," http://www.hrw.org/sites/default/files/related_material/financial-statements-2013.pdf.

40. Amnesty International of the USA, Inc., "Financial Statements, Year Ending December 31, 2012," http://www.amnestyusa.org/pdfs/aiusa2013-fs.pdf.

41. Amnesty International Limited, "Report and Financial Statements for the Period 1 January 2012 to 31 December 2012," http://www.amnesty.org/en/who-we-are/accountability/financial-reports.

42. Anna Freud and Dorothy Burlingame, *War and Children* (New York: Medical War Books, 1943).

43. I am deeply indebted to my friend and colleague Alex Weingrod for reminding me of the central role humility has played in much of anthropological analysis. Ever since Bronislaw Malinowski set forth as one of the central tasks of anthropology the understanding the native's point of view we have recognized that this is hardly a simple endeavor, whether the "native" is a Trobriand chief or the commander of the armed forces of a modern state.

SELECTED BIBLIOGRAPHY

Abani, Chris. *Song for Night: A Novella.* New York: Akashic Books, 2007.

Adichi, Chimamanda Ngozi. *Half of a Yellow Sun.* New York: Knopf, 2006.

Aduaka, Newtown I. *Ezra.* DVD. Vienna: Amour Fou Filmproduktion, 2007.

Adult Wars, Child Soldiers. New York: UNICEF, 2000.

Amis, Martin. *Koba the Dread: Laughter and the Twenty Million.* New York: Vintage, 2003.

Anderson, Benedict. *Imagined Communities: Reflections on the Origins and Spread of Nationalism.* London: Verso, 1991.

Ansell, S. T. "Legal and Historical Aspects of the Militia." *Yale Law Journal* 26 (1917): 471–479.

ANZAC. "Boy Soldiers." http://www.anzacs.net/BoySoldiers.htm.

Archard, David William. "Children's Rights." In *The Stanford Encyclopedia of Philosophy (Winter 2010 Edition)*, edited by Edward N. Zalta. http://plato.stanford.edu/archives/win2010/entries/rights-children.

Army and Navy Chronicle. Vol. 1. Washington, DC: B. Homans, 1835.

Arthur, Max. *Forgotten Voices of the Great War.* London: Lyons Press, 2004.

Ashley, Berhard. *Little Soldier.* New York: Scholastic Press, 2007.

Baldick, Robert. *The Memoires of Chateaubriand.* New York: Knopf, 1961.

Bandele, Biyi. *Burma Boy.* London: Jonathan Cape, 2007.

Banks, Angela. "The Growing Impact of Non-state Actors on the International and European Legal System." *International Law FORUM du droit international* 5 (2003): 293–299.

Beah, Ishmael. *A Long Way Gone: Memoirs of a Boy Soldier.* New York: Farrar, Straus and Giroux, 2007.

Beever, Anthony. *The Fall of Berlin 1945.* New York: Penguin, 2002.

Bergström, Christer, Andrey Dikov, and Vladimir Antipov. *Black Cross Red Star: Air War over the Eastern Front: Everything for Stalingrad.* Vol. 3. Hamilton, MT: Eagle Editions, 2006.

Bernal, Victoria. "Equality to Die For? Women Guerilla Fighters and Eritrea's Cultural Revolution." *PoLAR: Political and Legal Anthropology Review* 28, no. 2 (2000): 61–76.

Berwanger, Eugene H. *The British Foreign Office and the American Civil War.* Lexington: University Press of Kentucky, 1994.

Bevan, Tom. *Doing His "Bit": A Story of the Great War.* London: Thomas Nelson, 1917.

Biddescomb, Alexander Perry. *Werewolf: The History of the National Socialist Guerilla Movement, 1944–1946*. Toronto: University of Toronto Press, 1998.

Blackstone, William. *Commentaries of the Laws of England*. Vol. I. Philadelphia: Robert Bell, 1771.

Blattman, Christopher. "Making Reintegration Work for Youth in Northern Uganda." Survey of War Affected Youth, November 2007. http://chrisblattman.com/documents/policy/sway/SWAY.ResearchBrief.Reintegration.pdf.

Bluebond-Langner, Myra. *The Private Worlds of Dying Children*. Princeton, NJ: Princeton University Press, 1978.

Bowman, Travis. *Hercules of the Revolution*. Davidson, NC: Bequest, 2009.

Brogi, Paolo. "Il ponte sull'Aniene intitolato a Ugo Forno, eroe dodicenne del 1944." *Corriere della Sera*, June 10, 2010. http://roma.corriere.it/roma/notizie/cronaca/10_giugno_5/ponte-intitolato-go-forni-brogi-1703146566178.shtml.

Buell, Augustus C. *A History of Andrew Jackson*. Vol. I. New York: Charles Scribner's Sons, 1904.

Burrows, Edwin G. *Forgotten Patriots: The Untold Story of American Prisoners during the Revolutionary War*. New York: Basic Books, 2008.

Card, Orson Scott. *Ender's Game*. New York: Tom Doherty Associates, 1991.

Castlemon, Harry. *Frank on a Gun Boat*. Philadelphia: Porter & Coates, 1864.

"Children and Armed Conflict: Report of the Secretary General." UN General Assembly, Security Council, A/68/878-S/2014/339, May 15, 2014. http://unispal.un.org/UNISPAL.NSF/0/AD785413FF8594C685257D090069FD10.

Child Soldiers International. "Child Soldiers Global Report 2001—Iran. 2001." http://www.refworld.org/docid/498805f02d.html.

Clausewitz, Carl von. *On War*. Princeton, NJ: Princeton University Press, 1989.

Clem, John Lincoln. "From Nursery to Battlefield." *Outlook*, July 4, 1914, 546–547.

Cohn, Ilene. "The Protection of Children and the Quest for Truth and Justice in Sierra Leone." *Journal of International Affairs* 55, no. 6 (2001): 1–34.

Colliers, Paul, and Anke Hoeffler. "Greed and Grievance in Civil War." *Oxford Economic Papers* 56, no. 4 (2004): 563–595.

Collier, Paul, and Nicholas Sambanis, eds. *Understanding Civil War: Evidence and Analysis*. Vol. I—*Africa*. Washington, DC: World Bank, 2005.

Comber, Chris. "Worthing War Memorial Roll of Honor." 2006. http://www.roll-of-honour.com/Sussex/WorthingST.html.

Committee on Armed Services. *Inquiry into the Treatment of Detainees in US Custody*. Washington, DC: U.S. Senate, 2008. http://www.armed-services.senate.gov/imo/media/doc/Detainee-Report-Final_April-22–2009.pdf.

Conley, Mary A. *From Jack Tar to Union Jack: Representing Naval Manhood in the British Empire, 1870–1918*. Manchester: Manchester University Press, 2009.

Conrad, Joseph. *Heart of Darkness*. 1899. Reprint, Mineola, NY: Dover, 1990.

Coontz, Stephanie. *Marriage, a History: How Love Conquered Marriage*. New York: Penguin, 2006.

———. *The Way We Never Were: American Families and the Nostalgia Trap*. New York: Basic Book, 1992.

Cooper, Matthew. *The Phantom War: The German Struggle Against Soviet Partisans 1941–1944.* London: McDonald and James, 1979.

Coppard, George. *With a Machine Gun to Cambrai.* London: HMSO, 1969.

Coulter, Chris. *Bush Wives and Girl Soldiers.* Ithaca, NY: Cornell University Press, 2008.

Cox, Caroline. "Boy Soldiers of the American Revolution: The Effects of War on Society." In *Children and Youth in a New Nation*, edited by James Marten, 13–28. New York: New York University Press, 2009.

Crozier, Frank. *The Men I Killed.* London: Michael Joseph, 1937.

Cutler, Frederick Morse. *The History of Military Conscription with Special Reference to the United States.* Worcester, MA: Clark University, 1922.

———. "Military Conscription, Especially in the United States." *Historical Outlook* 14, no. 5 (May 1923): 170–175.

Dandridge, Danske. *American Prisoners of the Revolution.* Charlottesville, VA: Michie Company, 1910.

Davis, David Brion. *Inhuman Bondage: The Rise and Fall of Slavery in the New World.* New York: Oxford University Press, 2006.

Dawidowicz, Lucy S. *The War Against the Jews 1933–1945.* New York: Holt, Rinehart and Winston, 1975.

de Graaf, Anne. *Son of a Gun.* Grand Rapids, MI: Eerdmans, 2012.

Demos, John. *A Little Commonwealth: Family Life in Plymouth Colony.* Oxford: Oxford University Press, 1999.

Denov, Myriam. *Child Soldiers: Sierra Leone's Revolutionary United Front.* Cambridge: Cambridge University Press, 2012.

De Simone, Cesare. *Roma, città prigioniera: i 271 giorni dell'occupazione nazista: 8 settembre '43—4 giugno '44.* Milan: Mursia, 1994.

Dolgin, Janet. "Transforming Childhood: Apprenticeship in American Law." *New England Law Review* 31 (1997): 1113–1191.

Domski, R. "The Aims of Jewish Youth, 1940." Archive Ref JM/215/1. Jerusalem: Yad Vashem, the Holocaust Martyr's and Heroes Authority. http://www.yadvashem.org/odot_pdf/Microsoft%20Word%20-%20599.pdf.

Dongala, Emmanuel. *Johnny Mad Dog.* New York: Farrar, Straus and Giroux, 2005.

Dormann, Knut. "The Legal Situation of 'Unlawful/Unprivileged Combatants.'" *International Review of the Red Cross* 85 (2003): 45–74.

Drumble, Mark. *Reimagining Child Soldiers in International Law and Policy.* New York: Oxford University Press, 2012.

Dunér, Bertil. "Rebellion: The Ultimate Human Right?" *International Journal of Human Rights* 9 (2005): 247–269.

Edgerton, Robert. *Mau Mau: An African Crucible.* New York: Free Press, 1989.

Elkins, Caroline. *Imperial Reckoning: The Untold Story of Britain's Gulag in Kenya.* New York: Henry Holt, 2005.

Evans, Susan. *Mothers of Heroes, Mothers of Martyrs: World War I and the Politics of Grief.* Montreal: McGill-Queens University Press, 2007.

Evans, William. "Peter Francisco: The American Soldier," *William and Mary Quarterly* 13, no. 4 (1905): 213–216.

Fast, Howard. *The Incredible Tito: Man of the Hour.* New York: Lev Gleason, 1944.

Faust, Drew Gilpin. *This Republic of Suffering: Death and the American Civil War.* New York: Vintage, 2008.

Forbes, Edna. *Johnny Tremain.* 1943. Reprint, New York: Dell, 1980.

Ford, Henry Allen. *Poems of History.* New York: William Shepard, 1883.

Forna, Aminatta. *The Memory of Love.* New York: Atlantic Monthly Press, 2010.

Fortescue, J. W. *A History of the British Army.* Vol. 1. London: Macmillan, 1899.

Frakt, David R. "Closing Argument at Guantanamo: The Torture of Mohammed Jawad." *Harvard Human Rights Journal* 22 (2009): 401–423.

Freeman, Dale. *Oliver Optic 1822–1897, Children's Author.* Boston: University of Massachusetts Joseph P. Healey Library Publications, 2004. http://scholarworks.umb .edu/cgi/viewcontent.cgi?article=1010&context=hlpubs.

Freud, Anna, and Dorothy Burlingame. *War and Children.* New York: Medical War Books, 1943.

Friedman, Lawrence. *The History of American Law.* 3rd ed. New York: Touchstone, 2005.

Gilbert, Ed. *Frontier Militiaman in the War of 1812: Southwestern Frontier.* Oxford: Osprey, 2008.

Goldhagen, Daniel Jonah. *Hitler's Willing Executioners: Ordinary Germans and the Holocaust.* New York: Vintage, 1997.

Goldensohn, Lorrie, ed. *American War Poetry: An Anthology.* New York: Columbia University Press, 2006.

Goldman, Jasper. "Warsaw: Reconstruction as Propaganda." In *The Resilient City: How Modern Cities Recover from Disaster,* edited by Lawrence J. Vale and Thomas J. Camanella, 135–138. New York: Oxford University Press. 2005.

Gouge, William. *Of Domestical Duties.* 1622. Reprint, Pensacola, FL: Chapel Library, 2006.

Gould, Benjamin. *Investigations in the Military and Anthropological Statistics of American Soldiers.* New York: Hurd and Houghton, 1869.

Green, Albert G., ed. *Recollections of the Jersey Prison Ship.* New York: P. M. Davis, 1831.

Grinspan, John. "The Wild Children of Yesteryear." *New York Times,* May 31, 2014.

Grossman, Chaika. *The Underground Army.* 1965. Translated by Shmuel Berri. New York: Holocaust Library, 1987.

Gullace, Nicoletta. *The Blood of Our Sons.* London: Palgrave Macmillan, 2002.

——. "White Feathers and Wounded Men: Female Patriotism and the Memory of the Great War." *Journal of British Studies* 36, no. 2 (April 1997): 178–206.

Gutman, Israel. *Resistance: The Warsaw Ghetto Uprising.* New York: Houghton Mifflin, 1994.

——. "Youth Movements." In *Encyclopedia of the Holocaust,* edited by Israel Gutman, 1697–1703. New York: Macmillan, 1990.

Habila, Helon. *Measuring Time.* New York: Norton, 2007.

Hacker, David J. "Recounting the Dead." *New York Times, Opinionator* (blog), September 20, 2011. http://opinionator.blogs.nytimes.com/2011/09/20/recounting-the -dead/#more-105317.

Hackman, Jorge, and Marko Leht. "The Myth of Victimhood and the Cult of Authenticity: Sacralizing the Nation in Estonia and Poland." In *Rethinking the Space for Religion: New Actors in Central and Southeast Europe on Religion, Authenticity and Belonging*, edited by Catherina Raudvere, Kryzstof Stala, and Trine Stauning Willert, 126–162. Lund, Sweden: Nordic Academic Press, 2013.

Haltof, Marek. *Polish Film and the Holocaust: Politics and Memory.* New York: Berghahn, 2012.

Happold, Matthew. "The Age of Criminal Responsibility for International Crimes under International Criminal Law." In *International Criminal Accountability and the Rights of Children*, edited by Karin Arts and Vesselin Popovski, 69–84. The Hague: Hague Academic Press, 2006.

———. "Child Soldiers: Victims or Perpetrators?" *University of La Verne Law Review* 29 (2008): 56–87.

Harris, Adrienne M. "The Lives and Deaths of a Soviet Saint in the Post-Soviet Period: The Case of Zoia Kosmodem'ianskaia." *Canadian Slavonic Papers* 53, nos. 2–4 (2011): 273–304.

———. "Memorializations of a Martyr and Her Mutilated Bodies: Public Monuments to Soviet War Hero Zoya Kosmodemyanskaya, 1942 to the Present." *Journal of War and Culture Studies* 5, no. 1 (2012): 73–90.

Haste, Cate. *Keep the Home Fires Burning: Propaganda in the First World War.* London: Allen Lane, 1977.

Hertz, Robert. *Death and the Right Hand.* Translated by Rodney Needham and Claudia Needham. Glencoe, IL: Free Press, 1960.

Hoffman, Danny. *The War Machines: Young Men and Violence in Sierra Leone and Liberia.* Durham, NC: Duke University Press, 2011.

Honwana, Alcinda. *Child Soldiers in Africa.* Philadelphia: University of Pennsylvania Press, 2006.

———. *Okusiakala ondalo yokalye: Let Us Light a New Fire: Local Knowledge in the Postwar Healing and Reintegration of War-Affected Children in Angola.* Luanda, Angola: Christian Children's Fund, 1998.

Howard, George Elliot. *A History of Matrimonial Institutions Chiefly in England and the United States, with an Introductory Analysis of the Literature and the Theories of Primitive Marriage and the Family.* Chicago: University of Chicago Press, 1904.

Hugo, Victor. *Les Misérables.* London: Hurst and Blackett, 1862.

Hull, Susan. *Boy Soldiers of the Confederacy.* New York: Neale, 1905.

I Can Still Smell the Dead: The Forgotten Human Rights Crisis in the Central African Republic. New York: Human Rights Watch, 2013.

Illustrated Centennial Record. New York: Phillips & Hunt, 1885.

"India's Child Soldiers." New Delhi: Asian Center for Human Rights, 2013. http://www.achrweb.org/reports/india/JJ-IndiasChildSoldiers2013.pdf.

Iweala, Uzodinma. *Beasts of No Nation.* New York: Harper Perennial, 2005.

Jablonski, Carla, and Leland Purvis. *Resistance.* New York: First Second, 2010.

Jal, Emmanuel. *War Child: A Child Soldier's Story.* New York: St. Martin's, 2009.

James, Allison, and Adrian James. *Key Concepts in Childhood Studies*. London: Sage, 2012.

James, William Dobein. *A Sketch of Brigadier General Francis Marion and a History of His Brigade*. Charleston: Gould and Milet, 1821.

Jarrett-Macauley, Delia. *Moses, Citizen and Me*. London: Granta, 2005.

Johnson, Walter. "On Agency." *Journal of Social History* 37, no. 1 (2003): 113–124.

Jourdan, Luca. "Mayi-Mayi: Young Rebels in Kivu, DRC." *Africa Development* 36, nos. 3–4 (2011): 89–111.

Kaeuper, Richard W. *Chivalry and Violence in Medieval Europe*. Oxford: Oxford University Press, 2001.

Kahn, David. *Hitler's Spies: German Military Intelligence in World War II*. New York: Da Capo Press, 2000.

Kaldor, Mary. *New and Old Wars: Organized Violence in a Global Era*. Cambridge: Polity Press, 1989.

Kaplan, Danny. "Commemorating a Suspended Death: Missing Soldiers and National Solidarity in Israel." *American Ethnologist* 35, no. 3 (2008): 413–427.

Kaplan, Robert. "The Coming Anarchy: How Scarcity, Crime, Overpopulation and Disease Are Rapidly Destroying the Social Fabric of Our Planet." *Atlantic Monthly*, February 1, 1994. http://www.theatlantic.com/magazine/archive/1994/02/the -coming-anarchy/304670/.

Katzlander, Howard. "PW Baby Cage: Captured Wehrmacht GIs between the Ages of 12 and 17 Get Special Indoctrination in Democracy at This PW School Sparked by a Yank Pfc." *Yank: The Army Weekly* 4, no. 18 (October 19, 1945): 16–17.

Keegan, John. *The Face of Battle*. New York: Barnes & Noble, 1976.

Keesee, D. M. *Too Young to Die: Boy Soldiers of the Union Army 1861–1865*. Huntington, VA: Blue Acorn Press, 2001.

Keller, Bill. "Echo of '41 in Minsk: Was the Heroine a Jew?" *New York Times*, September 15, 1987. https://www.nytimes.com/1987/09/15/world/echo-of-41-in-minsk -was-the-heroine-a-jew.html?pagewanted=3&src=pm.

Kendall, Amos. *The Life of Andrew Jackson*. New York: Harper & Brothers, 1843.

Kershaw, Ian. *The End: The Defiance and Destruction of Hitler's Germany, 1944–1945*. New York: Penguin, 2011.

Kessel, John. "Creating the Innocent Killer: *Ender's Game*, Intentions, and Morality." *Foundation, the International Review of Science Fiction* 33, no. 90 (Spring 2004). http://tentoinfinity.com/2013/10/18/creating-the-innocent-killer-by-john -kessel/.

Kilcullen, David. *Out of the Mountains: The Coming Age of the Urban Guerilla*. New York: Oxford University Press, 2013.

Kilmer, George L. "Boys in the Union Army." *Century* 70 (1905): 269–275.

King, Charles. "Boys of the War Days." In *A Photographic History of the Civil War*, vol. 8, edited by Francis Trevelyan Miller, 190–196. Springfield, MA: Patriot Press, 1911.

Knopp, Guido. *Hitler's Children*. Stroud, UK: Sutton, 2004.

Kourouma, Ahmadou. *Allah Is Not Obliged*. New York: Anchor, 2007.

Kramer, Paul. *The Blood of Government: Race, Empire, the United States, and the Philippines.* Chapel Hill: University of North Carolina Press, 2006.

Kreidberg, Marvin R., and Merton G. Henry. *History of Military Mobilization in the United States Army, 1775–1945.* Washington, DC: Government Printing Office, 1955.

Kucherenko, Olga. *Little Soldiers: How Soviet Children Went to War, 1941–1945.* New York: Oxford University Press, 2011.

Lakhani, Kalsoon. "Pakistan's Child Soldiers." *Foreign Policy,* March 29, 2010. http://afpak.foreignpolicy.com/posts/2010/03/29/pakistans_child_soldiers.

Lemmings, David. "Marriage and the Law in the Eighteenth Century: Hardwicke's Marriage Act of 1753." *Historical Journal* 36, no. 2 (1996): 339–360.

Lepore, Jill. "Bound for Glory: Writing Campaign Lives." *New Yorker,* October 20, 2008. http://www.newyorker.com/arts/critics/atlarge/2008/10/20/081020crat_atlarge_lepore.

Life of Luther C. Ladd, Who Fell in Baltimore, April 19, 1861 Exclaiming All Hail to the Stars and Stripes. Concord, NH: P. B. Cogswell, 1862.

Lister, David. *Die Hard, Aby.* Barnsley, South Yorkshire: Pen & Sword Books, 2005.

The Little Drummer Boy, Clarence McKenzie: The Child of the 13th Regiment New York State Militia and the Child of the Mission Sunday School. New York: Reformed Protestant Dutch Church, 1861.

Lossing, John Benson. *Pictorial History of the Civil War in the United States of America.* Philadelphia: George W. Childs, 1866.

"Luther C. Ladd, a Massachusetts Volunteer, Killed at Baltimore (First Victim of the War)." *Harpers Weekly* 5, no. 231 (June 1, 1861).

Macmillan, Lorraine. "The Child Soldier in North-South Relations." *International Political Sociology* 3 (2009): 36–52.

Maguire, Peter. *Law and War: An American Story.* New York: Columbia University Press, 2000.

Mann, Howard. "International Law and the Child Soldier." *International and Comparative Law Quarterly* 36 (1987): 32–50.

Martin, Joseph Plumb. *Private Yankee Doodle.* Fort Washington, PA: Eastern National, 2002.

Martins, Catrina. "The Dangers of the Single Story: Child-Soldiers in Literary Fiction and Film." *Childhood* 18, no. 4 (2011): 434–446.

Martyn, Peter. "Warsaw 1989 to September 2001: Successive Statuary and Monument Memorialization for the National Capitol." In *Power and Persuasion: Sculpture in Its Rhetorical Context,* ed. Ursula Szulakowska, 225–248. Warsaw: Institute of Art of the Polish Academy of Sciences, 2004.

Marwick, Roger D., and Euridice Charon Cardona. *Soviet Women on the Frontline in the Second World War.* New York: Palgrave Macmillan, 2012.

Massachusetts Register No. 94. Boston: Adams, Sampson, 1862.

McPherson, James. *Battle Cry of Freedom: The Civil War Era.* Oxford: Oxford University Press, 2003.

———. *Ordeal by Fire: The Civil War and Reconstruction.* New York: Knopf, 1982.

Meacham, Jon. *American Lion: Andrew Jackson in the White House.* New York: Random House, 2009.

Mead, Margaret, and Martha Wolfenstein. *Childhood in Contemporary Cultures.* Chicago: University of Chicago Press, 1955.

"Memoir of Major Thomas Young: A Revolutionary Patriot of South Carolina." *Orion: A Monthly Magazine of Literature and Art* 3, nos. 2–3 (1843). http://sc_tories.tripod .com/thomas_young.htm.

Merry, Sally. "Human Rights Law and the Demonization of Culture (and Anthropology along the Way)." *PoLAR: Political and Legal Anthropology Review* 26, no. 1 (1999): 55–77.

Meyer, Hubert. *The 12th SS: The History of the Hitler Youth Panzer Division.* Vol. 1. Mechanicsburg, PA: Stackpole Books, 2005.

Mintz, Steven. *Huck's Raft: A History of American Childhood.* Cambridge, MA: Harvard University Press, 2004.

Montgomery, Heather. *An Introduction to Childhood: Anthropological Perspectives on Children's Lives.* West Sussex, UK: Wiley-Blackwell, 2009.

Moore, Frank, ed. *Rebellion Record.* Vol. 1. New York: Putnam, 1862.

"More Youth at Guantánamo Than U.S. Claimed." University of California–Davis, News and Information Center, June 7, 2011. http://www.news.ucdavis.edu/ search/news_detail.lasso?id=9918.

Morpurgo, Michael. *War Horse.* New York: Scholastic Press, 2011.

Mosse, George L. *Fallen Soldiers: Reshaping the Memory of World Wars.* Oxford: Oxford University Press, 1990.

Murdock, Eugene C. "New York's Civil War Bounty Brokers." *Journal of American History* 53, no. 2 (1966): 259–270.

Murphy, Libby. "Gavroche and the Great War: Soldier *Gouaille* and the Legend of the *Poilu.*" *Journal of War and Culture* 2, no. 2 (2009): 121–133.

Musgrove, Richard Watson. *History of the Town of Bristol, Grafton County, New Hampshire.* Vol. 1. Bristol, NH: R. W. Musgove, 1904.

Myer, John E. B. *Child Protection in America: Past, Present, and Future.* New York: Oxford University Press, 2006.

———. "A Short History of Child Protection in America." *Family Law Quarterly* 42, no. 3 (2008): 449–463.

Nadal, Bernhard J. *The Christian Boy-Soldier: The Funeral Sermon of Joseph E. Darrow Preached in Sands Street Methodist Episcopal Church, Brooklyn, on the 27th of October, 1861.* New York: Steam, 1862.

Napoli, Donna Jo. *Fire in the Hills.* New York: Penguin, 2006.

New York State Annual Report of the Attorney General. Albany: J. B. Lyon, 1919.

Nguyen, Ken. *War Witch.* DVD. Montreal: Telefilm, 2012.

Nichols, R. H., and F. A. Wray. *The History of the Foundling Hospital.* London: Oxford University Press, 1935.

Ofele, Martin W. *True Sons of the Republic: European Immigrants in the Union Army.* Santa Barbara, CA: Praeger, 2008.

Optic, Oliver. *The Soldier Boy; or, Tom Somers in the Army*. New York: Hurst, 1864. http://www.gutenberg.org/ebooks//14595.

Orwell, George. *Homage to Catalonia*. New York: Harcourt, 1969.

Parkinson, Curtis. *Domenic's War*. Toronto: Tundra Books, 2006.

Parton, James. *The Life of Andrew Jackson*. Vol. 1. New York: Mason Brothers, 1860.

Perlis, Rivka. *The Pioneering Zionist Youth Movements in Nazi-Occupied Poland* [in Hebrew]. Tel Aviv: Kibutz Hameuchad, 1987.

Peterson, Edward N. *The Many Faces of Defeat*. New York: Peter Lang, 1990.

Pizzaro, Judith, Roxanne Cohen Silver, and JoAnn Prause. "Physical and Mental Health Costs of Traumatic War Experiences among Civil War Veterans." *Archives of General Psychiatry* 63, no. 2 (2006): 193–200.

Pugh, Gillian. *London's Forgotten Children: Thomas Coram and the Foundling Hospital*. Stroud, UK: Tempus, 2007.

Quaifem, M. M. "A Boy Soldier under Washington: The Memoir of Daniel Granger." *Mississippi Valley Historical Review* 16, no. 4 (1930): 538–560.

Raban, Havka Folman. *They Are Still with Me*. Translated by Judy Grossman. Western Galilee, Israel: Ghetto Fighters Museum, 2001.

Rampel, Gerhard. *Hitler's Children: The Hitler Youth and the SS*. Chapel Hill: University of North Carolina Press, 1989.

Rapp, Steven. "The Compact Model in International Criminal Justice: The Special Court for Sierra Leone." *Drake Law Review* 5 (2008): 11–49.

Register of Enlistment into Military Bands and Lists of Boys Sent to the Training Ships Goliath and Exmouth: 1858–1902. SMSD/178. London: London Metropolitan Archives, n.d.

Reid, Richard. *War in Pre-colonial Eastern Africa*. Athens: Ohio University Press, 2007.

Renshaw, C. A. *England's Boys: A Woman's War Poems*. London: Erskine MacDonald, 1916.

Report Made to the Senate Relative to the Enlistment of Boys from the Reform School into the Army of the United States. Providence, RI: Hiram H. Thomas, 1865.

Report of the Committee Appointed to Enquire into the Subject of Boy Enlistment. London: Harrison and Sons, 1876.

Report of the Secretary General on the Establishment of a Special Court for Sierra Leone. UN Doc S/2000/915. New York: United Nations, October 4, 2000.

Review of Department of Defense Detention Operations and Detainee Interrogation Techniques (Church Report). Washington, DC: U.S. Department of Defense, March 3, 2005. http://www.cfr.org/publication/11092/church_report.html.

A Review of the FBI's Involvement in and Observations of Detainee Interrogations in Guantanamo Bay, Afghanistan, and Iraq. Washington, DC: U.S. Department of Justice, 2008. http://www.justice.gov/oig/special/s0805/final.pdf.

Rhode Island Historical Society. *Providence Reform School Records: 1850–1885*. N.d. http://www.rihs.org/mssinv/Mss214sg3.htm.

Richards, Paul. *Fighting for the Rain Forest*. Portsmouth, NH: Heinemann, 1996.

Rinaldi, Richard. *The United States Army in World War I—Order of Battle*. Takoma Park, MD: Tiger Lily, 2005.

Ronen, Avihu. "'Youth Culture' and the Roots of the Idea of Resistance in the Ghetto (Youth Movements in Zaglembie during the Holocaust)" [in Hebrew]. *Zionism: Studies in the History of the Zionist Movement and of the Jewish Community in Palestine* 16 (1991): 141–165.

Rose, Lionel. *The Erosion of Childhood: Child Oppression in Great Britain 1860–1918*. London: Routledge, 1991.

Rosen, David. *Armies of the Young: Child Soldiers in War and Terrorism*. New Brunswick, NJ: Rutgers University Press, 2005.

Rubin, Ben. "The Rhetoric of Revenge: Atrocity and Identity in the Revolutionary Carolinas." *Journal of Backcountry Studies* 5, no. 2 (2010): 1–46.

Saro-Wiwa, Ken. *Sozaboy*. New York: Longman, 1994.

Sauvaire, Jean-Stéphane. *Johnny Mad Dog*. DVD. Paris: MNP Enterprise, 2008.

Schlesier, Karl H. *Flakhelfer to Grenadier: Memoir of a Boy Soldier, 1943–1945*. Lexington, KY: K. H. Schlesier, 2011.

Scott, G., and S. Reich. "Think Again: Child Soldiers: What Human Rights Activists Never Tell You about Young Killers." *Foreign Policy*, May 22, 2009. http://www .foreignpolicy.com/articles/2009/05/21/think_again_child_soldiers.

The Scouts Book of Heroes. London: C. Arthur Pearson, 1919.

Second Report of the Provost Marshal General to the Secretary of War on the Operations of the Selective Service System to December 20, 1918. Washington, DC: Government Printing Office, 1919.

Selesky, Harold. *A Demographic Survey of the Continental Army That Wintered at Valley Forge, Pennsylvania, 1777–1778*. Washington, DC: National Park Service, 1987. http://www.nps.gov/vafo/historyculture/demographic-survey.htm.

———. *War and Society in Colonial America*. New Haven: Yale University Press, 1990.

Senlavskala, Elizabeth S. "Heroic Symbols: The Reality and Mythology of War." *Russian Studies in History* 37, no. 1 (1998): 61–87.

Sevier, Elizabeth. *Resistance Fighter: A Teenage Girl in World War II France*. Manhattan, KS: Sunflower University Press, 1998.

Shraver, Maxim D. *An Anthology of Jewish-Russian Literature*. Vol. 1. Armonk, NY: M.E. Sharpe, 2007.

Sibley, David. *The British Working Class and Enthusiasm for War, 1914–1916*. London: Routledge, 2005.

Silvester, Victor. *Dancing Is My Life*. London: Heinemann, 1958.

Singer, Peter. *Children at War*. Berkeley: University of California Press, 2006.

Soyinka, Wole. *Of Africa*. New Haven: Yale University Press, 2009.

Sparrow, Robert. "Killer Robots." *Journal of Applied Philosophy* 24 (2007): 62–77.

Starinov, A. K. *Behind Fascist Lines: A Firsthand Account of Guerilla Warfare during the Spanish Revolution*. New York: Ballantine Books, 2000.

Steinbock-Pratt, Sarah. "The Lions in the Jungle: Representations of Africa and Africans in American Cinema." In *Africans and the Politics of Popular Culture*, edited by Toyin Falola and Augustine Agwuele, 214–236. Rochester, NY: University of Rochester Press, 2009.

Stewart, Richard W., ed. *The United States Army and the Forging of a Nation, 1775–1917.* Vol. 1. Washington, DC: U.S. Army Center for Military History, 2005.

Stone, Lawrence. *The Family, Sex and Marriage in England 1500–1800.* London: Harper and Row, 1977.

Stryker, William S., ed. *Official Register of the Officers and Men of New Jersey in the Revolutionary War.* Trenton, NJ: William Nicolson, 1872.

Tec, Nehama, and Daniel Weiss. "A Historical Injustice: The Case of Masha Bruskina." *Holocaust and Genocide Studies* 11, no. 3 (1997): 366–377.

Thavanet, Dennis. "The Michigan Reform School and the Civil War: Officers and Inmates Mobilized for the Union Cause." *Michigan Historical Review* 13, no. 1 (Spring 1987): 21–46.

Trafficking in Persons Report. Washington, DC: U.S. Department of State, 2004. http://www.state.gov/g/tip/rls/tiprpt/2004/34021.htm.

Tumarkin, Maria. *The Living and the Dead: The Rise and Fall of the Cult of World War II in Russia.* New York: Basic Books, 1995.

———. "Productive Death: The Necropedagogy of a Young Soviet Hero." *South Atlantic Quarterly* 110, no. 4 (2011): 885–899.

Tussaud, John. *The Romance of Madame Tussaud's.* New York: George H. Duran, 1920.

Tynan, Katharine. *Late Songs.* London: Sidgwick & Jackson, 1917.

UN War Crimes Commission. *Law Reports of the Trials of War Criminals.* Vol. 8. London: HMSO, 1949.

United States Marine Corps Commandant's Professional Reading List—All Hands. Quantico, VA: Library of the Marine Corps, 2013.

Utas, Mats. "Victimcy, Girlfriending, Soldiering: Tactic Agency in a Young Woman's Social Navigation of the Liberian War Zone." *Anthropological Quarterly* 78 (2005): 403–430.

Van Bueren, Geraldine. *International Law on the Rights of the Child.* Boston: Martinus Nijhoff, 1995.

Van Emden, Richard. *Boy Soldiers of the Great War.* London: Headline, 2005.

Veale, Angela. *From Child Soldier to Ex-fighter.* Pretoria, South Africa: Institute for Security Studies, 2003.

Vigh, Henrik. *Navigating Terrains of War: Youth and Soldiering in Guinea-Bissau.* New York: Berghahn, 2000.

Waletsky, Josh. *The Partisans of Vilna: The Untold Story of Jewish Resistance during World War II.* DVD. Washington, DC: Ciesla, 1986.

Warner, Ezra. *Generals in Blue: Lives of the Union Commanders.* Baton Rouge: Louisiana State University Press, 1964.

Warriner, Edwin. *Old Sands Street Methodist Episcopal Church of Brooklyn, New York: An Illustrated Centennial Record* (New York: Phillips & Hunt, 1885).

Weiss, Thomas G. "Principles, Politics, and Humanitarian Action." *Ethics and International Affairs* 13, no. 1 (1999): 1–22.

Wertsch, James V. *Voices of Collective Remembering.* Cambridge: Cambridge University Press, 2002.

Wessels, Michael. *Child Soldiers: From Violence to Protection.* Cambridge, MA: Harvard University Press, 2006.

West, Harry G. "Girls with Guns: Narrating the Experience of War of FRELIMO's 'Female Detachment.'" *Anthropological Quarterly* 73, no. 4 (2000): 180–194.

Westall, Robert. *The Machine Gunners.* 1975. Reprint, London: Pan Macmillan, 2001.

Wiącek, Elżbieta. "In the Labyrinth of Memory: Cultural Representations about the Warsaw Rising of 1945 in Polish Film and Media Narration." *History Research* 2, no. 6 (2012): 398–414.

Wiley, Bell Irvin. *The Common Soldier in the Civil War. Book II: The Life of Johnny Reb.* New York: Grosset and Dunlop, 1943.

Wilson, Richard. "Children and War in Sierra Leone: A West African Diary." *Anthropology Today* 20 (2001): 21–22.

Witte, John. "Honor Thy Father and Thy Mother? Child Marriage and Parental Consent in Calvin's Geneva." *Journal of Religion* 86, no. 4 (2006): 580–605.

Woolf, Virginia. *Three Guineas.* In *The Selected Works of Virginia Woolf,* 781–924. Hertfordshire, UK: Hare, 2007.

Yvorel, Jean-Jacques. "De Delacroix à Poulbot, l'image du gamin de Paris." *RHEI: Revue d'histoire de l'enfance irrégulière* 4 (2002).

Zwick, Edward. *Blood Diamond.* DVD. Burbank, CA: Warner Brothers, 2006.

INDEX

ABOUT THE AUTHOR

DAVID M. ROSEN is a professor of anthropology and law at Fairleigh Dickinson University in Madison, New Jersey. He has carried out research in Sierra Leone, Kenya, Israel, and the Palestinian territories. He is the author of *Armies of the Young: Child Soldiers in War and Terrorism* (Rutgers University Press, 2005), *Child Soldiers: A Reference Handbook* (ABC-CLIO, 2012), and numerous scholarly articles on the issue of child soldiers, including "War" in *Oxford Bibliographies Online: Childhood Studies*, edited by Heather Montgomery (New York: Oxford University Press, 2012); "Who Is a Child? The Legal Conundrum of Child Soldiers," *Connecticut Journal of International Law* 25 (Fall 2009): 81–118; and "Child Soldiers, International Humanitarian Law, and the Globalization of Childhood," *American Anthropologist* 109, no. 2 (June 2007): 296–306. He resides in Brooklyn, New York.

CPSIA information can be obtained at www.ICGtesting.com
Printed in the USA
LVOW07s2229150316

479324LV00004B/207/P